Higher Education Revolutions in the Gulf

Over the past quarter century, the people of the Arabian Peninsula have witnessed a revolutionary transformation in higher education. In 1990, there were fewer than ten public universities that offered their Arabic-language curricula in sex-segregated settings to national citizens only. In 2015, there are hundreds of public, semi-public and private colleges and universities. Most of these institutions are open to expatriates and national citizens; a few offer gender-integrated instruction; and the language of instruction is much more likely to be in English than Arabic.

Higher Education Revolutions in the Gulf explores the reasons behind this dramatic growth. It examines the causes of the sharp shift in educational practices and analyses how these new systems of higher education are regulated, evaluating the extent to which the new universities and colleges are improving quality. Questioning whether these educational changes can be sustained, the book explores how the new curricula and language policies are aligned with official visions of the future. Written by leading scholars in the field, it draws upon their considerable experiences of teaching and doing research in the Arabian Gulf, as well as their different disciplinary backgrounds (linguistics and economics), to provide a holistic and historically informed account of the emergence and viability of the Arabian Peninsula's higher education revolutions.

Offering a comprehensive, critical assessment of education in the Gulf Arab states, this book represents a significant contribution to the field and will be of interest to students and scholars of Middle East and Gulf Studies, and essential for those focused on higher education.

Fatima Badry is Professor of Linguistics in the Department of English at the American University of Sharjah in the UAE. Her research interests include language acquisition, bilingualism, education policy and globalization and the impact of global English on Arab identity.

John Willoughby is Professor of Economics at American University. After teaching at the American University of Sharjah, he has devoted his time to studying labor migration and educational issues in the GCC.

Routledge advances in Middle East and Islamic studies

1 **Iraqi Kurdistan**
Political development and
emergent democracy
Gareth R. V. Stansfield

2 **Egypt in the Twenty First
Century**
Challenges for development
Edited by M. Riad El-Ghonemy

3 **The Christian–Muslim Frontier**
A zone of contact, conflict or
cooperation
Mario Apostolov

4 **The Islamic World-System**
A study in polity-market
interaction
Masudul Alam Choudhury

5 **Regional Security in the Middle
East**
A critical perspective
Pinar Bilgin

6 **Political Thought in Islam**
A study in intellectual boundaries
Nelly Lahoud

7 **Turkey's Kurds**
A theoretical analysis of the PKK
and Abdullah Ocalan
Ali Kemal Özcan

8 **Beyond the Arab Disease**
New perspectives in politics and
culture
Riad Nourallah

9 **The Arab Diaspora**
Voices of an anguished scream
*Zahia Smail Salhi and
Ian Richard Netton*

10 **Gender and Self in Islam**
Etin Anwar

11 **Nietzsche and Islam**
Roy Jackson

12 **The Baha'is of Iran**
Socio-historical studies
*Dominic Parvis Brookshaw and
Seena B. Fazel*

13 **Egypt's Culture Wars**
Politics and practice
Samia Mehrez

14 **Islam and Human Rights in
Practice**
Perspectives across the *Ummah*
*Edited by Shahram Akbarzadeh
and Benjamin MacQueen*

15 **Family in the Middle East**
Ideational change in Egypt, Iran
and Tunisia
*Edited by Kathryn M. Yount and
Hoda Rashad*

16 **Syria's Kurds**
History, politics and society
Jordi Tejel

17 **Trajectories of Education in the Arab World**
Legacies and challenges
Edited by Osama Abi-Mershed

18 **The Myth of the Clash of Civilizations**
Chiara Bottici and Benoit Challand

19 **Chaos in Yemen**
Societal collapse and the new authoritarianism
Isa Blumi

20 **Rethinking Israeli Space**
Periphery and identity
Haim Yacobi and Erez Tzfadia

21 **Navigating Contemporary Iran**
Challenging economic, social and political perspectives
Edited by Eric Hooglund and Leif Stenberg

22 **Music, Culture and Identity in the Muslim World**
Performance, politics and piety
Edited by Kamal Salhi

23 **Dissident Writings of Arab Women**
Voices against violence
Brinda Mehta

24 **Higher Education Revolutions in the Gulf**
Globalization and institutional viability
Fatima Badry and John Willoughby

Higher Education Revolutions in the Gulf

Globalization and institutional viability

Fatima Badry and John Willoughby

Routledge
Taylor & Francis Group
LONDON AND NEW YORK

First published 2016 by Routledge

2 Park Square, Milton Park, Abingdon, Oxfordshire OX14 4RN
52 Vanderbilt Avenue, New York, NY 10017

Routledge is an imprint of the Taylor & Francis Group, an informa business

First issued in paperback 2019

British Library Cataloguing-in-Publication Data
A catalogue record for this book is available from the British Library

Library of Congress Cataloging-in-Publication Data
Badry, Fatima.
Higher education revolutions in the Gulf : globalization and institutional viability / Fatima Badry and John Willoughby.
   pages cm. – (Routledge advances in Middle East and Islamic studies ; 24)
   Includes bibliographical references and index.
   1. Education, Higher–Persian Gulf Region. 2. Educational change–Persian Gulf Region. 3. Education and globalization–Persian Gulf Region.
   4. Gulf Cooperation Council. I. Willoughby, John, 1949– II. Title.
   LA1431.4.B34 2015
   378.536–dc23   2015010477

ISBN: 978-0-415-50565-9 (hbk)
ISBN: 978-0-367-86698-3 (pbk)

DOI: 10.4324/9780203796139

Typeset in Times New Roman

Contents

List of tables   viii
Preface   x
Acknowledgments   xv
List of abbreviations   xvii

1 Introduction: the political and socio-economic emergence of the
   Arabian Gulf   1

2 The global expansion of higher education: alternative
   perspectives   12

3 Globalization of education and the GCC   28

4 The multi-model approach to privatization: questions of
   sustainability   54

5 GCC public universities: growing pains   97

6 Assessing quality: adopting Western standards of accreditation 134

7 Reforming higher education in Saudi Arabia: reasons for
   optimism   153
   AMANI K. HAMDAN

8 Arabic in higher education: questions of national identity and
   pragmatism   179

9 Higher education revolutions: short-term success versus
   long-term viability?   204

Index   228

Tables

1.1	Economic indicators of the GCC (2010)	2
1.2	GCC demographic composition	3
1.3	Changes in the rate of adolescent pregnancy (number of births to women ages 15–19 per 1,000 women ages 15–19)	6
1.4	Educational attainment in the GCC: expected years of schooling	7
2.1	Share of students in tertiary education by region (1970–2007)	13
2.2	Share of students in tertiary education by income status of country	13
2.3	Gross enrollment rates in tertiary education	14
3.1	Categorizing cross-border collaboration	32
3.2	Members of the Association of American International Colleges and Universities	35
3.3	Enrollment in tertiary educational institutions in the Gulf	44
3.4	Inbound and outbound mobility rates of GCC tertiary students	46
3.5	Top five destinations of outward bound student from the Gulf (2012)	47
3.6	Top five home countries of inward bound students to the Gulf (2012)	48
3.7	Regional origin of inbound tertiary education students in the small GCC states (2012)	48
4.1	Classification of the private universities in the GCC	56
4.2	List of private higher education institutions in Doha, Qatar	59
4.3a	Dubai's colleges and universities	66
4.3b	Dubai's HEIs outside the free zones	69
4.4	Private universities and colleges in the Sultanate of Oman	72
4.5	Private higher education institutions of Bahrain (2000–6)	76
4.6	Private institutions in Kuwait (2002–8)	78
4.7	Private universities in the Northern Emirate	83
4.8	The branch and private universities in the Emirate of Abu Dhabi (UAE)	84
5.1	The first state universities in the Gulf	98
5.2	Degree programs in Kuwait's public HEIs	100

5.3	Qatar University	101
5.4	The UAE federal public universities	103
5.5	Abu Dhabi's public, non-federal HEI	106
5.6	Colleges in the public institutions in Oman	108
5.7	Oman's higher education governing bodies	109
5.8	Bahrain public HEIs	110
5.9	Scientific and technological capacities in world regions (percentage of world total, 1995)	123
5.10	Global Competitiveness rankings (2012–13)	124
5.11	Public expenditure on education as a percentage of GDP	124
5.12	Comparative analysis of perceived significance versus satisfaction	126
5.13	Main research centers in the GCC	128
6.1	Government higher education accreditation and assessment agencies: IQAAHE members	138
6.2	ABET accreditation of engineering, computer science and information systems programs in the GCC	139
6.3	Gulf institutions with AACSB accreditation	140
7.1	Growth of universities in KSA (2005–14)	157
7.2	Growth of colleges in KSA (2005–14)	157
7.3	Public universities in KSA	158
7.4	Private universities in KSA	159
7.5	Private colleges in KSA	160

Preface

Our interest in writing this book ultimately stems from personal experiences. We both joined the faculty of the American University of Sharjah (AUS) just as it was beginning in the late 1990s. One of us is still there 17 years later.[1] The establishment of AUS and University City was the dream of the ruler of Sharjah, Dr. Sheikh Sultan bin Muhammad Al-Qasimi. This dream became a reality in a remarkably short period of time.[2] Both the AUS and the University of Sharjah in University City opened in the fall of 1997 even before all buildings were completed. The faculty who arrived in September 1997 had to be housed in hotels and share the campus, still under construction, with roaming camels for the first few months.

Both students and faculty were well aware that they were participating in a risky venture. It was not at all certain that the AUS would succeed, and the sense of entering into uncharted territory led us to label ourselves "Pioneers" and "Settlers."[3] Those who arrived in the first year were the pioneers. The settlers followed in the second year. The divisions between the two cohorts seemed rather stark at first. Indeed, the settlers often joked that our edgy veteran colleagues suffered from PTSD – Pioneer Traumatic Stress Disorder.

As this lame witticism indicates, the beginning years at the AUS were difficult. We on the faculty had uprooted ourselves and traveled long distances to what seemed like a remote location. All of us wanted this experiment to succeed. On the other hand, we found ourselves struggling with important questions of education policy as well as being involved in conflicts related to the distribution of power and authority. The uncertainty and riskiness of our decision to relocate only added to the fraught work environment.

Part of this anxiety was no doubt caused by our own perceptions of the location in which this high-stakes educational experiment was taking place. The societies of the Arabian Peninsula have not been known as places that are open to social and intellectual experimentation. Most of us wondered to what extent a new and different university devoted to the promotion of critical thinking would have the political support necessary for its survival. What would happen if the ruler who sponsored the university withdrew his backing for this controversial project? Would we be able to create a meritocratic academic culture that would allow us to judge student accomplishment according to academic quality and not pre-existing social standing? Would the integration of the sexes in the classroom and on campus prove too controversial? Would our willingness to move away from our home academic base doom us to living in an educational backwater? Could we survive the heat? Could we raise our children in this new environment?

The sense that a GCC polity would not welcome an ambitious academic enterprise staffed by foreign newcomers did not just stem from orientalist stereotypes. Some Western faculty considered students' weak English proficiency and their insufficient knowledge about Western culture a sign of lack of sophistication and, sometimes worse, a sign of stupidity. Many Arabs from other countries had their own stereotypical misconceptions. The view from Egypt, Lebanon and many other countries was (and is) that the Gulf States are culturally backward, but lucky enough to be endowed with great, but somehow undeserved, wealth. These perspectives often bred a condescending attitude to the surrounding society not that different from the way many European intellectuals view barbarian America. In any event, there we were – an assortment of faculty with different backgrounds, prejudices and expectations, working together in a new, unformed institution, in a remote territory, in a society of which most if not all of us had limited and inaccurate knowledge. Participating in the creation of any institution is always stressful; however, our situation was unusually unique.

Despite or perhaps because of these difficulties, we in the faculty had the mandate from the president of the university to create a liberal arts undergraduate institution on the American model. Our first task was to establish a remedial educational program for beginning students whose language and study skills required them to take special foundation courses before being allowed to take university-level courses.[4] At the same time we were all involved in formulating a general education curriculum, creating majors, establishing reasonable and rigorous standards of academic quality, supporting a robust but regulated student life, developing a Faculty Organization Plan to create a faculty senate, instituting rules and procedures that would permit the non-arbitrary retention and termination of faculty; and establishing a library that could support the academic work of students and faculty alike. Many felt that it was necessary to develop these institutions quickly, and this gave rise to inevitable conflicts and frequent administrative restructurings. Finally, it is important to note that geopolitical crises increased the uncertainty of working on this project in the Gulf. The 9/11 catastrophe revealed fissures within the faculty and student body.[5] For some, Sharjah became an uncomfortable place to live and work.

The sense that we were standing on a precipice that could give way at any moment, along with the prospect of losing a tenured academic position at American University in Washington, DC, caused one of the co-authors (John Willoughby) to resign his associate professorship at the AUS and return to the United States. The other co-author (Fatima Badry) remained at the AUS, became chair of the department of English while serving on important faculty and administrative committees. In both cases, our experiences at the AUS generated an academic interest in the study of GCC societies. Our own research increasingly explored issues related to education in the Gulf. One author (Fatima Badry) began to examine the opportunities and threats posed by the increasing insistence of educational authorities that nearly all higher educational instruction had to be delivered in English. Her discussions with students led her to examine the impact of a Western higher education model in English on the identity of Arab millennials. The other author (John Willoughby) started to investigate the links between the AUS experience and higher educational transformation throughout the region. There were similarities in our two research projects. While supporting the principles of liberal arts higher education, both of us were (and are) uneasy with the authoritarian ways in which educational reform has often been implemented. Both of us were (and are) worried about the educational and geopolitical implications of an uncritical adoption of Western educational models. Because our own research raised as many questions as answers, and because we thought our different analytical frameworks could be usefully combined, we decided to join forces to write this study.

The goals of higher education revolutions

The main title of our book, *Higher Education Revolutions in the Gulf*, underlines our belief that the changes we have observed in the organization and delivery of higher educational services constitute a revolution in the tertiary educational system of each GCC state. Although the policy changes and institution formation processes in Oman, the competing emirates of the UAE, Qatar, Bahrain and Kuwait are distinct, all are significant and deserve the *revolution* label. The competitive environment in which higher education is offered, the regulatory environment that organizes and evaluates university and college operations, and the curricula that confront incoming students have profoundly changed throughout the region. On the other hand, countries and emirates have not implemented identical programs. Both available financial resources for educational restructuring and educational philosophies differ significantly across the region, and any study of higher education in the Gulf must take account of this heterogeneous reality. There is no single GCC revolution in higher education. Rather, the changes we observe are interconnected, but significantly different to warrant the term *revolutions* rather than *evolution*.

The subtitle of our book, *Globalization and Institutional Viability*, signals that we have decided to embark on two distinct, but interconnected research projects. The first is providing an analytical account of the recent history of higher education in the five small GCC states. When did governments begin to implement higher educational reforms in response to globalization pressures? What new institutions began to form? What is the best way to describe the changes we are observing? This contemporary historical account required us to develop appropriate categories that would allow us both to describe clearly how higher education has changed and to explore the distinct evolutionary tendencies embodied in these institutional changes.

The second research project uses the history we have developed to consider the viability of the new worlds of GCC higher education. Not all revolutions work; not all radical reforms are well designed. As the first section of the introduction suggested, the political and social environment in which these educational changes were implemented is challenging. Although the experience is recent, we believe we have enough information to make a preliminary assessment. On the other hand, what do we assess? The appropriateness of the new curricula? The quality of the educational services? The financial stability of the new institutions? The governance systems of universities and colleges? The quality of the regulatory environment? The social legitimacy of these educational projects? The implications of using many Western and expatriate administrators and faculty to implement these policy changes? The educational and social meaning of requiring English to be the sole language of sophisticated academic discourse? As the list of questions suggest, the term viability has many different meanings.

We chose to be ambitious, rather than restrained. To the extent possible, we have tried to answer as many of these questions as we can. Our goal is to provide a comprehensive overview of the changes and challenges that have occurred within the higher education sectors of the GCC, and we hope that this effort is useful for policy-makers and academics alike. While initially we planned to limit this book to the smaller GCC states of Bahrain, Kuwait, Oman, Qatar and the UAE, because we felt higher education developments in the Kingdom of Saudi Arabia were somehow different from those developments in the rest of the GGC, a paper presented by Professor Amani Hamdan, from the University of Dammam, KSA, at the Conceptualizing the Global University conference, held at the American University of Sharjah, in May 2014, made us realize that there are many parallel developments. We invited Professor Hamdan to contribute a chapter to this book to give the reader a comprehensive representation of higher education developments in all of the GCC.

Just as our interest in the formation and organization of the American University of Sharjah led us to place this experience in a regional context, our study of educational reform in the GCC as a whole has forced us to consider the global context of higher educational transformation. While there are many distinctive features of GCC society that give the establishment of new universities and colleges in the region specific characteristics and problems, the same claim could be made for many other regions of the world that are creating new tertiary educational policies and institutions. The GCC shifts have clearly not taken place in a vacuum. What we observe in the region are not idiosyncratic expressions of exotic societies. For this reason, we decided to begin our book with a consideration of recent global trends in higher education.

It is our hope that this ambitious project allows scholars, educational policy-makers, and, indeed, the students who have experienced and are experiencing the new educational institutions being developed in the GCC an opportunity to reflect on and assess the transformed educational institutions of the region. When we began working in the American University of Sharjah, we did not realize that we would be part of an important historic movement to remake higher education in the Arabian Peninsula. The 17 years that now separate us from the launch of that ambitious initiative put us in a position to make a first comprehensive assessment of the revolutions in which we have participated.

Notes

1 During these 17 years, the AUS has undergone several changes to become one of the leading universities in the region. A major factor in its success should be attributed to its president and patron, the ruler of Sharjah, Dr. Sheikh Sultan bin Muhammad Al-Qasimi. An avid historian and playwright himself, he has given the AUS the space to grow to achieve his vision of developing higher education and culture in the region.
2 The university opened less than one year after construction began.
3 Badry arrived in January 1998 and was thus a pioneer. Willoughby arrived in fall 1998 and joined the second-year cohort of settlers.
4 During the first two years, faculty teaching English were more than 50 percent of all faculty.
5 In the aftermath of 9/11 some faculty became very apprehensive about living in an Arab country and abruptly resigned from their positions. American faculty felt generally uneasy in the classroom not knowing whether or not to discuss the issue with their Arab/Muslim students.

Acknowledgments

We would like to thank our families, colleagues and friends who supported us during the writing of this book. At times, it seemed like it would never get to a close! But here we are. We are indebted to many across the GCC who gave so much of their time to talk to us and answer our questions about their experiences as administrators or faculty in GCC higher education. In particular we thank, from the UAE, Dr. Amr Abdelhamid, special advisor on higher education to the ruler of Sharjah; former Zayed University provosts, Dr. Dan Johnson and Dr. Larry Wilson; Dean Dan Keating, NYIT Abu Dhabi campus; in Kuwait, President Dr. Nizar Hamzeh, Dean Rawda Awwad and Dr. Ralph Palliam from AUK and Dean Kassem Saleh from Kuwait University; Dr. Abdelatif Sellami from the Qatar Foundation and Dr. Rizwan Ahmad, chair, Department of English, QU. We would also like to acknowledge participants and organizers of two conferences on the global university at the AUS, in particular Professors Kevin Gray and Stephen Keck. The conferences brought together researchers from the Gulf to discuss the state of tertiary education in the region and were thus very stimulating. We would like to also acknowledge our indebtness to two leaders of the American University of Sharjah who are alas no longer with us. Dr. Samih Farsoun, the first dean of the College of Arts and Sciences, was instrumental in both of our joining the AUS, and the third chancellor of AUS, Dr. Peter Heath, wrote important essays on higher education in the region and was always willing to discuss these issues with us. We also recognize the first chancellor of the AUS, Dr. Roderick French, who has always supported us and who provided useful insights to an earlier manuscript on higher education in the GCC.

During a Fulbright grant during the Fall 2010 semester at Zayed University, John Willoughby had many discussions with several colleagues about the challenges of providing high quality education at Zayed University. Particular thanks to former Dean John Seybolt for his hospitality.

Many academics at American University provided support for this long-term and somewhat idiosyncratic (for an economist) research project. These include Professors Maria Floro, Tom Husted, Robert Feinberg, Alan Isaac, Mieke Meurs, Jim Mittelman, Brett Williams, and Jon Wisman. In addition, Professor U.J. Sofia, Associate Dean of the College of Arts and Sciences, helped John Willoughby attain important financial assistance for travel to the region. Mr.

Glen Arnold of the Department of Economics also provided important assistance in obtaining research funding at American University, Washington, DC. Academics and scholars from other institutions were also very helpful. In particular, Professor Julia Wrigley of the Graduate Center of the City University of New York introduced John Willoughby to important sociological literature on the globalization of education. The important historical perspective of Professor James Onley of Exeter University was also invaluable, as was the expertise of Professor Mary Ann Tetreault. Professors Jeanie Hofer, Greg Gelles and Benjamin L. Dow of the Missouri University for Sciences and Technology provided insights on building collaborative academic relations with universities in Oman and Kuwait and Dr. Imad Elhaj offered important information on higher education reforms in Kuwait.

Fatima Badry received an AUS faculty research grant that covered travel expenses and payments of research assistants to collect data. As a visiting scholar to Georgetown University and American University in Washington, DC during two consecutive summers, she was able to access invaluable library resources and benefit from interactions with faculty. Thank you all for your welcome and generosity. Many thanks to our graduate assistants, Elena Syzmanska-Saleem, Katherine Barrus and Sobia Afzal, for your hard work at AUS. In DC, three additional students provided important research assistance during this long project. Mr. Marwan Ayad and Mr. John Escobar did useful research on labor market conditions in the region, and Ms. Fatema Al Hashemi provided valuable assistance in sharpening our understanding of the contemporary history of higher education in Bahrain and Kuwait. Thank you all.

Finally, without the support of our families we could not have completed this project. John Willoughby's wife, Professor Mary Ann Fay of Morgan State University, provided him constant support and shared in the frustrations and senses of accomplishment associated with both building a new university and raising a family. Many of her ideas and insights about the GCC region and higher education are in this book.

Fatima Badry's husband, Iskandar Zalami, shared his insight and was always ready to respond to non-stop questions about labor policies in the GCC. Daughters Dina and Rania were a continuous source of inspiration and during the writing of the book granddaughter Sophia came to this world and gave new meaning to life.

This book is dedicated to our families.

Every effort has been made to report publicly available data as accurately as possible. However, given the changing nature of everything in the region, some figures may no longer be accurate. We apologize for any unintended omissions or errors.

Abbreviations

AACSB	Association to Advance Collegiate Schools of Business
ABET	Accreditation Board for Engineering and Technology
ADEC	Abu Dhabi Educational Council
ADEE	Association for Dental Education in Europe
ADNOC	Abu Dhabi National Oil Company
ALC	Academic Leadership Council
APEX	Accelerated Program for Excellence
AUB	American University of Beirut
AUC	American University in Cairo
AUD	American University of Dubai
AUK	American University of Kuwait
AUM	American University of the Middle East
AUS	American University of Sharjah
BEC	Basic Education Curriculum
BIBF	Bankers Institute of Banking and Finance
CA	Classical Arabic
CAA	Commission for Academic Accreditation (UAE)
CHERS	Centre for Higher Education Research and Studies
CHES	Centre for Higher Education Statistics
CLIL	Content and Language Integrated Learning
DEC	Dubai Educational Council
DHC	Dubai Healthcare City
DIAC	Dubai International Academic City
DIFC	Dubai International Financial Center
DKV	Dubai Knowledge Village
EDC	Education Cluster
EIB	Emirates Industrial Bank
ESA	Educated Spoken Arabic
ESSEC	Ecole Superieure des Sciences Economiques and Commerciales
FNC	Federal National Council
GCC	Gulf Cooperation Council
GUST	Gulf University for Science and Technology
HBKU	Hammad Bin Khalifa University

HCT	Higher Colleges of Technology
HEI	Higher Education Institution
HERU	Higher Education Review Unit
ICT	Information and Communication Technologies
IGOs	International Governmental Organizations
INQAAHE	International Network for Quality Assurance Agencies in Higher Education
JAB	Joint Advisory Board
KACST	King Abdulaziz City for Science and Technology
KASP	King Abdullah Scholarship Program
KAUST	King Abdullah University of Science and Technology
KFUPM	King Fahd University for Petroleum and Minerals
KHDA	Knowledge and Human Development Authority
KSA	Kingdom of Saudi Arabia
KU	Kuwait University
KUSTAR	Khalifa University of Science, Technology and Research
LAU	Lebanese American University
MIST	Masdar Institute of Science and Technology
MIT	Massachusetts Institute of Technology
MoHE	Ministry of Higher Education
MOOCS	Massive Open Online Courses
MSA	Modern Standard Arabic
MSCHE	Middle States Commission on Higher Education
NCAAA	National Commission for Assessment and Accreditation
NCAHE	National Centre for Assessment in Higher Education
NERI	The National Education Review Initiative
NES	National Economic Strategy
NGOs	Non Governmental Agencies
NYU	New York University
NZTEC	New Zealand Tertiary Education Consortium
OAAA	Oman Academic Accreditation Authority
OECD	Organization for Economic Co-operation and Development
PAAET	The Public Authority for Applied Education and Training
PI	The Petroleum Institute
PISA	Program for International Student Assessment
PNU	Princess Nora University
PPPM	Policy, Planning and Performance Management
PSUAD	Paris-Sorbonne University at Abu Dhabi
PUC	Private University Council
QAAET	Quality Assurance Authority for Education and Training
QFIS	Qatar Faculty of Islamic Studies
QU	Qatar University
RCSI	The Royal College of Surgeons in Ireland
RQPI	RAND–Qatar Policy Institute
SACS	Southern Association of Colleges and Schools

SEC	Supreme Educational Council
SFS-Q	School of Foreign Service in Qatar
SQU	Sultan Qaboos University
SRC	Senior Reform Committee
STEM	ScienceTechnology, Engineering and Mathematics
TIEC	Texas International Education Consortium
TIMMS	Trends in International Mathematics and Science Study
UAEU	United Arab Emirates University
UM5A-AD	University Mohammed V-Agdal Abu Dhabi
UMSL	University of Missouri-St. Louis
UNDP	United Nations Development Programme
UoB	University of Bahrain
UOJ	University of Jazeera
UoS	University of Sharjah
UOWD	University of Wollongong Dubai
UQAIB	University Quality Assurance International Board
WCMCQ	Weill-Cornell Medical College-Qatar
ZU	Zayed University

1 Introduction

The political and socio-economic emergence of the Arabian Gulf

The present-day Arabian Gulf states of Bahrain, Kuwait, Oman, Qatar and the United Arab Emirates (UAE) share a common history, geography, social structure, culture and language. The peoples of the region were among the first to embrace Islam, and this religion continues to play a major role in shaping the practices and evolution of Gulf societies. In addition, the region is subject to similar environmental conditions of little rain and extreme summer heat. This has meant that, with the exception of parts of Oman, most of the Arabian Gulf region does not have a history of pre-capitalist settled agricultural production. Instead, many of the Gulf peoples were semi-nomadic herders, pearl divers and traders organized around different tribal groups. In addition, small trading centers on the Gulf and Indian Ocean played an important role in organizing pre-modern oceanic trade between Persia, South Asia, East Africa and the Arab world. Finally, the annual Haj pilgrimage meant that a relatively large number of religious pilgrims regularly passed through the region. Despite this openness to trade and the movements of people, unfavorable climatic conditions meant that this region remained very poor and lacked much of the physical and social infrastructure that could promote development.

The poverty of the Arabian Gulf territories was further exacerbated by the period of European imperial domination. With the important exceptions of what is now Saudi Arabia and Oman, representatives of the British Empire forged a series of treaties with the ancestors of the contemporary ruling families of the region. In return for the acceptance of British hegemony in the Gulf, the British rulers recognized the authority of these tribal leaders. The result was the increased political and economic isolation of the Arabian Gulf region. For much of British imperial rule, the present-day Gulf Cooperation Council (GCC) states or "trucial states" were overseen by the colonial government of India.

The advent of oil production, the rise of Arab nationalism and the decline of British influence have led to profound economic, social and political transformations in the last 65 years. Living standards improved at an unprecedented rate, as revenues from oil exports funded the construction and maintenance of an impressively modern physical infrastructure. This led to the importation of vast numbers of skilled and unskilled expatriate labor from the rest of the Arab world, Asia and, to a lesser extent, Europe and North America. In addition, all of the

DOI: 10.4324/9780203796139-1

Arabian Gulf states attained independence and established a unique form of absolutist monarchical governments that maintained their power and popular legitimacy through aggressive development programs and the distribution of oil rents to their tribal/national constituencies.

The GCC region is the wealthiest region in the Arab world and enjoys some of the highest per capita GDPs worldwide. Its wealth is tied to its oil and gas natural resources, although some regions such as the Emirate of Dubai have succeeded in diversifying their economy as their oil resources started to dwindle. Although oil exploration and exploitation began in the early twentieth century, most of the benefits went to British and American oil companies. It was not until the 1970s that the Gulf states began to reap the benefits from their oil wealth, which by the early 1990s became under total state control (Metz, 1993). Today, the economies of the six member states of the GCC are heavily reliant on the hydrocarbons industry. Oil and gas exports account for a large proportion of total exports in all of the GCC states and play an even more crucial role in financing government activity (see Table 1.1).[1]

The nations of the Arabian Gulf that evolved from this process are not identical. A key factor differentiating the countries from each other is their degree of wealth. Qatar, Kuwait and the UAE (especially the Emirate of Abu Dhabi) have very high per capita incomes, while Bahrain and Oman are poorer. Because of these important economic differences, Bahrain and Oman are somewhat less dependent on expatriate labor and have relatively more nationals working in less remunerative jobs in the private sector (see Table 1.2).

Until the early 1980s, Arabs outside the Arabian Peninsula held a stereotypical view of Gulf Arabs as nomads living a life of camel herding and pearl diving in tribal sheikhdoms under harsh desert conditions. The centers of the Arab world were cities such as Algiers, Baghdad, Beirut, Damascus, Cairo, Casablanca or Tunis that stood for the image of modernity in the Arab world. Oil wealth in the Gulf region changed all that. Today, cities such as Dubai or Doha represent the image of what Arabs could achieve if they could only get their house in order. Dubai holds world records for the tallest buildings, largest

Table 1.1 Economic indicators of the GCC (2010)

Country	GDP per capita (PPP, US dollars)	Export revenue of oil and gas as % of total export revenue	Revenue from oil and gas exports as % of total government revenue
Bahrain	23,101	72.3	69.0
Kuwait	41,240	81.7	86.2
Oman	22,390	86.1	65.6
Qatar	136,248	64.7	74.8
Saudi Arabia	20,189	81.8	83.1
United Arab Emirates	60,175	80.6	30.5

Source: Cherif and Hasanov (2014: 45).

Table 1.2 GCC demographic composition

Country	Total population	Nationals	Non-national	% of population under 25*
Saudi Arabia (2013)	29,994,272	20,271,058 (68%)	9,723,214 (32%)	51
UAE (2010 estimate)	8,264,070	947,997 (17%)	7,316,073 (83%)	31
Kuwait (2012 estimate)	3,268,431	1,128,381 (34%)	2,140,050 (65%)	38
Oman (2010)	2,803,000	1,785,304 (64%)	1,128,381 (36%)	52
Qatar (2014)	2,269,672	278,000 (12%)	1,828,983 (88%)	34
Bahrain (Census 2010)	1,234,571	568,399 (46%)	666,172 (54%)	44

Sources: for Saudi Arabia: Saudi Arabia Population 2014 – *World Population Review*, worldpopulationreview.com/countries/saudi-arabia-population (accessed March 31, 2014) and Cental Department of Statistics and Information, www.cdsi.gov.sa/english/. For the UAE, National Bureau of Statistics, Uaestatistics.gov.ae.www.uaestatistics.gov.ae/ReportPDF/Population%20Estimates%202006%20-%202010.pdf and www.escwa.un.org/popin/members/uae.pdf. For Kuwait, *World Population Review*. For Oman, *Oman Times of Oman*, April 22, 2014, www.escwa.un.org/popin/members/oman.pdf. For Qatar, Ministry of Development and Statistics, qsa.gov.qa. For Bahrain, www.cio.gov.bh/CIO_ARA/English/Publications/Census/2011%2009%2018%20English%20Census%202010%20Summary%20%20Results%20-%20Review%201.pdf.www.cio.gov.bh/CIO_ARA/English/Publications/Census/2011 09 18 Final English Census 2010 Summary Results – Review 1.pdf.

firework displays, biggest screen and busiest airport in the world. It has won the right to host the World Expo in 2020 and Doha, Qatar will host the World Cup in 2022. The UAE, Qatar and Kuwait, are at the forefront of providing financial help to their poorer, less fortunate "Arab brothers" and in so doing yielding tremendous influence on the politically aware Arab scene, despite their relatively small populations.

The tribal groupings have become modern nations and their cities are "world hubs for transnational flows of people, goods, and capital." The new political entities of the Gulf are "each carved out of shared tribal territory and identical histories" (Cooke, 2014: 5) that are gradually being differentiated by the adoption of national symbols taken from the common past (an oryx, a pearl, a coffee pot, a dhow or an incense burner, or a falcon). In embracing modernity and globalization, the GCC states attempt to maintain their tribal heritage as part of their modern identity. The need to highlight their past signals their uniqueness and serves to assert their prestigious standing in societies where they have become minorities. As Cooke puts it, the return to tribal identity:

> signals racial privilege, social status, and exclusive entitlement to a share in national profits. Indeed, the rubbing up of the tribal against the modern in today's Gulf states does not represent a clash of conflicting values, but, rather, the desired effect of common aspirations.
>
> (Cooke, 2014: 10)

There are many ways that this return is accomplished through preserving the national dress for both women and men in public spaces, national museums and heritage villages, traditional sports, national celebrations with appeal to tribal ceremonies and symbols, to promoting local dialects. An iconic representation of this combination of the tribal and the modern is best captured in women's dress. Young Gulf women wearing the latest Western designer fashions being revealed under the "Sheela" (long, black, cape-like traditional dress) with the latest makeup, and luxury brand accessories. While some have interpreted these combinations in dichotomies as engendering some sort of "cognitive dissonance" young women see their behaviors as a marriage of the two worlds they are part of. A Saudi writer aptly captures this convergence when she says "where the old world and the new are tight as two lovers" (Alim, 2007: 217, as cited in Cooke, 2014).

The birth of the GCC and the contemporary challenges facing the region

The Cooperation Council for the Arab States of the Gulf, generally referred to as the Gulf Cooperation Council (GCC), was established in 1981 as a regional intergovernmental union. Its members are the Kingdom of Bahrain, the Kingdom of Saudi Arabia, the Sultanate of Oman, the United Arab Emirates (UAE), the State of Kuwait and the Emirate of Qatar. They are all located on the Arab side of the Arabian/Persian Gulf. The council was formed in reaction to the Iranian Revolution and aimed to establish institutions that would facilitate cooperation between its members in political, military, economic and social domains. Its ultimate goal was to unify member states' economic, monetary, commercial and financial policies. The GCC has accomplished some of its goals, as there are no custom duties among GCC states, citizens do not need a passport to travel across state boundaries and GCC businesses enjoy equity investments and have special access to all GCC ports (Metz, 1993). The monetary union, however, has proved more difficult and has been put on hold. Politically, the GCC members are not always in agreement, as witnessed by the 2014 rift between Qatar and the rest of the GCC members in response to political events in Egypt.

Due to its strategic location and oil wealth, US interests in the region have intensified sometimes at the expense of the United Kingdom. The Palestinian–Israeli conflict, the Iranian Revolution, the Iraqi invasion of Kuwait and subsequent Gulf Wars, the 9/11 attacks and the resulting US-led Afghanistan and Iraq wars have all impacted the GCC (Peterson, 2014). In addition, the events surrounding the Arab Spring led to mass protests in Bahrain, which awakened and intensified sectarian strife. Oman also experienced smaller protests, and most of the GCC governments responded to these political challenges by increasing social benefits while cracking down on some dissident groupings. Finally the failures of the 2011 Arab Spring uprisings against the autocratic and authoritarian regimes in the rest of the Middle East and North Africa region have further unsettled the Arabian Gulf and led the surviving regimes to find ways to tighten their grips on power even more. In particular, the collapse of state authority in much of Syria and the Arab Sunni regions of Iraq have allowed xenophobic "Islamist" movements to establish a presence that clearly threatens Gulf rulers' efforts to intensify liberal political economic intercourse with the world economy while maintaining the region's distinct political and cultural practices.

Despite these shocks, there is reason to believe that the monarchies of the region will maintain their authority. Bank *et al.* (2014) discuss four major factors which may explain the longevity of the monarchies in the Arabian Peninsula. These include external political and military support from Western powers, mainly the United States, the United Kingdom and France; the oil wealth that allows the rulers to perpetuate a rentier economy by distributing rents to privileged groups/tribes and ensuring their continued loyalty; the inclusion of family and elite tribal members in their cabinets (Shoura system); and the reliance on religion and other tribal traditions to maintain legitimacy.

A key factor promoting the stability of the region is that oil wealth continues to improve material living standards, health and educational outcomes. The United Nations Development Program (UNDP) reports that all but one of the GCC countries are classified in the highest category of human development, and the exception, Oman, has experienced one of the most rapid improvements in material living standards, health and education in the world. One further indication of the dramatic social transformations of the region has been sharp changes in demographic behavior. In the mid-1980s, a large number of adolescent women were bearing children. By 2013, the proportion of young mothers between the ages of 16 and 19 had dropped sharply. The shrinkage in the rate of adolescent pregnancy is especially dramatic for Oman, the UAE and Saudi Arabia (see Table 3.1). This means that the youth bulge which is presently a feature of many of GCC societies will eventually recede. Although more than 50 percent of the population of Oman and Saudi Arabia is under 25, and the figures for the other GCC countries are in the 30 percent range, most of the data indicate a rise in the marriage age for women and a fall in family size. Present trends indicate that the GCC family will look more like the small nuclear families of advanced capitalist societies in the next generations.

A major demographic challenge facing all countries of the GCC is the continued reliance on expatriate labor. Indeed, the decade of relatively high oil prices that has just come to an end (2005–14) increased most of the GCC's reliance on expatriate labor. In other words, what was supposed to be a temporary measure to promote development has become a quasi-permanent feature of the GCC. Moreover, the extensive use of foreign labor has tended to "de-Arabize" much of the region, since the relative number of South Asian workers (as opposed to workers from other parts of the Arab world) has steadily increased. Tens of thousands of professional expatriate families now call the GCC their home. They have formed families, raised children, and seen their adult children now work and form families of their own in the region. Thus, the GCC countries are increasingly diverse, but remain highly segmented. Only national citizens can gain direct access to the revenues from oil and petroleum exports through state welfare programs and government employment, although the incomes of the whole region remain dependent on these essential energy exports. As we shall see, this dual reliance on exports from a very narrow set of petroleum-based commodities and "temporary" migrant labor has unleashed political and social anxieties that are very important to our understanding of the transformation of higher education in the region. A Booz & Co. report which is based on the Arab organization of labor reveals that in 2007, the GCC countries still relied heavily on foreigners despite attempts to nationalize the workforce. Figures of this dependence vary depending on the source consulted and the year but they remain very high, ranging from 91.6 percent in the UAE, 82.2 percent in Kuwait,

Table 1.3 Changes in the rate of adolescent pregnancy (number of births to women aged 15–19 per 1,000)

Country	1985	2000	2010
Bahrain	51.6	18.3	14.7
Kuwait	67.6	26.6	15.1
Oman	117.2	43.5	13.6
Qatar	71.5	22.8	15.1
UAE	116.8	27.6	29.9
Saudi Arabia	118.1	37.3	11.6

Source: UNDP (2014).

75.8 percent in Bahrain, 74.5 per cent in Oman and 62.3 percent in Qatar (Al Munajjed and Sabbagh, 2011). By 2014, and despite all the efforts of nationalization of the workforce, dependence on expatriates shows no sign of weakening.

The evolution of education

The transformation in the region is especially evident in the spheres of education. Bahrain, Kuwait and Qatar attained near universal attendance of children in primary and secondary education by 1985, while Oman and the United Arab Emirates made rapid progress to reach this benchmark by 2013. In Oman today the expected years of formal education is 13.6 years and literacy rates are between 80 and 95 percent. In the UAE, literacy rates are around 90 percent.

Most GCC states had to develop their educational system from elementary to university in the last 40 years. Before independence there were hardly any schools in the GCC. The very few schools that existed in Bahrain and Kuwait were focused on Islamic education. By the 1970s early educational systems were focused on eradicating illiteracy and spreading basic education to reach all citizens with the help of teachers and administrators from Iraq, Lebanon, Syria, Palestine, Jordan and Egypt (see Table 1.4).

In the last four decades more attention has been given to the quality of education and the establishment of the first national universities. By the beginning of the millennium all states emphasized the role of education in meeting the challenges of the twenty-first century and helping them to become knowledge societies. GCC governments launched their first national universities modeled on other Arab universities and staffed by Arab academics that were open to their citizens only. The end of the twentieth century witnessed mounting criticisms of the "Arab university" as being unable to produce graduates equipped with the twenty-first century skills required by the labor market.

Analyzing the higher education transformations of the GCC

Because the small GCC states supply crucial energy commodities to the world economy, are highly open to trade, investment and labor flows, have unusual royalist political systems, and appear to maintain distinct practices, there is a

Table 1.4 Educational attainment in the GCC: expected years of schooling

Country	1985	2000	2013
Bahrain	13.0	13.6	14.4
Kuwait	12.2	15.5	14.6
Oman	5.9	10.9	13.6
Qatar	12.5	12.6	13.8
UAE	9.8	12.0	13.3

Source: UNDP (2014).

tendency to view the region as an idiosyncratic world unto itself. We argue, on the contrary, that Gulf society should be interpreted through a comparative framework that links the socio-political practices to that of the rest of the world. Most of our analysis focuses on the small states of the GCC (Bahrain, Kuwait, Oman, Qatar and the UAE), although we do include a chapter on Saudi Arabia contributed by Professor Amani Hamdan. In some chapters, we tend to pay somewhat more attention to developments in the United Arab Emirates. This is necessary for several reasons. First, the higher education reform efforts largely began in Dubai and Sharjah. Second, university and college enrollments have grown most rapidly in the UAE. Third, the different emirates of the UAE have engaged in a great variety of experiments that are part of all the models of educational reform that we explain and analyze. And finally, the availability of data on higher education released by the private and public institutions of the UAE allow us to develop a more complete and accurate assessment of the higher education reform process for the whole region.

We begin our study of the dramatic transformations in GCC higher education by placing these developments in the broader context of global educational trends. Chapter 2 documents the rapid quantitative expansion of higher education throughout the globe and notes that an increasingly large proportion of college students receive their education outside of the advanced capitalist world. There is no reason to think that this growth will slacken. We show that there is a consensus amongst policy-makers that a dynamic and good society requires a robust tertiary education system. We conclude Chapter 2 by exploring the different economic, sociological and political perspectives that explain why national commitments to higher education are so strong and uniform. This analysis alerts us to the reality that higher education reform takes place on a contested terrain, since different stakeholders place contradictory demands on their national universities and colleges.

Chapter 3 continues our comparative framework by examining the process of educational globalization. In the first part of this chapter, we define the quantitative and qualitative aspects of globalization. This analysis leads us to highlight the crucial importance that educational developments in Asia play in intensifying the influence of Western academic institutions. The second part of this chapter applies this analysis to the GCC. We show that the higher education systems of the Arabian Gulf are unusually extraverted. Large numbers of students travel across borders to earn their academic degrees, and the nations (and emirates) of the GCC have aggressively adopted many of the educational policies and practices of Western universities and colleges.

In Chapter 4 we argue that this drive to adopt American and British academic practices lies behind the extraordinary expansion in the numbers of private and semi-private universities and colleges over the past two decades. In this chapter, we provide a comprehensive country-by-country survey of the emergence of the non-state educational sector. (In the case of the United Arab Emirates, this analysis is done on an emirate-by-emirate basis.) This historical review allows us to identify distinct models of educational transformation. We demonstrate that while the drive to restructure and privatize parts of higher education is common to the whole GCC, the results are regionally distinct because of the distinct regulatory choices that national and emirate ruling authorities have made.

Chapter 5 chronicles the birth of public higher education institutions in the GCC and provides a general overview of the major GCC national universities. The purpose of the chapter is to analyze the impact of the reforms that public universities and colleges have undergone in the last decades to assess their potential for achieving stated national visions. The assessment reveals that national universities' reforms share several characteristics. Most GCC public institutions have attempted to follow an American model of higher education from its structure to its curricula and language without aligning themselves with secondary education outcomes. They have relied on foreign experts to plan, implement and assess the reforms and set utilitarian goals based on a human capital approach to education that emphasizes professional education. The top-down approach to education reform is based on short-term politico-economic considerations that have in fact resulted in universities as teaching institutions rather than centers of research, thus falling short of the nations' visions to transform themselves into leaders among the advanced knowledge societies.

In Chapter 6 we continue our analysis of the quality of higher education in the GCC by highlighting the issues of accreditation and regulation. We argue through the use of institutionalist economic reasoning that the establishment of a competitive system of private higher education institutions requires the creation of robust, governmental regulatory practices. With the exception of those GCC states that have encouraged the importation of "turnkey" branch campuses, the governments of the region have implemented their accreditation and supervisory institutions by adopting Western standards of higher education regulation. We demonstrate that almost every state has created an intensive accreditation process that involves institutional self-studies and site visits and reports by outside experts. In Bahrain and Oman, these assessment documents are publicly available, and this has allowed us to offer a preliminary evaluation of the higher education quality. We are able to examine issues related to governance, faculty working conditions, and student preparation. We find that the quality of some of the smaller colleges that focus on providing business and information technology degrees is often low. On the other hand, those institutions that make a serious commitment to establishing multi-disciplinary liberal arts education are more likely to be successful.

In Chapter 7, our guest author, Dr. Amani K. Hamdan, describes the exceptional growth of higher education in Saudi Arabia during the last decade. She discusses the achievements, challenges and opportunities inherent in a booming higher education sector, with emphasis on analyzing the viability and alignment of recent educational reforms with national goals (be they economic, socio-cultural or linguistic development). Many of Dr. Hamdan's arguments and criticisms parallel our own; the higher educational challenges the Kingdom of Saudi Arabia (KSA) faces are similar to those we have outlined in our analysis of the other GCC states. On the other hand, the Saudi experience is institutionally distinct. We cannot assume that the educational advances and setbacks we observe in the smaller GCC states will be associated with similar developments in Saudi Arabia.

In Chapter 8, we address the reasons behind the low status of Modern Standard Arabic (MSA) in education and its declining use among millennials for academic purposes and in written communication. The chapter analyzes linguistic, socio-economic and globalization factors interfering with the promotion of MSA as the medium of knowledge production despite numerous policy decisions and official statements affirming that Arabic is a central component of national and Pan-Arab identity. We argue that efforts to improve Arabic literacy development in MSA must recognize and deal with the diglossic feature of Arabic and associated attitudes, unify its language planning efforts, modernize its teaching methodologies based on the specific typology of the language and its writing system and aim for a balanced dual language policy that places equal value on Arabic and English in society.

In our concluding chapter, we revisit the main question that led to the writing of this book: can the extensive educational reforms, by themselves, lead to the societal, economic and political transformations of the GCC countries to become leaders in the twenty-first century? There is no doubt that today's GCC educational systems have opened the doors to education for many groups in the GCC societies that otherwise would have had limited access to higher education (e.g., women and resident expatriates). In addition, the introduction of private institutions has forced public institutions to become more accountable in order to remain competitive in a rapidly changing environment. At the same time, the nature of the reforms adopted raises important questions as to whether they can achieve the goals stated in the GCC countries' visions of the future, namely in terms of their ambition to become leaders in the knowledge economy, their claim to be at the vanguard of protecting and developing the Arabic language and their desire to preserve their Arab traditions and cultural identity. Based on our analysis of the reforms, we argue that the Western-directed reforms rest on assumptions that limit their capacity to achieve their expected long-term goals because these substantial changes in higher education are not grounded in their local contexts and are not embedded in a comprehensive transformation of the socio-political environments in which they are implemented.

Note

1 The petroleum reserves of the six GCC member states were estimated by the US Department of Energy to be 500.5 billion barrels, or about 30 percent of the world's total reserves in 2010. These six nations also possessed 21 percent of the world's natural gas reserves (US Energy Information Agency, 2014). According to the *BP Statistical Review* (as cited by Cherif and Hasanov, 2014), the expected lifetime ranges from six years for Bahrain, to 63 years, 79 years and 89 years for Saudi Arabia, the United Arab Emirates and Kuwait, respectively (Cherif and Hasanov, 2014: 46). Other sources reported in Table 1.1 give slightly lower figures but within the same ranges.

References

Al Munajjed, M. and Sabbagh, K. (2011). *Youth in GCC Countries: Meeting the Challenge*. Booz & Co., Inc. Ideation Center Insight. Available at: www.youthpolicy.org/library/wp-content/uploads/library/2011_Youth_GCC_Countries_Meeting_Challenge_Eng.pdf (accessed May 27, 2015).

Bank, A., Richter, T. and Sunik, A. (2014). Durable, yet different: Monarchies in the Arab Spring. *Journal of Arabian Studies: Arabia, the Gulf, and the Red Sea*, 4(2): 163–179.

Cherif, R. and Hasanov, F. (2014). Soaring of the Gulf falcons: Diversification in the GCC oil exporters in seven propositions. IMF Working Paper 14/177. Available at: www.imf.org/external/pubs/ft/wp/2014/wp14177.pdf (accessed February 3, 2015).

Cooke, M. (2014). *Tribal Modern: Branding New Nations in the Arab Gulf*. Berkeley: University of California Press.

Metz, H.C. (ed.) (1993). *Persian Gulf States: A Country Study*. Washington, DC: GPO for the Library of Congress. Available at: http://countrystudies.us/persian-gulf-states/ (accessed February 3, 2015).

Peterson, J.E. (2014). The Arabian Peninsula in modern times: A historiographical survey of recent publications. *Journal of Arabian Studies: Arabia, the Gulf, and the Red Sea*, 4(2): 244–274.

United Nations Development Programme (2014). *Human Development Report 2014, Sustaining Human Progress: Reducing Vulnerabilities and Building Resilience*. New York: UNDP.

US Energy Information Agency (2014). *2010 World Proved Reserves*. Available at: www.eia.gov/countries/index.cfm?view=reserves (accessed February 3, 2015).

2 The global expansion of higher education

Alternative perspectives

The century-long expansion of higher education

Higher education is one of the most rapidly growing sectors of the world economy today. Between 1815 and the period shortly after World War I, there was very little growth in the number of young adults attending colleges or universities, but starting in the 1920s, the number of students began to expand at an intensifying rate in the advanced capitalist world. By 1940, there were approximately five million university students worldwide. By 1960, this number had doubled to ten million (Schofer and Meyer, 2005). Fifty years later, in 2010, more than 177 million students were attending colleges and universities in all of the world's regions (UNESCO Institute for Statistics, 2012: 228). This increase represents a 5.9 percent annual growth rate in enrollments. If this rate of growth continues, the tertiary education population of students will nearly double every 12 years. To highlight the extraordinary nature of the trend, Schofer and Meyer point out that, today, there are approximately as many students attending colleges and universities in Kazakhstan as there were in the entire globe a century ago (Schofer and Meyer, 2005: 3).

It is important to stress that nearly all regions of the world have been a part of this process. Western Europe, North America and Japan have the most tertiary students per capita – approximately 350 students per every 10,000 people – but Eastern Europe, after experiencing relatively slow growth in college education during the Communist period, has largely caught up to its Western neighbors. After the major OECD nations, Eastern Europe, the Arab world and Latin America have the highest share of college and university students in the total population. In addition, the student population of the East Asian and Pacific region is growing very rapidly. According to UNESCO, the student body in China has expanded by 19 percent per year during the first decade of this century. There are exceptions to these trends. India, Pakistan and Bangladesh's student bodies have grown more slowly, and sub-Saharan Africa has the lowest proportion of college students in its population, although growth is so rapid that UNESCO estimates that the number of students will double every 8.4 years (UNESCO Institute for Statistics, 2009).

This growth is associated with significant regional changes in the composition of the university student body. There has been a sharp rise in the share of students

DOI: 10.4324/9780203796139-2

Table 2.1 Share of students in tertiary education by region (1970–2007)

	1970	1980	1990	2000	2007
Sub-Saharan Africa	1	1	2	2	3
Arab states	2	3	4	6	5
South and Southwest Asia	10	8	9	12	12
East Asia and the Pacific	14	15	21	24	31
Latin America and Caribbean	6	10	11	11	12
Central Asia	3	3	2	2	2
Central and Eastern Europe	18	18	14	13	14
North America and Western Europe	48	42	37	29	23

Source: UNESCO Institute for Statistics (2009: 12).

outside the advanced capitalist world but what is particularly noteworthy is that the East Asian and Pacific region now have the largest number of college and university students in the world. The Arab world's share of students has increased from 3 to 5 percent, which in itself represents a significant increase for a region with a relatively small share of the world's population (see Table 2.1).

An examination of a country's level of development is equally revealing. College education is no longer limited to high income countries. Indeed, the fastest growth of students is in countries with lower middle income status. These regions of the world economy have, in general, experienced sharp rises in educational attainment at the primary and secondary level. Thus, it is not surprising that such changes have led to an explosion in the size of the tertiary student population. Having said this, there is little doubt that within each region under consideration, a disproportionate share of tertiary students comes from more privileged economic backgrounds. Thus, while global educational expansion suggests a certain levelling across nations, class divisions within societies are often widening (see Table 2.2).

Another way to consider the expansion of higher education is to consider enrollment rates. UNESCO uses the term gross enrollment rates to determine the proportion of university-age students in the total relevant age group. It is difficult to devise a precise measurement of enrollment rates from country to country, since the appropriate age range can differ from region to region, and students sometimes take multiple courses of study. Nevertheless, these tables show the

Table 2.2 Share of students in tertiary education by income status of country

	1970	1980	1990	2000	2007
Low income	4	4	4	5	6
Lower-middle income	22	24	29	35	42
Upper-middle income	17	22	21	21	22
High income	57	50	46	39	30

Source: UNESCO Institute for Statistics (2009: 13).

same trends we have already considered, while also revealing that the advanced capitalist world has a much higher share of young adults participating in tertiary education. The Arab world gross enrollment rate is slightly below the world average, even though the per-capita share of college students is somewhat higher. This is because of the much higher share of young adults in the total population of this region (see Table 2.3).

Finally, the other striking feature of the expansion of higher education is the increasing participation of women in most of the world's regions. Indeed, the faster college enrollment is growing, the more important is the rising share of female students. For example, the number of female and male students in colleges and universities in the Arab world is approximately equal, while in slower-growing areas such as India, there is still a significantly larger presence of male students in higher education institutions. For the world as a whole, 51 percent of all higher education students are women (UNESCO Institute for Statistics, 2010: 69). In 1970, female enrollment in colleges and universities was only 80 percent of male enrollment. In the Arab world, this was less than 40 percent (UNESCO Institute for Statistics, 2010: 69). Given the region's reputation as an area troubled by extreme forms of male domination, it is significant that women's participation in post-secondary education mirrors this global trend. This is especially true for the Gulf, often thought to be the most patriarchal sub-region of the most patriarchal region of the world. Higher education data, at least, should lead us to re-examine this stereotype.

Unless there is a sharp disruption in the trajectory of the world economy, it is reasonable to expect that this intensive growth in university education will continue. The poorer countries of the world lag significantly behind the richer countries when one examines the share of young adults who are attending post-secondary institutions. As income levels rise and perhaps begin to converge with those of the West, we can expect that student participation will rise as well. Moreover, more rapid population growth in most regions of the non-Western world (with the notable exception of China) should further fuel the growth of university education in lower middle income countries.

Table 2.3 Gross enrollment rates in tertiary education

	1970	*1980*	*1990*	*2000*	*2007*
North America and Western Europe	30	37	49	64	71
Central and Eastern Europe	–	–	–	41	62
Latin America and Caribbean	6	13	17	23	34
Central Asia	–	–	–	23	31
East Asia and Pacific	3	5	7	15	26
Arab states	–	–	–	20	23
South and West Asia	4	4	6	9	11
Sub-Saharan Africa	1	2	3	4	6
World	9	12	13	19	26

Source: UNESCO Institute for Statistics (2009: 14).

Different perspectives on the mission and purpose of higher education

The extraordinary growth in higher education everywhere in the world suggests that contemporary socio-economic evolution creates both an intensifying demand for higher education and pressures to create institutions that are roughly similar to universities and colleges in the advanced capitalist world. Most governments, international governmental organizations (IGOs) and non-governmental organizations (NGOs) view the establishment of a robust system of universities and colleges as an essential part of a credible economic development strategy. Today, increasing proportions of national adult populations groups subscribe to this approach and link their children's social and economic advance to receiving recognized higher education credentials. This near universal consensus on the value and importance of university training can best be understood by reviewing the social scientific literature on the roles of higher education in contemporary society.

There are four distinct arguments that we need to consider in order to obtain a full picture of the roles that higher education is hypothesized to play in today's society. The dominant claim is economic and bases itself on neoclassical economic growth theory. The second two are social and political and focus on the connection between higher education, the socio-economic integration of commercial societies and the imperatives of a capitalist world order. These three perspectives concentrate on different social processes, but taken together, provide a coherent analytic description of the assumed purposes of higher education and the reasons for both its stunning growth and the tendency for its institutions to converge. Finally, the fourth framework articulates a humanistic vision of higher education as a good in and of itself rather than as an instrument that facilitates the achievement of some other socio-economic goal. The argument that higher education has intrinsic value has ancient roots. It deserves consideration because the perspective has helped create an academic culture which, even if under attack, still plays an important role in guiding policy-makers and academic administrators.

Higher education as a producer of human capital and enhancer of economic growth: an economic perspective

In today's supra-territorial/global world, higher education reforms are subject to different and sometimes conflicting pressures. These pressures are both global and local but are all aimed at improving university graduates' chances of "successful participation in a global knowledge-based economy" (Rhoads and Liu, 2009: 272) and empowering them to contribute to their nation's development (Farag, 2010; Hennock, 2010). The assumption that education is the motor of economic and social development is generally taken for granted by development experts as well as by lay persons (Farrell and Fenwick, 2007; Olssen and Peters, 2005; Zaher, 2009). International government organizations (IGOs), such as the

Organization for Economic Cooperation and Development (OECD), the United States Agency for International Development (USAID), the World Bank (WB), and high-profile think-tanks such as the RAND Corporation play an important role in setting education agendas at national levels and "have become policy activists in their own right" (Rawolle and Lingard, 2008: 736). For example, the OECD's PISA tests have become an internationally accepted standard in assessing educational outcomes. As Spring (2009: 57) points out, "by becoming an international standard, PISA has the direct potential for determining the curriculum content in the areas tested." Another OECD goal is to develop a world culture of education by encouraging sharing of ideas on all matters relating to education from building designs, to research and policy. The influence of IGOs is felt worldwide. Even for high income countries such as those in the Arabian Gulf that do not need international financial aid, the "World Bank's comparative advantage as both a knowledge broker and an observer of international experience" remains influential (Salmi, 2009: 68).

Underlying the focus on education as a motor of development, is human capital theory and neo-liberal policy. This framework posits a strong correlation between education and development (Fagerlind and Saha, 1989; Farrell and Fenwick, 2007; Mazawi, 2007). Human capital theory emerged as a dominant paradigm in development studies in the second half of the twentieth century, partly through the work of Nobel prize laureate economists Theodore Schultz (1961) and Gary Becker (1964). Schultz states the case most dramatically when he concludes one of his most famous articles with the statement: "Truly, the most distinctive feature of our economic system is the growth in human capital. Without it, there would only be hard manual work and poverty except for those who have income from property" (Schultz, 1961: 17).[1]

The economic growth and progress made by the "emergent" countries of East Asia are often cited as evidence to validate the link between investing in education, human labor productivity and development. As a result of this widespread belief that investing in education is like investing in the creation of technologically sophisticated capital goods, developing countries have been allocating significant percentages of their budget to improve both the quantity and quality of their educational systems. The argument is that the benefits of education influence both individuals and their societies. At the individual level, education offers several advantages, including better employment opportunities, social mobility and knowledge acquisition, which ultimately lead to economic gains. At the level of society, education helps in generating new ideas and technologies necessary for progress, encouraging research and development, and creating new products.

It is important to realize that this view of higher education as a promoter of rapid economic growth and social advancement is relatively new. The link between formal higher education and rapid economic growth was not always obvious. It can be traced back to the aftermath of World War II and the Cold War period when the importance of developing scientific–military–industrial complexes that relied heavily on highly educated scientific and technical workers was clear to nearly everybody. If anything, the link between economic dynamism and higher education in the early twenty-first century has intensified. Production and innovation centers in Silicon Valley or Bangalore, India depend on a steady stream of academically trained, technologically savvy workers – even if some of the important founding entrepreneurs of software or social media companies dropped out of college.

It is also important to point out that the pressures of economic globalization have intersected with human capital theory, leading to calls for the development and reform of higher education worldwide. The reality of intensified international competition and the need to keep up with and develop new technologies have led many commentators to support the development of a modernized higher educational system that can produce creative workers. Without this capability, policy-makers fear that countries or whole regions will fail to adapt to technological imperatives and become economically irrelevant. We witness this anxiety everywhere, from the politically fraught efforts to reform education in the United States to critics of Arab societies who also focus on real and alleged failures in the delivery of education. This is one reason why the first Arab Human Development Reports stressed the need to improve the education system in general and the higher educational system in particular in order to create a dynamic knowledge economy (United Nations Development Programme, 2002).

Is this consensus about the economic importance of higher education well-founded? As our earlier empirical review of the growth of college and university enrollments indicated, the expansion of economic activity and education attainment are closely connected to each other. College graduates consistently earn a wage premium over workers who stopped formal education after primary or secondary school. The most recent comprehensive study of this issue argues that individuals who receive a college degree get a higher return on their or their families' investment than college graduates of earlier generations. This does not mean that all regions of the world get benefits from educational attainment in the same way. This same comprehensive study provides evidence that suggest that countries which rely on natural resource exports receive a smaller economic return from educational investments than equivalent investments in other countries (Psacharopoulos and Patrinos, 2010: 112). The Middle East and North Africa region, for example, experiences the lowest rate of return for educational investments in the globe.[2]

With respect to promoting economic growth, universities are also often associated with stimulating the agglomeration of scientific and technical workers who cluster in those regions where economic innovation is most dynamic. These empirical observations, however, do not necessarily prove the validity of the specific claims of human capital theory. This is because the actual direction of causation is not clear. Is higher education improving the prospects for growth or is growth causing the expansion of higher education?

A further ambiguity in human capital theory is that the actual higher education systems we observe are normally not structured to maximize economic growth. One common finding in the economic development literature, for example, is that many societies systematically under-invest in primary education and over-invest in the tertiary sector. An efficient allocation of investment funds across educational levels should lead to an equal social rate of return across all sectors (primary, secondary and tertiary).[3] Economists measure rates of return by estimating the increases in income generated by educating future workers with respect to the public and private costs associated with creating and maintaining these educational institutions (Psacharopolous and Patrinos, 2010).

As we pointed out earlier in this chapter, increases in income can accrue to those who receive the education and to those who receive higher incomes as a result of the presence of more highly educated and productive workers. Thus, it is by no means easy to determine the correct level of net benefits caused by investments in education. Nevertheless, most studies of returns from education have reached similar conclusions. Primary education normally generates the highest rate of return, followed by secondary education, which is, in turn, followed by tertiary education. This implies that there is a stronger case for the public funding of basic education of children than there is for the more advanced education of young adults, and that there is a bias in favor of the professional-managerial class when governments allocate educational expenses.[4] It is important to note that this analysis does not necessarily imply that public funding for tertiary education should be cut. On the other hand, it does suggest that the expansion of this type of funding should be associated with an even greater commitment to the financial support of elementary and high schools.

An additional resource allocation issue concerns the choice of degrees by university students. A common complaint throughout the world is that too many students choose liberal arts majors rather than specializing in STEM (Science, Technology, Engineering and Mathematics) degrees. One might expect that the problem of students choosing the "wrong" degree concentration would correct itself over time. The higher incomes offered by technical occupations would overcome students' desires to take less mathematically demanding subjects. In reality, this adjustment to market signals seems to be glacial. In the first place, many entry-level college students might be unable to major in applied scientific subjects because of inadequate primary and secondary education or a personal disinclination to study mathematics and science.[5] In the second place, the flow of professional workers across national borders can make it less urgent to train indigenous scientific personnel. High income societies can recruit talented workers from other parts of the world to fill skill gaps, and immigration policy is often structured to encourage the recruitment of such workers from the developing world (Cervantes and Guelleo, 2014). Even if local workers are available in higher income countries, the opportunity to hire workers more willing to accept a lower salary is a further impediment to the sort of domestic market-based adjustment we have discussed.

This problem can lead to a global under-investment in scientific training within higher education institutions, since poor countries can lose their most talented students to rich societies, and rich governments can put less funding into the scientific training of their best and brightest. Unless there are countervailing factors, economic globalization might not lead to an optimally constructed higher education system.

This critique implies that the actual ways in which higher education is expanding are not completely explained by the requirements for skilled technical workers suggested by human capital theory. Given well-documented employment problems in the labor market for college-educated workers in many different countries, it seems likely that universities and colleges are both more and less than institutions that promote the effective expansion of value or the accumulation of capital. They are less than servants promoting the maximization of economic growth because national education policies and universities do not always produce workers in the "correct" mix of skills. They are more than pro-growth capitalist institutions because the purposes of the university cannot be limited to the promotion of economic growth. As economist Nicholas Barr notes, one key problem associated with human capital theory is that we still are unable to measure what good higher education is (Barr, 2008). While human capital theory contains important insights, we clearly need to go beyond economic theory to understand higher education's actual purposes in contemporary society.

Higher education and the construction of the meritocratic nation: a sociological perspective

The last section suggests that human capital theory has an important but limited ability to explain the expansion of the university system. While there is undoubtedly a strong case to be made for specialized training in order to promote economic development and while one can also draw on standard economic theory to explain why the state must be involved in organizing and promoting such training, it does not follow that the university system we observe today efficiently produces the trained workers that a modern economy needs (Meyer *et al.*, 2006). To be more precise, human capital theory does not seem to have an explanation for the mismatch between the occupations available and graduate qualifications that universities regularly produce throughout the world.

One can go back to the beginning of the university system to note that the initial purpose of the University of Al-Karaouine in Morocco or Al Azhar University in Egypt or the University of Bologna, the first medieval university of Europe, was to train clerics, theologians and legal scholars (CollegeStats.org., 2009). While this imperative had little to do with developing new productive technologies, it had much to do with promoting social and political integration. Spreading the same belief systems and state-sponsored legal system throughout a political entity can create greater cultural unity and thus had clear political utility for political leaders who wished to consolidate a region under their rule. Moreover, training highly educated workers who would be able to interpret and implement a unified legal system could facilitate the expansion of commercial activity and allow some talented students from humble backgrounds to enter into the elite. Thus, even the non-scientific universities of this pre-modern period could promote economic growth by facilitating the expansion of trade.

The mission of the university evolved with the emergence of more secular states during the late nineteenth and early twentieth centuries, which, based on the "imagined community" of the nation, stimulated an expansive phase of higher education formation (Anderson, 1983). Universities began to slowly distance themselves from their religious foundations, but not their legalistic origins. They became locations where professionals like lawyers, doctors, business people, scientists and engineers could be trained to build the modern nation and economy. This transformation in the university's mission meant that relying on aristocratic and mercantile elites became less and less viable. Modern nation-state building required the creation of a meritocratic society of a greater number of qualified professionals who could both organize increasingly complex production and distribution systems and use rationalist techniques to mediate conflict and legitimate new social practices.

Increasing numbers of individuals who did not have the social legitimacy of nobility needed to communicate and cooperate with each other. They needed to be accredited as worthy members of an educated elite, and universities were uniquely placed to provide this service. Accrediting a graduate's understanding of rationalist methods of inquiry and certifying the acquisition of particular skills is not just important for internal national development, but the construction of the international economy as well. Higher education both responds to populist demands for social mobility within the nation and global demands for the creation of knowledgeable workers who can communicate effectively with similarly trained workers. Thus, higher education promotes both national integration and the integration of the nation with its international surroundings even if the skill sets produced by this education do not optimize economic growth.

It is important to note that this analysis suggests that university formation is a transnational process. Although the oldest universities in the world began in the Arab world and Iran, modern, secular universities first emerged in Europe and North America, then spread to other outposts of the advanced capitalist world, such as Japan, then moved onto the colonized and semi-colonized periphery, to become a truly global phenomenon in our "post-modern," globalized world. The nation-building process did not produce unique higher educational systems, but rather ones that are surprisingly similar or isomorphic. "Clearly there are world-wide models for higher education, and these models render higher education as essential to the successful nation-state. And in fact higher education spreads in rather standardized forms where the nation-state system spreads" (Meyer *et al.*, 2006: 15).

The attraction of this perspective is that the decision to develop higher education institutions by the state or elites and the decision by individual families to send their sons and daughters to tertiary educational institutions are not just a product of economic calculations. Obtaining a university education comes to be associated with social legitimation, prestige and the projection of individual power. For parents and students, successfully completing a degree signals that the graduated student can use high-level symbolic discourse to make their way in the professional world. For a government, sponsoring the formation of internationally recognized educational institutions within one's territory signals to the global community that the nation or region is able to participate successfully in the global economy. For elites, sponsoring a prestigious university confirms one's position in society today and associates one's name with future generations of successful professionals. If the human capital framework emphasizes the importance of capital accumulation, this perspective on the university as a social institution which promotes national and international integration emphasizes the importance of communication and display (Veblen, 1899). Given the central need to prepare a new professional-managerial class for the complexities of a commercial society, it is not surprising that higher education might be "too large" from the perspective of human capital theory or that students choose those specializations that improve their ability to communicate with other members of the elite, rather than enhance their understanding of science or engineering.

This framework also provides an explanation that human capital cannot provide for the rise of those disciplines such as music or literature or philosophy or sociology that have little to do with improving commodity production. Higher education provides a framework for members of the academy to create and communicate meaning and purpose for society as a whole. Higher education gives legitimacy to those who wish to analyze and critique social structures and social practices, and there is no reason to think that such activities are always compatible with the prevailing social order, even if that order helps create the conditions that allow the university to prosper.

Higher education and the reproduction of the global capitalist order: educational globalization as the extension of Western domination

The economic and sociological perspectives outlined in the previous two sections argue that colleges and universities are institutions that both provide skills and social legitimation. They provide credentials that signal to employers and others that this graduate is a worthy member of society. Moreover, this assessment does not just depend on the acquisition of particular skills, but also on the association of the graduate with a rationalist worldview that facilitates communications within and across societies. College students throughout the world experience the life of studying, reasoning and exploring social and cultural limits. This creates a transnational social stratum that can perhaps understand each other more easily than they can members of their own society who do not gain access to universities. The expansion of university education creates a new and powerful mechanism of national and global social differentiation.

Not only do graduates carry specific knowledge and a general worldview, but they also occupy a specific social position as the monitors and managers of the key political economic organizations of society. This insight introduces a class theoretic and world systems framework inspired by authors such as Marx and Wallerstein to our understanding of the purpose and role of university education (Ginsburg *et al.*, 1990). The emphasis is not only on the appropriate acquisition of technical and social skills useful for the management of sophisticated production and distribution systems, but also on the more difficult to quantify need to manage and legitimate the increasingly complex set of hierarchical social processes associated with more sophisticated and interconnected economies. Moreover, the meritocratic ideology permits children from the "lower orders" to become part of the middle class that manages and enjoys a part of the surplus created by an increasingly productive capitalist workforce, which includes themselves.

According to this view, educational institutions in general and higher educational institutions in particular reproduce and legitimate class structures by facilitating the differentiation of the population. The original class analysis of Bowles and Gintis, for example, contrasted the emphasis of teachers of middle class schools to foster creativity to the tendency of teachers in working class schools to emphasize discipline (Bowles and Gintis, 1977). Within higher education, the same could be said of less prestigious colleges and trade schools that concentrate on training students for technical occupations, while those higher-order universities focus on inculcating the more general worldview and symbolic reasoning skills necessary for the management and legitimation of the social order.

When examining higher educational institutions in the Third World or on the periphery of the world capitalist system, one can combine world systems theory with this class analysis (Wallerstein, 2005). Globalization creates a dynamic in which the needs of a developing country are subordinated to the demands of an evolving capitalist order. This might not only be true for indigenous production processes which are deemed too inefficient or backward to compete effectively within the world economy, but also for national educational institutions that do not teach in the appropriate language or resist the offering of Western degree programs or disdain the use of Western expert consultants.

Not only does this dynamic mean that universities organize themselves in a similar manner, but also that the actual education content becomes more and more similar. The point is not to maximize national economic welfare or even economic growth, but to insert a nation more effectively into the world system of capitalist production by creating a similarly educated, but subordinated, technocratic elite.

Theories that legitimate higher education because it enhances human capital actually relegate national educational institutions to "consumers status in the global knowledge economy" (Collins and Rhoads, 2009: 186) and perpetuate their dependence on the West rather than transform them into producers of emancipatory knowledge.[6] As Olssen and Peters argue:

> The premise of knowledge as capital … universalizes policies and obscures country and regional differences. It also denies the capacity of local traditions, institutions and cultural values to mediate, negotiate, reinterpret and transmute the dominant model of globalization and the emergent form of knowledge capitalism on which it is based.
>
> (Olssen and Peters, 2005: 330)

The Marxist/world systems critique of human capital theory carries within it a claim that higher education should not exist to serve the dominant political economic order.

This critique of actually existing higher education institutions as a tool for intensified political economic subordination to the global capitalist order has important policy implications. Fagerlind and Saha (1989) discuss how the success of investment in education depends on the objectives it sets for itself. When outcomes are evaluated in terms of instrumental goals, such as preparing the citizen to be economically more productive, data may be interpreted as supporting the achievement of these goals. However, when education is assessed in terms of knowledge production, values and attitudes consistent with a nation's strategic aspirations, the results are open to debate (Pennycook, 2000). Others argue that educational reforms sometimes serve "a new form of western imperialism that has as its purpose the incorporation of populations within the formerly called 'Second and 'Third worlds' into a regime of global government" to yield "docile" populations (Tikly, 2004: 173).

Higher education, the disinterested pursuit of knowledge and the creation of more capable global citizens

Less radical discussions of the place of higher education would not accept this critique of higher education. Nevertheless, there are many advocates for the expansion of higher education who similarly argue that higher education is good in and of itself because it is a location where emancipatory knowledge and truth can be produced. Indeed, it is claimed that the intellectual practices of higher education should be spread to society as a whole so that critical thinking and a commitment to rationalist discourse becomes pervasive.[7] Students (and especially advanced graduate students) are supposed to absorb an ethos that stresses the disinterested pursuit of knowledge, the sharing of research findings with the rest of the academic community, the extensive and detailed use of references to acknowledge the work of other scholars, and the adherence to rigorous standards of proof that include the use of logic and evidence to validate one's arguments. Finding the truth is, within the academy, the ultimate goal motivating academic workers, and the highest academic awards are received by those scholars and intellectuals who are judged to be the most rigorous and original researchers in their fields. Moreover, higher institutions that receive the highest ranks normally include those scholars who do the most high-profile research, whether or not these investigations promote economic growth, facilitate national integration, or more effectively respond to the needs of the global economy.

An educational institution that promotes the disinterested pursuit of knowledge often fits uneasily within the established order.[8] A wide range of fields in the liberal arts do not directly facilitate commodity production, directly support the development of technocratic professional classes, or legitimate current structures of global inequality and class differentiation. While a majority of professors are not particularly politically engaged, the culture of academic freedom means that it is expected that institutions will protect and tolerate those scholars who provide political, social or cultural critiques of the world around them.[9] Students, as well, often take advantage of their new-found autonomy to embrace ideas and movements which place them in opposition to the status quo. Thus, we often observe the paradoxical protests of students who – as a result of their higher education – are likely as adults to become part of the elite against whom they struggle.

A good case can be made that this idealized picture of academic culture has never really existed and is, in any event, under threat by globalization (we will be exploring these issues in future chapters). Nevertheless, it is also the case that the culture of the academy we have outlined still influences the practices of contemporary universities and colleges. The argument for the promotion of liberal arts and critical thinking can be justified either as a necessary general investment for the production of skilled labor, or as a necessary step in creating more capable, intelligent and moral citizens who can affect change in their own societies and have deeper appreciation of what it means to be human. These different perspectives do not necessarily contradict each other, but they are not identical. The human capital approach, for example, argues for the more perfect integration of the university into the global capitalist system, while this humanist alternative asserts that the university makes its own independent contribution to social welfare that does not necessarily contribute to the maintenance of our present economic system.

Any analysis and evaluation of higher education reforms should take note of the fact that there is often no universal consensus over the purpose of higher education. Whatever its goals and intentions, it is likely that a revivified higher education system will produce "outputs" that were not intended by the reformers. Training a larger number of professional workers, for example, who can innovate and fulfill the demands of a modern society might also inadvertently produce a core of "non-productive" critical thinkers who have the ability both to contribute to and to destabilize a society. For these scholars, the function of higher education is not to allow students to become more productive workers or legitimate their social standing or consolidate and stabilize an unequal national and global order. Rather, the practices of higher education are seen as encouraging social practices of rational scholarship that are good in and of themselves. The production of competent students and rigorous creative investigations into all realms of the natural and social world needs no extrinsic justification.

A brief conclusion

These different explanations of the purposes of higher education suggest that universities and colleges remain contested terrains throughout the world, since government officials, business interests, advisors in international organizations, university administrators, faculty, students and parents all attempt to impose their contradictory visions on the inevitably embattled academic institution. The struggle over the future of the university will take different forms in different parts of the world. Thus, we postpone our discussion of this issue until we analyze more deeply the particular of these alternative explanations of higher education's purpose in the Arabian Gulf context.

What is clear, however, is that – despite the inevitable controversies – social support for the continued expansion of higher education remains strong. Having a robust system of universities and colleges is associated with a prosperous, well-ordered society; a dynamic, technologically advanced economy; and a more creative, fulfilled population. On the one hand, these ambitious expectations place unreasonable political pressures on all academic institutions. On the other hand, these desires for a good society do not signal a disenchantment with college education, but rather a desire for its continual restructuring and expansion.

Notes

1 Thomas Piketty in his recent work, *Capital in the Twenty-First Century* (2014), argues that human capital is distinct from capital since the ownership of human skills cannot be transferred in the same way that physical and financial assets can. This alerts us to the possibility that students acquire knowledge for a variety of reasons, some of which are not based on market-based cost–benefit analysis.
2 This might not be related to natural resource abundance, but instead to poor quality investments and dysfunctional job markets for college graduates.
3 The most recent data from Psacharopoulos and Patrinos tells us that the social rate of return for primary education was 18.9 percent; for secondary school completion, 13.1 percent, and for tertiary or higher education, 10.8 percent (Psacharopoulos and Patrinos, 2010).
4 As Psacharopoulos and Patrinos note, "The degree of public subsidization increases with the level of education, which has regressive income distribution implications" (Psacharopoulos and Patrinos, 2010: 112).
5 This is not just a matter of lacking mathematical skills. A bigger problem is the creation of mass science phobia amongst young students. It is common, for example, for young Emirati adults to claim that they (the national Arab population) are bad in science, while Asians are better. This opinion is especially pronounced in women, who have somehow been made to think they are not smart enough to do well in these subjects. This argument is based on one of the author's personal encounters with students while teaching at Zayed University.
6 See review of this research perspective in Tikly (2004); Ensor (2004); Fagerlind and Saha (1989); Farrell and Fenwick (2007); and Olssen and Peters (2005).
7 There are many authors who make this argument, and the political visions of the authors who maintain that universities should promote rigorous discourses which promote virtue and scientific rigor are wide-ranging. See Bloom (2008), Bok (2003) and Aronowitz (2000) for conservative, corporate liberal and radical versions of this humanistic argument.
8 Many academic administrators are very aware of the conflict between the promotion of commercialized knowledge and the development of general knowledge that is often critical of the social and cultural order (see Stein, 2004). Recent studies suggest that the higher education institutions in the United States are becoming more influenced by commercial imperatives. See Slaughter and Rhoades (2004), Aronowitz (2000) and Rhoads and Carlos (2006).
9 Pierre Bourdieu was particularly well known for championing those academics who used their analytic powers to critique the political economic order being created by globalization (see Bourdieu, 2003).

References

Anderson, B. (1983). *Imagined Communities: Reflections on the Origin and Spread of Nationalism*. London: Verso.

Anyon, J. (2011). *Marx and Education*. New York: Routledge.

Aronowitz, S. (2000). *The Knowledge Factory: Dismantling the Corporate University and Creating True Higher Learning*. Boston: Beacon Press.

Barr, N. (2008). Financing higher education: Lessons from developed economies, options for developing economies. In Liu, J.Y. and Pleskovic, B. (eds.). *Higher Education and Development: Annual World Bank Conference on Development Economics*. Washington, DC: World Bank.

Becker, G.S. (1964). *Human Capital: A Theoretical and Empirical Analysis, with Special Reference to Education*. New York: National Bureau of Economic Research.

Bloom, A. (2008). *The Closing of the American Mind*. New York: Simon & Schuster.

Bok, D. (2003). *Universities in the Marketplace: The Commercialization of Higher Education*. Princeton: Princeton University Press.

Bourdieu, P. (2003). *Firing Back: Against the Tyranny of the Market 2*. New York: The New Press.

Bowles, S. and Gintis, H. (1977). *Schooling in Capitalist America: Educational Reform and the Contradictions of Economic Life*. New York: Basic Books.

Cervantes, M. and Guelleo, D. (2014). The brain drain: Old myths, new realities. *OECD Observer*, December 11. Available at: www.oecdobserver.org/news/archivestory.php/aid/673/The_brain_drain:_Old_myths,_new_realities.html (accessed December 11, 2014).

CollegeStats.org (2009). Top ten oldest colleges in the world: Ancient colleges. Available at: http://collegestats.org/2009/12/top-10-oldest-universities-in-the-world-ancient-colleges (accessed December 11, 2014).

Collins, C.S. and Rhoads, R.A. (2009). The World Bank, support for universities, and asymmetrical power relations in international development. *Higher Education*, 59 (2010): 181–205.

Ensor, P. (2004). Contesting discourses in higher education curriculum restructuring in South Africa. *Higher Education*, 48(3): 339–359.

Fagerlind, I. and Saha, L. (1989). *Education and National Development*, 2nd edn. New York: Pergamon.

Farag, I. (2010). Going international. In Mazawi, A.E. and Sultana, R.G. (eds.). *Education and the Arab "World": Political Projects, Struggles and Geometries of Power*. New York: Routledge, 284–298.

Farrell, L. and Fenwick, T. (2007). Educating a global workforce. In Farrell, L. and Fenwick, T. (eds.). *Educating the Global Workforce: Knowledge, Knowledge Work and Knowledge Workers*. London: Routledge, 13–26.

Ginsburg, M.B., Cooper, S., Raghu, R. and Zegarra, H. (1990). National and world systems explanations of educational reform. *Comparative Education Review*, 34.

Hennock, M. (2010). University of Hong Kong looks to the West in curricular redesign. *The Chronicle of Higher Education, Curriculum*, July 19. Available at: http://survey.csuprojects.org/uploads/yc/u1/ycu1J8aFygYxu-tgusYQLg/U-of-Hong-Kong-Looks-to-the-West-in-Curricular-Redesign.pdf (accessed May 29, 2015).

Mazawi, A.E. (2007). "Knowledge society" or work as "spectacle": Education for work and the prospects of social transformation in Arab societies. In Farrell, L. and Fenwick, T. (eds.). *Educating the Global Workforce: Knowledge, Knowledge Work and Knowledge Workers*. London: Routledge, 251–267.

Meyer, J.W., Ramirez, F.O., Frank, D.J. and Schofer, E. (2006). Higher education as an institution. Center on Democracy, Development, and the Rule of Law, Working Paper #57. Stanford: Stanford University.

Olssen, M. and Peters, M.A. (2005). Neoliberalism, higher education and the knowledge economy: From the free market to knowledge capitalism. *Journal of Education Policy*, 20: 313–345.

Pennycook, A. (2000). Language ideology and hindsight: Lessons from colonial language policies. In Ricento, T. (ed.). *Ideology, Politics and Language Policies: Focus on English*. Philadelphia: John Benjamins, 49–65.

Piketty, T. (2014). *Capital in the Twenty-First Century*. Cambridge, MA: Harvard University Press.

Psacharopoulos, G. and Patrinos, H.A. (2010). Returns to investment in education: A further update. *Education Economics*, 12: 111–134.

Rawolle, S. and Lingard, B. (2008). The sociology of Pierre Bourdieu and researching education policy. *Journal of Education Policy*, 23: 729–741.

Rhoads, R.A. and Carlos, A.T. (eds.) (2006). *The University, State, and Market: The Political Economy of Globalization in the Americas*. Stanford: Stanford University Press.

Rhoads, R.A. and Liu, A. (2009). Globalization, social movements, and the American university: Implications for research and practice. In Smart, J.C. (ed.). *Higher Education: Handbook of Theory and Research*. Netherlands: Springer, 273–315.

Salmi, J. (2009). *Challenge of Establishing World Class Universities*. Herndon: World Bank. Available at: http://site.ebrary.com/lib/aus/Doc?id=10281477&ppg=86 (accessed December 10, 2011).

Schofer, E. and Meyer, J.W. (2005). The world wide expansion of higher education. Center for Democracy, Development and the Rule of Law, Working Paper #32. Stanford: Stanford University.

Schultz, T.W. (1961). Investment in human capital. *American Economic Review*, 51: 1–17.

Slaughter, S. and Rhoades, G. (2004). *American Capitalism and the New Economy: Markets, State, and Higher Education*. Baltimore: The Johns Hopkins University Press.

Spring, J. (2009). *Globalization of Education: An Introduction*. London: Routledge.

Stein, D.G. (ed.). (2004). *Buying In or Selling Out? The Commercialization of the American Research University*. New Brunswick: Rutgers University Press.

Tikly, L. (2004). Education and the new imperialism. *Comparative Education*, 40: 173–198.

UNESCO Institute for Statistics (2009). *Global Education Digest 2009: Comparing Education Statistics across the World*. Montreal: UNESCO Institute for Statistics.

UNESCO Institute for Statistics (2010). *Global Education Digest 2010: Comparing Education Statistics across the World: Special Focus on Gender*. Montreal: UNESCO Institute for Statistics.

UNESCO Institute for Statistics (2012). *Global Education Digest 2012: Opportunities Lost: The Impact of Grade Repetition and Early School Leaving*. Montreal: UNESCO Institute for Statistics.

United Nations Development Programme (2002). *Arab Human Development Report 2002: Creating Opportunities for Future Generations*. New York: UNDP.

Veblen, T. (1899). *The Theory of the Leisure Class*. New York: Macmillan.

Wallerstein, I. (ed.) (2005). *The Modern World System in the Longue Duree*. Boulder: Paradigm Publishers.

Zaher, S. (2009). The human right to education in Arab countries. In Mazawi, A.E. and Sultana, R.G. (eds.). *Education and the Arab "World": Political Projects, Struggles, and Geometries of Power*. London: Routledge.

3 Globalization of education and the GCC

This chapter has two purposes. In Part I, we define more precisely what we mean by the globalization of higher education. We examine whether or not there are intensifying international flows of students and academic personnel in the present period, and whether or not higher educational institutions or practices are becoming more uniform throughout the world. These investigations allow us to engage in more specific regional comparisons as well as to consider more precisely the role of the West and the United States in particular, in this globalization process. In Part II, we demonstrate that the GCC region's universities and colleges have become unusually extraverted and that American and Commonwealth higher education institutions are important drivers of this educational opening to the West. We conclude by explaining why the GCC has placed so much emphasis on Western-oriented educational reform.

Part I: conceptualizing and describing the global globalization of higher education

The international growth of higher education and globalization

The presence of common global conditions promoting the growth of higher education does not necessarily imply that tertiary education is becoming globalized. We need to carefully consider what we mean by educational globalization and how we might measure this phenomenon. When we use the phrase globalization of education, we are referring to at least two processes:

1 The increasing intensity in the flow of students, faculty and educational administrators across international borders.
2 The tendency for this commerce to create similar educational institutions through:
   a the adoption of Western models of higher education as benchmarks; and
   b the acceptance of Western quality assessment standards to measure educational outputs.

The assumption that that the intensifying flow of students and faculty must lead to social homogenization is similar to the claims of postwar modernization

DOI: 10.4324/9780203796139-3

theory as well as Marx and Engel's prediction in *The Communist Manifesto* that the chaotic and violent rise of European capitalism would create "a world after [Europe's] own image" (Marx and Engels, 1969). Thomas Friedman has more recently celebrated this hypothesis with his pronouncement that "The world is flat" (Friedman, 2007).

These dramatic, sweeping hypotheses can both clarify and obscure. On the one hand, our discussion of the different social scientific frameworks that explain the global rise of tertiary education revealed that administrators overseeing the establishment of new universities and colleges will normally attempt to replicate the policies and practices of successful higher educational establishments that already exist. On the other hand, the decision to allow the creation of new higher education institutions is always political. Colleges and universities cannot exist without the approval and regulation of the state, and it would be surprising if the structures and processes that organize political life had no effect on the educational practices of the university. Global forces might explain the expansion of higher education throughout the world, but they do not by themselves explain the institutional characteristics of the actually existing universities and colleges in each region of the world.

Have international exchanges of students and academics intensified?

We begin this discussion by considering intensified international educational exchange globally. This phrase refers to changes in the share of students and other academic personnel moving across borders in order to receive or provide educational services. Given the enormous growth in the number of college students in all parts of the world, we would expect that there would be more international students and more faculty and administrators working in countries that are not their own. There are three possible scenarios we could consider: growth and global educational introversion; growth and global education extraversion; and growth and globally neutral growth. The first category refers to the possibility that higher educational growth is associated with a *decline* in the share of students and academics participating in academic institutions outside their country. The second refers to the possibility that internal educational growth is associated with an *increase* in the share of "globalizing students and academics." Finally, globally neutral higher educational growth describes a situation in which the numbers of students and academics studying and working in institutions outside the country expands at a similar rate to the domestic growth of colleges and universities.[1] All of these scenarios are plausible. Higher education enrollment could be growing so rapidly in some countries that the share of students able to be absorbed in external exchange programs actually declines. On the other hand, it may be that the creation of new institutions is intimately connected to the establishment of international educational alliances that facilitate the flow of a higher proportion of students and faculty across borders. Expansion, however, does not necessarily mean that the flows of students and academic personnel are intensifying. To examine this question, we examine whether or not there is an increasing *proportion* of students and academics attending and working for foreign academic institutions.

Students' and academics' mobility

There are no comprehensive data sets that track the movements of academic personnel across national borders. On the other hand, UNESCO does collect considerable information on the movements of students. The overall results on student mobility suggest that higher education growth has been globally neutral. As the UNESCO Global Education Digest of 2009 states:

> The global outbound mobility ratio was 1.8%. This means that approximately 2 out of every 100 tertiary students left their home countries to study. Moreover, this figure has barely changed since 1999 (1.9%). So, despite the dramatic rise in absolute numbers, the global share of mobile students has largely remained the same. Globally, student mobility has kept apace with student enrolment.
>
> (UNESCO Institute for Statistics, 2009: 37)

This broad measure of international student mobility is interesting, but misleading. Certain sectors of the world have experienced introverted growth; others continue on an extraverted path; and the overall conclusion of neutral growth is partly a result of changes in national borders that make international mobility seem greater than it actually is. When we disaggregate the world, the neutral growth regions are North America, East Asia and the Pacific, Latin America and the Caribbean, and East and Central Europe. On the other hand, more extraverted growth has taken place in Central Asia, sub-Saharan Africa, and the Arab world. Finally, Western Europe has been experiencing introverted higher education growth.[2]

The data also reveal two other important trends. Increasing numbers of women are becoming internationally mobile students, and a higher share of this mobility is taking place within a region, as opposed to across regions. With respect to gender, women represent nearly half of all internationally mobile students. With respect to international mobility within a region, two trends stand out. A large proportion of mobile Central Asian students are receiving their education within the Russian Federation, while increasing numbers of Chinese students are attending tertiary institutions in the region: Australia, New Zealand and Japan. This has meant that the share of mobile students coming to the United States has declined from about one-fourth of the total to one-fifth over the past decade (UNESCO Institute for Statistics, 2009: 36–48). In the Central Asian case, we might label this false or misleading educational globalization since presumably this movement of students across new international borders mimics the borderless flow of students during the Soviet era. On the other hand, the Arabian Peninsula in particular is associated with increasing the relative numbers of college students crossing borders to pursue higher education. The GCC, as we shall demonstrate, likely possesses the most globally extraverted higher educational system in the world.

The globalization of institutions

It is difficult to investigate empirically the evolution of educational institutions, since the questions we are asking tend not to generate quantitative or numerical information. Despite this problem, it is still possible to determine if:

* Higher educational institutions from the advanced capitalist world are increasingly establishing cross-border presences.
* Higher education institutions are increasingly subject to common methods of assessment.
* Academic curricula are becoming more homogeneous.
* English is becoming a common language of instruction.
* A global corps of administrators and professors largely trained in the advanced capitalist world has emerged to run colleges and universities in a similar way.
* Personnel policies and academic governance have become more similar.

Indeed, describing and analyzing the institutional details of educational globalization can give us a much better sense of the ways in which international interconnections are and are not being constructed. Our goal in this section is to provide a general commentary on international trends in order to situate educational developments in the Gulf in the appropriate global context. We list in Table 3.1 a list of the key methods of cross-border collaboration that can influence and potentially make uniform global educational practices.

The cross-border presence of Western universities and colleges

We begin by considering the cross-border presence of universities and colleges. Futao Huang provides a useful categorization scheme to guide our consideration of this issue (Huang, 2007).

According to Huang, colleges and universities can establish online learning programs, academic partnerships with local institutions, franchise arrangements and/or branch campuses. Online programs, until recently, were delivered by the less prestigious for-profit sector of Western European and North American universities and had limited academic credibility. The rise of Massive Open Online Courses (MOOCS) and the offering of online degree programs by established Western universities is a phenomenon that is too recent for us to discuss in this volume. For this reason, we will only focus on the creation of cross-border academic partnerships, including the establishment of branch campuses.

What is most common is the establishment of academic partnerships, which range from support in curricular development, to assistance in overseeing administrative operations and the hiring of academic personnel, to the development of

Table 3.1 Categorizing cross-border collaboration

Types of cross-border collaboration	Specific policy
Facilitating mobility	Teacher exchange*
	Student exchange**
	Assistance in the hiring of faculty
	Assistance in the hiring of administrators
Curriculum development	General assistance in the development of curriculum
	Offering of joint courses
Offering bi-national degrees	Offering of a degree that carries the name of the foreign institution
	Permitting a foreign institution to create a branch campus that allows all students to receive degrees that carry the name of the foreign institution

Notes
* More often than not, professors from the foreign institution travel to the Gulf university or college to offer administrative or teaching services rather than the reverse.
** More often than not, students from the Gulf institutions will travel to the foreign institution to take a year of course work or finish degree requirements rather than the reverse.

degree programs closely identified with the prestigious foreign institution. For example, Huang describes the development of joint degree programs in China where the growth is substantial by stating:

> At present, the transnational programs that are provided by foreign institu-tions in China consist of two types: non degree-conferring programs and degree programs leading to degrees of foreign universities or universities of Hong Kong (a special administrative district of China). For example, in 1995, there were only two joint programs that could lead to foreign degrees; by 2004, the number of joint programs provided in Chinese higher educa-tion institutions in collaboration with foreign partners had reached 745, and by June 2004 joint programs qualified to award degrees in foreign or Hong Kong universities amounted to 169.
>
> (Huang, 2007: 427)

Huang points out that these joint programs have mainly linked prestigious Western institutions with the most well-known state universities in China. While there are some science and engineering programs, the greatest number of these endeavors has focused on professional academic programs in business and man-agement in order to "prepare professionals for work in multinational corpora-tions or firms engaged in international commerce" (Huang, 2007: 428).

The explosion of joint academic programs in China and elsewhere in the region combined with the increasing numbers of students documented above means that a larger share of students in Asia and, as we shall see, in the Gulf are being exposed to common academic programs (Naidoo, 2009). What is even more striking is the emergence of national educational strategies that combine the encouragement of student mobility and the creation of cooperative arrangements in order to create centers of innovation or "knowledge societies." These trends are most noticeable in China, Malaysia, the small city-states of Singapore and Hong Kong, and the GCC.

Singapore is undoubtedly the leading pioneer of this linkage of higher education reform to the restructuring of a region's economic position in the world economy. Knight describes this strategy in the following passage:

> The focus on tertiary education is clear as it aims to improve the quality and capacity of Singapore's higher education sector by focusing on three strategies such as inviting and providing financial support for "world class universities" to establish programs, research partnerships, and a branch campus in Singapore; recruiting 150,000 international students from Asia and beyond by 2015, and modernizing the domestic higher education institutions (HEIs) through international partnerships with elite universities from around the world.
>
> (Knight, 2011: 226)

Certainly, the Singapore approach has transformed the city-state's educational system. By 2009, 12 branch campuses had been established and "1,120 cross-border educational arrangements were operational" (Knight, 2011: 226).

This educational hub trend is also clear in Malaysia, although Knight characterizes the Malaysian initiative as a low-rent version of Singapore's. The developers of a hub labeled Educity plan to invite eight international universities to offer programs in fields such as business, multimedia, engineering, logistics, hospitality and medicine. The hope is that Malaysia's lower-cost education will continue to attract large numbers of foreign students, since Malaysia also has a reputation for offering educational services that are closely linked to foreign educational institutions (Knight, 2011: 226–228).

Naidoo (2009) shows that for Asia and the Gulf, at least, both the quantity and intensity of international educational partnerships are increasing. One can also examine this phenomenon from the perspective of the institutions exporting educational programs and campuses. In this case, it is also clear that important cross-border collaborations are growing most intensively for English-language universities and colleges. As Naidoo notes:

> Australia is by far the most active exporter of program mobility. With 1,569 education programs and 37 institutions operating in the program mobility landscape, the overall "intensity" of Australia's activity was 42.4 programs per institution, compared with 12.7 programs for U.K.-based institutions. In absolute terms, the United States is the third most active exporter of TNHE [transnational higher education] programs followed by New Zealand and Canada.
>
> (Naidoo, 2009: 322)

The intense participation of educational institutions in Australia and New Zealand highlights the importance of Asia in the construction of cross-border educational agreements. As we shall see, many of the Gulf countries have also required new universities and colleges to establish collaboration agreements with foreign institutions. Many of these arrangements do not receive much attention from international observers, but it is clear that they play a key role in the processes of accreditation and regulation within the GCC.

The rise of the American university model

The spread of the American university model worldwide is a strong argument for cross-border homogenization of higher education. These ventures began in the 1860s and intensified after the 1990s. The American-style liberal arts education continues to be initiated by political, economic and, in the early stages, religious elites. On the one hand, the American universities themselves are normally independent and thus cannot be characterized as a branch campus of a particular university in the United States. On the other hand, most of the overseas American-inspired institutions attempt to become accredited by agencies based in the United States and are chartered by one of the state governments of the United States. A good starting point in investigating the phenomenon of overseas American colleges and universities is to turn to the Association of American International Colleges and Universities. Founded in 1971, this body was designed to help these institutions to share information that might enhance the educational standards and missions of each college and university. The headquarters of the Association is presently in Beirut because the President of the American University of Beirut (Peter Dorman) currently heads the Association. The list of members of the Association gives a good sense of the significance of the movement to establish US-inspired higher education institutions (see Table 3.2). Table 3.2 is not, however, a complete list of all institutions that claim the American label since the American University of Kuwait and the American University of Dubai do not belong to this association.

   The list of institutions in this table tells us something about the factors behind the recent drive to create American-style liberal arts education. The earliest institutions (of the nineteenth and early twentieth centuries) were often founded by Christian organizations. The primary impetus behind this movement was often not to proselytize directly, but to create an institution that could provide important services to the surrounding community and thereby embed itself in it. The two Greek institutions in this list were originally placed in Anatolia and relocated to Greece after the collapse of the Ottoman Empire. On the other hand, the Lebanese institutions and American University in Cairo have survived regional and national turmoil and became quite important parts of the region's higher educational systems.

   The second wave of American universities came to Europe after World War II. Some institutions were founded to serve US expatriate communities and US soldiers. Others were created as centers to service the thousands of American

Table 3.2 Members of the Association of American International Colleges and Universities

Name	Date of founding	American accreditation and other information
American College of Thessaloniki (Greece)	1886 (originally in Anatolia and called Anatolia College)	Commission of Higher Education of the New England Association of Schools and Colleges (CIHE-NEASC) – 1997
American University of Bulgaria	1991	CIHE-NEASC – 2001
Central European University (Hungary)	1991	Postgraduate institution founded by Open Society
Franklin College (Switzerland)	1968	Middle States Commission on Higher Education (MSCHE)
American College Dublin (Dublin, Ireland)	1993	Applied to MSCHE Constituent part of Irish American University
John Cabot University (Rome, Italy)	1972	MSCHE
American International University in London	1972	MSCHE and Open University (UK)
American College of Greece	1875 in Smyrna, Anatolia, now in Athens. Offered first bachelor's degree in 1969	CIHE-NEASC
American University of Paris	1962 as Junior College. Offered four-year degree program in 1978	MSCHE
American University of Rome	1969 as institution for study abroad students from United States. Started four-year degree programs in 1986	MSCHE (2010) and Accrediting Commission for Independent Colleges and Schools (1992)
American University of Armenia	1991	Accrediting Commission for Senior Colleges and Universities of Western Association of Schools and Colleges in the US (WASC)
Al Akhawayn University in Ifrane (Morocco)	1995. Founded by Royal Decree in 1993	
American University of Sharjah	1997	MSCHE
Haigazian University (Beirut, Lebanon)	1955 as Haigazian College. Became university in 1996	
Lebanese American University	Originally American School for Girls in 1835. Became Lebanese American University in 1994	CIHE-NEASC (2010). Previously accredited by New York Board of Regents
American University in Cairo	1919. First four-year bachelor's degree granted in 1928	MSCHE
American University of Beirut	1866 as Syrian Protestant College. Became AUB in 1920	MSCHE (2004). Recognized by New York State Education Department since 1863
American University of Nigeria	2004	
Forman Christian College (Pakistan)	1864 as Lahore Mission College	
American University of Afghanistan	2006	

Source: website of Association of American International Colleges and Universities. Available at: www.aub.lb/aaicu/Pages/index.aspx (accessed November 6, 2013).

study abroad students. By the 1980s, most had established small, but sustainable, four-year degree programs and occupy a relatively insignificant niche within Western Europe's well-established higher education system.

Finally, a new wave of universities and colleges began to appear in the 1990s and 2000s. Two universities in Eastern Europe partially funded by George Soros and the Open Society Institute established themselves after the fall of Communism. A similar process of educational innovation occurred in Central Asia with the establishment of the American University of Armenia and the American University of Central Asia (in Kyrgyzstan). Around the same time, several Arab countries began to reorganize higher education and permit the establishment of private and non-profit institutions. This restructuring process led to the establishment of American-inspired institutions in Morocco, the UAE and Kuwait. Finally, there are signs that the American university movement is spreading to Afghanistan, Nigeria and the Kurdish area of Iraq. The Afghan and Iraqi cases are unique, in that the creation of these institutions intimately involved the highest levels of the Bush Administration. The Nigerian story is more typical: a well-placed politician used his influence to found the university and called on an American institution (in particular, the American University in Washington, DC) to help establish the institution.[3]

One surprising feature of the American university phenomenon is that the Muslim world in general and the Arab world and the GCC region in particular seem to be particularly open to this educational innovation. We speculate that this connection is largely due to the earlier successes of the American University of Beirut (AUB) and the American University in Cairo (AUC). By the 1970s, both institutions had established themselves as two of the most elite higher education institutions of the region. As a result, wealthy business people and government officials interested in educational innovation looked to the AUB and AUC as models that could be replicated. The AUB, in particular, has often played an important role in supporting regional higher education institutions that wish to establish liberal arts educational practices.

The elite branch campus phenomenon

While free-standing universities based on American curricular principles provide some evidence of institutional homogenization, one could still argue that these institutions create unique and idiosyncratic cultures that do not completely replicate the American experience of education. More recently, however, Gulf countries in particular, like Singapore, have begun to establish branch campuses of American and European institutions, and, in some cases, these institutions are required to provide the identical courses of study and the identical regulations so that students can claim their degree has the same prestige as the home campus. One advantage of this approach, from the point of view of the host country, is that the new institutions do not need to undergo intense reviews by national authorities. The administration in the home country campus provides the assurances necessary to ensure that a quality education is being provided. Since Qatar inaugurated this practice in the late 1990s, the elite branch campus movement has received quite a lot of attention, even if the actual enrollment of students is rather small. The most high-profile additions have been implemented by New York University (NYU), which has established campuses in Abu Dhabi and Shanghai as well as a series of study away locations for students in this evolving NYU global network. It is clear that, in this case, the Gulf has led this globalization movement, but it is unclear how significant this development is for global education, or even for higher education in the Gulf. We explore these issues in in more detail in Chapter 4.

Global rankings and homogenization

Regardless of the model being followed, higher education institutions are trying to establish elite centers of knowledge production and dissemination that are comparable to their Western counterparts. To achieve this goal, non-Western universities willingly subject themselves to Western assessment bodies in order to reach a higher global ranking. Securing a place in the top 500 rankings has become a major objective that universities are willing to do all it takes to reach it. This striving for prestige promotes institutional homogenization. As Marginson and van der Wende put it:

> Global university rankings have cemented the notion of a world university market arranged in a single "league table" for comparative purposes and have given a powerful impetus to intranational and international competitive pressures in the sector.
>
> (Marginson and van der Wende, 2007: 309)

Important rankings include the *Times Higher Education Supplement* and the US News and World Report. In addition to these Western agencies, Asian institutions such as Shanghai's Jiao Tong University are taking a leading role in imposing traditional Western standards on their own higher educational systems. GCC institutions have recently been active in trying to figure in the top ranked institutions worldwide but so far only two universities in the UAE and two in Saudi Arabia figure among the top 500 in the QS top universities rankings (QS, 2013).

Common language, curricula and academics

The combination of increasing cross-border collaborations with the adoption of common modes of ranking and accreditation has clear implications for the core of the academic project – providing degrees to qualified students who have undertaken a structured course of study. Whether it is joint degree programs with universities from the United States or the Commonwealth nations or global network branch campuses or the drive to obtain Western accreditation, these developments have meant that instruction is in English and nearly similar curricula, if not identical ones, are established. Even European universities such as the

Sorbonne Abu Dhabi have had to make adjustments to their language of instruction by offering some degrees in English rather than French. Fouache, the director of the Sorbonne Abu Dhabi, declared in response to the question why the physics bachelor's degree was not offered in French: "We are realistic.... In the field of science there isn't the market for French" (Swan, 2013).[4]

To ensure uniformity and the maintenance of quality, sponsoring Western institutions will also lead to the appointment of Western academic administrators to oversee these initiatives. Not surprisingly, these chancellors, academic vice presidents and deans will hire professors who have received their degrees from English-speaking countries. This does not necessarily mean that those hired must be citizens of the United States or British Commonwealth nations, but it does mean that those hired bring with them the templates and experiences of Western academic institutions.[5] The global dominance of Western graduate education in advanced academic training means that there are large numbers of potential academic workers on which to draw.

This analysis suggests that even in the absence of partnerships with Western institutions, ranking and accreditation processes can push independent higher education institutions in a similar direction. If one institution improves its standing by receiving Western accreditation, pressure is placed on competitive institutions to adopt similar standards. As we shall see, the spread of Western curricula and English language instruction in the GCC has often been promoted by government accrediting boards as well as accreditors usually drawn from the West to accredit programs. In many cases Western approval for an academic program or the existence of partnership agreements are required before receiving government certification. All of these trends provide strong support for the global homogenization hypothesis.

An important factor driving this phenomenon is the drive to improve one's standing in order to gain access to increasingly scarce funds. The fact that higher education spaces are increasing rapidly means that governments and universities feel compelled to search for new methods of financing. As Mok puts it:

> Educational restructuring and reforms taking place in Asia have been significantly influenced by the Western public management-oriented doctrines and neoliberalist ideologies and practices. Responding to the growing impact of globalization, we have found that all our selected Asian states ... have reviewed their education systems and launched reforms along the lines of marketization, privatization, and corporatization with intentions to improve their governance and management.
>
> (Mok, 2007: 440)

The emergence of new academic centers inevitably creates a new hierarchy of higher educational institutions and a decline in the prestige and influence of indigenous institutions which are left behind. It might be that the emergence of a more privileged, engaged group of faculty in elite colleges and universities is purchased by creating an enlarged group of proletarianized academics who have fewer rights and more contingent employment.

In addition, Mok argues that reforms in the elite institutions put greater emphasis on fundraising and getting grants, since governments increasingly expect them to be financially self-supporting. Some of Mok's Chinese academic informants viewed these pressures to be "like forcing a gentlewoman to be a prostitute" (Mok, 2007: 442). Mok's analysis tells us that there is an element of coercion in the institutional restructuring dynamic we have outlined. Not all faculty or students necessarily benefit from the drive to create prestigious, more Western-oriented academic programs, and Mok – by suggesting that educational internationalization is a polite word for educational imperialism – argues that this type of educational restructuring might not be in the national interest as well (Mok, 2007: 437).

Indeed, to the extent that educational globalization increasingly creates stark distinctions among colleges and universities in both home and host countries, the corporatization process described by Mok implies that the democratic and liberal traditions of the academy are not spreading. While the content and language medium of college education is becoming more similar, governance and administrative practices remain diverse. There is little evidence that participatory systems of Western academic governance are spreading globally. This global homogenization hypothesis may be partially correct, but not in the liberating way that its proponents often celebrate.

Part II: the Arab Gulf states in the vanguard of educational globalization

The globalization of higher education has affected colleges and universities in most of the world's regions. In this section, we argue that the GCC has played a central and unique role in both influencing trends in global higher education and allowing its own educational establishments to be transformed by Western educational institutions. While the number of Gulf university students is relatively small, the transformation of the regional educational landscape has been profound and attracted international attention. We document these trends by drawing on a variety of quantitative and qualitative sources. Our discussion also places these developments in the context of pressures to change higher education in the Arab world as a totality.

Educational reform and the general Arab efforts to create a knowledge economy

The expansion and globalization of higher education that we outlined in the previous chapter have not occurred spontaneously. As we noted earlier, politics plays a crucial role in determining how fast higher education will expand, what type of institutions will be created, how universities and colleges will be financed, and what types of regulatory environments will be functioning. These decisions are interconnected and require a vision of higher education that guides policy-makers and takes into account the financial constraints which inevitably face any government or potential private funder of tertiary institutions.

What is significant about contemporary policy debates about higher education is their uniformity. From Barack Obama's emphasis on creating an enlarged core of STEM high-tech workers to the World Bank's policy pronouncements on educational policy, the focus is on constructing universities and colleges that serve the alleged economic need for rapid technological change and high levels of growth.[6] In the Arab world, this ideology was most forcefully articulated in the first Arab Human Development Reports and partially adopted by GCC ministers of education.

Between 2002 and 2005, the UNDP released four highly publicized and controversial documents collectively entitled the Arab Human Development Report. Using the framework of the UNDP annual Human Development Report, scholars (primarily Arab) assessed the successes and failures of the development policies of the region. Included in the general framework of the study was an evaluation of the health, living standards and educational status of the Arab population. Beyond this empirical exercise, however, lay deeper, political issues: the authors wanted to determine if Arabs in the region had the ability to enjoy freedom and security so that they could regulate their own political economic destiny. The conclusions of these studies were both revolutionary and conservative. The volumes were revolutionary because the authors expressed contemptuous disdain for the dominant authoritarian and patriarchal cultures of the Arab world. The first Arab Human Development Reports clearly favored radical reform. Indeed, the authors provided the sort of secular critiques that anticipate the ideologies of the Arab Spring a little more than half a decade later. On the other hand, these same Arab Human Development Reports were conservative because their points of reference were largely the practices and institutions of the United States and Western Europe. Arab development would be successful if the governments of the region could establish institutions that recreated the conditions that promoted dynamic social and economic evolution in the West. Unlike the Arab radicals of the colonial and early post-colonial period, these twenty-first century analysts largely embraced capitalist globalization and thus called for a deeper integration with the political, economic and cultural forces of the West (UNDP, 2002, 2003, 2004, 2005).

The analysis of educational reform in the Arab Human Development Reports best exemplify the neo-liberal capitalist tendencies of the authors. The first report (published in 2002) is subtitled "Creating Opportunities for Future Generations." It identifies three shortcomings or gaps in Arab societies that must be overcome if human development is to reach its potential. These gaps persist in the arenas of:

- freedom;
- the empowerment of women; and
- knowledge.

The first two points clearly challenge contemporary political structures and social norms. This is the revolutionary side. Arab societies need to change or radically reform their political regimes, while challenging pervasive male privilege. On the other hand, the same report and the one that immediately follows mainly represent the knowledge gap as an economic failure (UNDP, 2002, 2003). The authors wish to exploit the challenges posed by economic globalization to create a more technically competent workforce. They do not stress higher education as an experience that fosters the capacity to engage in rational critiques of the social order or enhancing personal creativity. Rather, the focus is on the more effective use of science by an increased number of well-trained Arab professional scientists and engineers.

This concentration on the more effective dissemination and utilization of mathematics and science is not new. The first twentieth-century universities of the Arab world, such as Cairo University, were well known for their high-quality engineering programs (Cairo University, Faculty of Engineering, 2014). The authors of the Arab Human Development Report criticize the old Arab socialist regimes for focusing on the importation of knowledge without laying the basis for the emergence of an internally dynamic scientific infrastructure (UNDP, 2003: 5–6). This failure was certainly not the intention of the Nasser government and others like it (Cochran, 2013). The old policy might not have been successful, but the technocratic focus on building an Arab-centric competence in applied science to transform the productive base of society is similar.

What is different is the vision of how the higher education system should be organized. The focus is less on borrowing technology than on borrowing Western institutional templates. The authors call for a university system that is more autonomous from the state and open to the establishment of private higher education institutions which are not structured by the "unregulated profit motive" (UNDP, 2002: 61). While vaguely formulated, this apparently means the creation of independent governance boards for all universities, whether funded by the state or not. The members of what American educators would call the Board of Trustees or Board of Regents would include representatives from the state, business, civil society and academia. Notably absent in this formulation are representatives from trade unions, faculty and students. In addition, the authors seem to envisage the creation of a non-profit sector of private universities similar to what exists in the United States that would be accredited by an independent Arab organization that supervises this process.

It is important to note that, despite the emphasis on the importation of Western institutional structures, the authors of the Human Development Report, like their Arab nationalist forebearers, emphasize the need to create regional solutions to Arab deficiencies. The stress is on regional cooperation and the development of curricula and educational methods that unify the region as a cultural whole. For example, while recognizing the importance of developing English language competence, the Arab Human Development Report calls for the Arabization of science and the aggressive development of translation facilities that will permit the expansion of Arabic language instruction in a wide range of technical fields (UNDP, 2003: 7). As we shall see in later chapters, this emphasis on developing Arabic as a language of academic discourse differentiates the authors of these volumes from the actual reform efforts in higher education, which, in most other respects, closely follow the recommendations for institutional reform embedded in these reports.

The chief goal of these reforms is to construct a *knowledge society*. This entails, according to Abdel Latif Yusuff El Hamed – the then Director General and Chairman of the Arab Fund for Economic and Social Development – "transforming knowledge wealth into knowledge capital in order to generate new knowledge" (UNDP, 2003: v). This rather circuitous formulation stresses the need to create centers of knowledge production that are tightly integrated with expanded and technologically dynamic commodity production within the Arab world. The emphasis is on uncovering the commercial applications of science, but the authors do not restrict themselves to this domain. Developments in social sciences and the humanities – the authors claim – can also lay the basis for scientific advances (UNDP, 2003: 43). What is needed is the creation of a "knowledge culture" that embodies "values motivating the acquisition and use of knowledge" (UNDP, 2003: 38–39).

Since the publication of this report in 2003, Gulf societies in particular have rhetorically embraced the goal of creating a knowledge society. This is seen as a key part of a development strategy that can insert national intellectuals into systems of knowledge-based production. The technocratic goal is to create a skilled national workforce that can monitor and direct high technology industries. This requires more than the creation of an appropriate skill set. Perhaps more daunting is to overcome a rentier culture which, for understandable reasons, does not connect productive effort to the acquisition of high levels of income.

The GCC countries have adopted much of the pro-capitalist focus of the Arab Human Development Reports without the potentially revolutionary political critique. The leaders of every country in the region claim that they are trying to create a 'knowledge society" in which national citizens play a leading role. On the other hand, there are inevitable tensions between the Arab Human Development Reports' emphasis on freedom and political openness, and the GCC rulers' emphasis on social solidarity, security and the preservation of cultural identity. At about the same time that the first Arab Human Development Reports were written, the GCC Ministers of Education released a document entitled the "Comprehensive Development of Education in the Gulf Cooperation Council." While recognizing the need to be open to scientific knowledge, the document also stresses the need to use education to create "good citizens" who can more effectively participate in the new representative institutions being created in most GCC countries. Great importance is placed "on preserving Arabic and Islamic identity" that can "enhance the spirit of citizenship in the Council countries' youth" (Gulf Cooperation Council Ministers of Education, 2002).

The GCC report mixes conservative and radical perspectives in unique ways. On the one hand, the openness of youth to the worldwide web is decried for its negative effects on social and cultural developments in the GCC. On the other hand, the ministers condemn restrictions on women's employment and seem to call for the full integration of women into the labor market – without apparently realizing that such a development would more radically transform traditional society than any other measure. It is worth noting that despite this rhetoric, most universities are gender segregated and thus perpetuate cultural taboos that restrict women's ability to participate in the labor force and society at large.

Less attention is paid in the Arab Human Development Reports and the GCC Ministers of Education document to financial issues. Nevertheless, they are real, even in the wealthy oil-producing countries. The emphasis on the creation of alternative institutional models in the Arab Human Development Report provides a way for governments to commit themselves to the radical restructuring of higher education without funding all these new endeavors. By suggesting the use of private funding to create autonomous, non-profit universities and colleges, the way is open to break from complete reliance on the state sector and, as we shall see, permit the rise of for-profit tertiary educational institutions as well. This focus on the knowledge economy and the creation of a private or non-state sector of higher education prepares the way for the GCC to adopt Western institutional templates that intensify the integration of local universities and colleges with their counterparts in the Western English-speaking world.

Expansion in university enrollment and the increasing international mobility of students in the Gulf

The policy shift toward the promotion of Western-oriented higher educational reforms is closely connected to the rapid growth of GCC higher education. Over the past 15 years, enrollment in Gulf colleges and universities has expanded substantially in nearly all countries. (Incomplete Kuwaiti data suggest that this nation's tertiary educational experience might be something of an outlier.) Attendance in Qatar's colleges and universities has expanded most slowly, but even in this case, enrollment figures have nearly doubled. The United Arab Emirates represents the other end of the spectrum with increases in the tertiary level student population of more than four times (from approximately 21,000 in 1999 to about 122,000 in 2012). Even the lower income small countries of the region – Oman and Bahrain – have seen substantial increases in college-level education. Bahrain's enrollment figures have nearly tripled, while Oman's have more than doubled. Finally, Saudi Arabia stands apart because of the much greater number of young adults studying in its higher educational institutions. In 13 years the capacity of universities and colleges increased from 372,000 to 1,206,000 (see Table 3.3).

This expansion has generally affected both male and female students. In recent years, there seems to be a slightly more rapid increase in the numbers of male tertiary students attending colleges and universities in the GCC, but women's presence in higher education remains relatively higher than male participation in most countries. In Kuwait, Bahrain, Qatar and the UAE women are a clear majority of university students, while in Saudi Arabia and Oman, they represent about half of the student body. While in Oman we witness an increasing

Table 3.3 Enrollment in tertiary educational institutions in the Gulf

	1999	2004	2009	2012	% change (1999–2012)
Bahrain total	11,048	18,524	34,689	31,128	181.8
Bahrain women's enrollment (percentage)	6,630 (60.0)	11,684 (63.1)	18,859 (54.4)	18,489 (59.4)	184.3
Kuwait total	33,906	36,866			
Kuwait women's enrollment (percentage)	21,178 (62.5)	23,701 (64.3)			
Oman total	36,204	41,578	75,715	89,230	146.5
Oman women's enrollment (percentage)	14,827 (41.0)	21,555 (51.8)	36,670 (48.4)	45,002 (50.4)	203.5
Qatar total	8,880	9,287	13,133	17,266	94.4
Qatar women's enrollment (percentage)	6,380 (71.8)	6,633 (71.4)	8,426 (64.2)	11,247 (65.1)	76.3
UAE total	21,000	80,296	92,668	121,626	479.2
UAE women's enrollment (percentage)		48,346 (60.2)	53,325 (57.5)	67,410 (55.4)	
Saudi Arabia total	371,522	573,803	757,770	1,206,007	224.6
Saudi Arabia women's enrollment (percentage)	202,210 (54.4)	336,920 (58.7)	414,433 (54.7)	594,146 (49.3)	193.8

Sources: UNESCO Institute for Statistics, *Arab States: Regional Report* (Montreal, 2002); and UNESCO Institute for Statistics, Data Centre, "Enrolment in tertiary institutions, all programs, both sexes (number)," available at: http://data.uis.unesco.org/index.aspx?queryid=130&lang=en (accessed May 22, 2014).

Note
In some cases, the figures are as close to the designated year as possible.

feminization of the university student body, as the percentage of women students has increased from 41 to 50 percent, in Qatar and Saudi Arabia, the share of women in universities and colleges has declined. Between 1999 and 2012 the percentage of female students fell[7] from 72 to 65 percent in Qatar and from 54 to 49 percent in Saudi Arabia.

The rapid expansion of higher education in the GCC has been accompanied by the unusually higher international mobility of students in most GCC countries. While the outward mobility of college students is not a new trend for the region, the increasing numbers of non-national students attending universities and colleges within the region does represent a significant change. In terms of the outward mobility ratio, Bahrain, Kuwait, Oman and Qatar have more than 10 percent of their college students studying abroad. In the case of Saudi Arabia, which has the lowest outward mobility rate, the late King Abdullah's ambitious program promoting college education in the United States has increased the outward mobility of Saudi students significantly (from 1.9 to 5.2 percent). For a large country with sizeable domestic university establishments, this outward mobility figure is unusually high (see Table 3.4).

When we examine inward mobility data, the high numbers of non-national students who are "entering" Bahrain, Qatar, the UAE and perhaps Kuwait are striking. These data – especially for Bahrain, Qatar and the UAE – represent a decision by the authorities to create colleges and universities that cater to large numbers of non-national students who live within the country or are temporarily immigrating to pursue higher education. The universities and colleges of the region are becoming much more diverse and open to the international influences that expatriate students bring with them.[8]

When we examine the different regions that attract outbound and inbound students, we get a more precise picture of the type of intensified student mobility that is taking place. The outbound mobility ratios document what most qualitative studies have already claimed: that a key part of most of the Gulf's countries' education policy is to send some of its most talented national students to Western institutions for study. While Saudi Arabia and, to a lesser extent, Kuwait send many of their nationals to the United States for university study, the other GCC states still tend to "export" their students to the United Kingdom. This is especially true for Bahrain and Oman (see Table 3.5).

These data also reveal trends which receive less attention. Jordan is a very important destination for students in the Arabian Peninsula, and Jordanian colleges and universities have played a significant role in sponsoring and supporting degree programs in certain Gulf States. Finally, it is important to note that the UAE is an educational location for many students from the GCC region itself. Abu Dhabi, Dubai and Sharjah have all created tertiary educational institutions that attract other Gulf nationals for study.

It is also interesting to note that if we divide the population into three broad segments – students from the GCC, students from South Asia and students from other Arab states – we find that the largest numbers of expatriate students comes from other Arab states with South Asian student body being approximately

Table 3.4 Inbound and outbound mobility rates of GCC tertiary students

	Outbound rates 2007 (numbers)	Outbound rates 2012 (numbers)	Inbound rates 2007 (numbers)	Inbound rates 2012 (numbers)
Bahrain	14.1 (2,576)	13.1 (4,096)	3.8 (672)	8.5 (2,648)
Kuwait	17.1 (5,573)	(10,686)		(7,984)
Oman	7.7 (5,090)	11.0 (10,049)	0.6 (165)	2.4 (2,108)
Qatar	20.2 (1,492)	19.7 (3,410)	31.4 (2,487)	41.4 (7,154)
United Arab Emirates		7.0* (8,526)		44.5 (54,162)
Saudi Arabia	1.9 (17,067)	5.2 (62,535)	2.2 (13,687)	3.9 (46,566)

Sources: UNESCO Institute for Statistics, Data Centre, "Global flow of tertiary level students," available at: www.uis.unesco.org/Education/Pages/international-student-flow-viz.aspx (accessed May 22, 2014); UNESCO Institute for Statistics, *Global Educational Digest 2009: Comparing Educational Statistics across the World* (Montreal, 2009): 142.

Note
* Estimated by authors.

Table 3.5 Top five destinations of outward bound student from the Gulf (2012)

Bahrain	United Kingdom 1,112
	Jordan 673
	United Arab Emirates 467
	United States 424
	Saudi Arabia 269
Kuwait	United States 3,605
	United Kingdom 1,816
	Jordan 1722
	United Arab Emirates 963
	Bahrain 504
Oman	United Arab Emirates 5,186
	United Kingdom 1,202
	Jordan 1,079
	United States 521
	Australia 486
Qatar	United Kingdom 1,252
	United States 948
	United Arab Emirates 330
	Jordan 219
	India 214
United Arab Emirates	United Kingdom 3,089
	United States 2,031
	Australia 1,133
	India 748
	Canada 255
Top five destinations of small GCC states	United Kingdom 8,471
	United States 7,529
	United Arab Emirates 6,946
	Jordan 3,693
	Australia 1,619
Saudi Arabia	United States 33,066
	United Kingdom 9,773
	Australia 5,392
	Jordan 3,295
	Canada 3,168

Source: UNESCO Institute for Statistics, Data Centre, "Global flow of tertiary level students," available at: www.uis.unesco.org/Education/Pages/international-student-flow-viz.aspx (accessed May 22, 2014).

50 percent smaller. Eighty-four percent of the South Asian students (mainly from India and Pakistan) studying in the region are doing so in the United Arab Emirates. In the rest of the GCC, most expatriate students are from other GCC states or the rest of the Arab world, particularly the countries of the Levant, Iraq and Egypt (see Tables 3.6 and 3.7).

Both outbound and inbound mobility data suggest that all of the states in the GCC possess extraverted higher educational systems. Outbound students study in disproportionately large numbers in British and American institutions, while the UAE, Qatar and Bahrain rely on a large number of non-national students

Table 3.6 Top five home countries of inward bound students to the Gulf (2012)

Bahrain	Kuwait 504 Saudi Arabia 494 Pakistan 426 Jordan 211 Egypt 184
Kuwait	Saudi Arabia 753 Egypt 238 Iraq 157 Syria 140 Iran 135
Oman	India 504 United Arab Emirates 179 Iraq 171 Pakistan 163 Kuwait 132
Qatar	Egypt 836 Palestine 747 Jordan 638 Yemen 533 Pakistan 398
United Arab Emirates	India 7,310 Oman 5,186 Jordan 4,313 Palestine 3,816 Syria 3,525
Saudi Arabia	Yemen 5,539 Syria 2,669 Egypt 2,403 Pakistan 2,125 Palestine 2,104

Source: UNESCO Institute for Statistics, Data Centre, "Global flow of tertiary level students," available at: www.uis.unesco.org/Education/Pages/international-student-flow-viz.aspx (accessed May 22, 2014).

Table 3.7 Regional origin of inbound tertiary education students in the small GCC states (2012)

Region	Numbers
GCC states	7,628
South Asia	12,397
Other Arab states	24,186

Source: UNESCO Institute for Statistics, Data Centre, "Global flow of tertiary level students," available at: www.uis.unesco.org/Education/Pages/international-student-flow-viz.aspx (accessed May 22, 2014).

from the surrounding region for their enrollments. The inbound mobility data for Saudi Arabia and Oman are relatively low, and we do not have enough reliable information to make any claims about Kuwait. The large movements of students across national borders also place pressures on universities and colleges throughout the region to implement common educational practices and standards. We explore this issue in Chapter 6, which we devote to the issue of accreditation.

Part III: concluding analysis: the paradoxical context of educational globalization in the GCC: economic globalization and isolation of national workers

If we take into account the historical context, our findings that GCC colleges and universities are unusually influenced by global (or Western) trends in higher education is not surprising. None of the nation-states of the Arabian Peninsula had any experience with formal education before World War II and the discovery of oil. The United Kingdom was content to leave the social structures of the region untouched and impoverished as long as the tribal leaders respected British hegemony.

Given the initial dependence of the GCC on the outside world for its foreign exchange from the sale of oil and for the importation of labor and technology, it is not surprising that the globalizing patterns we have documented have continued and indeed intensified. We should, however, note the paradox in this finding. It is the historical insularity of the region that is responsible for its contemporary openness. Gulf society today is characterized by a tension between a sometimes xenophobic attachment to a somewhat invented tradition of cultural solidarity and Islamic piety and the drive to achieve complete capitalist modernity.

This contradiction is reinforced by the idiosyncratic workings of the Gulf labor market as well as the dynamics of business formation. On the one hand, no region in the world has grown more rapidly over the past several decades. On the other hand, this growth has been accompanied by an unprecedented isolation of the national population from direct participation in and management of the capitalist economy. With respect to the labor market, national citizens normally work in the state sectors with wages and benefits significantly higher than those which similarly qualified private sector workers would receive (Hertog, 2014). With respect to business formation, many citizens take advantage of the sponsorship system and laws restricting foreign ownership outside free trade zones to become relatively passive partial owners of the many enterprises that have formed in the Gulf.[9] In addition, the influx of expatriate labor to these businesses has allowed many nationals to profit directly from sponsorship fees that workers must pay in order to gain access to the labor market. Because these expatriate workers are tied to workplaces, this also means that foreign workers are employed at a lower wage than an unregulated labor market would produce, and this allows national business owners (and foreign owners of local businesses as well) to gain further benefits or rents from the Gulf economies.

While all countries of the Gulf display these features, it is the richest GCC states (Qatar and the UAE) that have the smallest presence of national citizens in the private sector. Kuwait, while also wealthy, operates somewhat differently, because its citizens play a bigger role in the management of a larger public sector. Finally, Saudi Arabian, Bahraini and Omani citizens are much more likely to work in the private sector. In the Bahraini case, more nationals are private sector workers than public sector workers. In the Saudi case, more than 60 percent of the total workforce (national and expatriate) is employed in one of the largest public sectors in the world (Hertog, 2014).

The emphasis on educational reform, which extends to the primary and secondary educational sectors as well, is particularly salient because of the failure of governmental efforts to force business owners to hire more national workers. While quotas and hiring targets have been imposed in most countries, Hertog reports that:

> They [hiring quotas] have been difficult to monitor, have led to evasion and in some cases corruption between businesses and labor administrations. Various forms of "phantom employment" of nationals are widespread across the region, and quotas have probably increased the informal employment of foreigners.
>
> (Hertog, 2014: 7)

The lesson drawn from this unsuccessful experience has been that quotas have failed because nationals do not have the appropriate skills to function effectively in a global economy or do not have incentives to do so. Because national citizens are unattractive employees (even to citizen business owners), quotas cannot force businesses to really use their labor services.

Despite their differences, all of the GCC governments are uneasy with these social arrangements. Drives to "nationalize" the private sector workforce by creating a new class of private sector national entrepreneurs, scientists, engineers, professionals and administrators are the center of each GCC country's labor long-run economic policy. Most of the policy-makers have diagnosed national citizens' lack of participation in capitalist economic life as an input issue. The public sector educational system in general and the national university system in particular are accused of failing to mold college students into workers who have the appropriate technical, social and linguistic skills. By creating a competitive higher education system, it is hoped that both the new colleges and universities and the older public universities will be able to produce a well-trained workforce of technicians who are competent in English and creative, critical thinkers. In other words, the answer to the pressures of economic globalization is more globalization in the education sector.

This analysis certainly has its persuasive aspects. It is the case that many national citizens have poor technical and work skills when they complete their formal education. On the other hand, most analysts who have studied this problem believe that the problem is deeper than "getting the education system right." On the demand side, many business owners (national and expatriate) would rather hire foreign workers who command lower wages and are easier to control through the sponsorship system. On the supply side, many national citizens prefer to work in a less onerous environment for higher incomes. To use economic jargon, the "reservation wage" of nationals is too high from the perspective of private sector employers.[10] This means that national workers are unwilling to accept a job below a certain wage. The richer the country, the higher the reservation wage will be.

Bahrain, Oman and Saudi Arabia have higher private sector participation because per capita income is lower in these countries and thus the reservation wage is lower. Moreover, because these countries are poorer in terms of per capita income, there is a greater economic concern about the long-term costs of continuing to rely on expatriate workers, who export a lot of their income to their home country in the form of remittances and who, more importantly, acquire job skills through private sector work that cannot be attained by nationals in these three countries. Thus, these three countries have most aggressively pursued policies that will nationalize the workforce.

Changing the wage gap between private-sector expatriate workers and public-sector national workers could, in principle, be accomplished by taxing private sector employers who hire expatriate workers, providing subsidies to employers who hire national workers, and both lowering the wage of public sector workers and cutting back on employment by the government. All of these measures are difficult to implement politically, except perhaps providing subsidies. Unfortunately, in the absence of reforms in the public sector, efforts to increase private sector wages and benefits for national workers are likely to be costly and not entirely successful.[11]

Given these political economic difficulties, even more pressure is placed on the educational system to produce high-skilled, creative national citizen workers. The hope is that by exposing the youth of the Gulf to Western educational practices and the English language that they will become attractive and eager employees. This instrumentalist view of higher educational reform is not unique to the GCC. Many countries (especially in the Arab world) worry about the skills and quality of the workforce that higher educational institutions are attempting to create. On the other hand, the GCC is unusual. No other region of the world faces the peculiar problems of economic isolation of national citizens that we have outlined in this section. As we have documented, this has led to reform efforts that have created a globally extraverted higher education system. Whether or not these reforms have been successful or are sustainable is one of the key issues we examine in the rest of this book.

Notes

1 Even these measures cannot completely capture the complexity of the educational globalization dynamic. It might be that some institutions within a country are globally extraverted, while others are introverted. We will argue later that this extraverted and introverted combination exists within some Gulf higher educational systems.

2 Between 1999 and 2007, the outbound mobility ratio rose by 1.1 percentage points in Central Asia, followed by 0.8 percentage points in sub-Saharan Africa, 0.5 percentage points in the Arab states and 0.4 points in South and West Asia. In contrast, the ratio fell by 0.5 percentage points in Western Europe over the same period (UNESCO Institute for Statistics, 2009: 37).

3 The American University in Washington, DC has no direct governance connection to any American university outside the United States. On the other hand, it has recently participated actively in helping the American University of Sharjah and American University of Nigeria establish themselves. This was done under the direction of an entrepreneurial president (Ben Ladner). His departure has led American University to partially withdraw from this aggressive international posture.

4 The only exception to this trend of establishing academic programs in English that we could find is the attempt of the Sorbonne in Abu Dhabi to offer a course of study in French.

5 See for example this sentence in calls for applications for faculty positions at an American university in the GCC region: "As a university formed on American models, [name of university] will give priority to candidates who have substantial experience in American models of higher education."

6 This is not the place to question in detail the hegemonic emphasis on the need to have an ever expanding economy as measured by GDP per capita. However, it is not clear to us that constant increase in material abundance is a realistic policy goal – especially in the advanced capitalist world. The growth imperative of capitalism should not be confused with the ever-present need of complex societies to constantly evolve in the face of new social and environmental challenges.

7 The definition of inward mobility makes it more difficult to interpret these numbers. UNESCO defines a student as being internally mobile if he or she attends a higher education institution but does not have permanent status. Thus, this increase of inward mobility can take place if students who have lived most of their life in the region attend university but do not have permanent resident status.

8 Many of the small businesses in the GCC economies are operated and partially owned by expatriate business people. However, in most cases, national citizens must have majority ownership in all businesses located outside the free trade zones. In many cases, nationals receive a majority ownership share and a pre-arranged share of profits in return for sponsoring the small business.

9 The term reservation wage refers to the minimum wage that workers will accept in order to enter a particular job.

10 Hertog notes that most subsidization schemes last for a limited duration. At that point, private sector employers are supposed to raise the wages of national citizens. This makes such policies much less attractive, especially since employers have no ability to prevent citizens from migrating to other sectors in search of higher wages and more comfortable working conditions.

References

Cairo University, Faculty of Engineering (2014). A brief history of Cairo University. Available at: www.eng.cu.edu.eg/CUFE/History/CairoUniversityShortNote/tabid/81/language/en-US/Default.aspx (accessed December 19, 2014).

Cochran, J. (2013). *Education in Egypt*. London: Routledge.

Friedman, T.L. (2007). *The World is Flat 3.0: A Brief History of the Twenty-First Century*. New York: Macmillan.

Gulf Cooperation Council Ministers of Education (2002). *Comprehensive Development of Education in the Gulf Cooperation Council Countries: A Study of the Directives in the Supreme Council Resolution on Education (The 23rd Session, Doha).* Available at: www.google.com/?gws_rd=ssl#q=Comprehensive+Development+of+Education+in+th e+Gulf+Cooperation+Countries:++A+Study+of+the+Directives+Stated+in+the+Supre me+Council+Resolution+on+Education:+The+Twenty-third+Session+ (accessed December 19, 2014).

Hertog, S. (2014). Arab Gulf states: An assessment of nationalisation policies. Gulf Labor Markets and Migration Research Paper, 1/2014. European University Institute and Gulf Research Center.

Huang, F. (2007). Internationalization of higher education in the developing and emerging countries: A focus on transnational higher education in Asia. *Journal of Studies in International Higher Education*, 11: 421–432.

Knight, J. (2011). Education hubs: A fad, a brand, an innovation? *Journal of Studies in International Education*, 15: 221–240.

Marginson, S. and van der Wende, M. (2007). To rank or to be ranked: The impact of global ranking in higher education. *Journal of Studies in International Education*, 11: 306–329.

Marx, K. and Engels, F. (1969). *Manifesto of the Communist Party. Selected Works, 1.* Moscow: Progress Publishers, 98–137.

Mok, K.H. (2007). Questing for internationalization of universities in Asia: Critical reflections. *Journal of Studies in International Education*, 11: 433–454.

Naidoo, V. (2009). Transnational higher education: A stock taking of current activity. *Journal of Studies in International Education*, 13: 310–330.

QS (2013). Top Universities in Africa and the Middle East. Available at: www.topuniversities.com/where-to-study/region/africa/top-universities-africa-middle-east (accessed February 10, 2015).

Swan, M. (2013). UAE schools and universities need to do more to bolster national identity. *The National*, April 20. Available at: www.thenational.ae/news/uae-news/education/uae-schools-and-universities-need-to-do-more-to-bolster-national-identity#ixzz2r0wDfGv4 (accessed February 10, 2015).

UNDP (United Nations Development Programme) (2002). *Arab Human Development Report 2002: Creating Opportunities for Future Generations.* New York: UNDP.

UNDP (United Nations Development Programme) (2003). *Arab Human Development Report 2003: Building an Arab Knowledge Society.* New York: UNDP.

UNDP (United Nations Development Programme) (2004). *Arab Human Development Report 2004: Towards Freedom in the Arab World.* New York: UNDP.

UNDP (United Nations Development Programme) (2005). *Arab Human Development Report 2005: Towards the Rise of Women in the Arab World.* New York: UNDP.

UNESCO Institute for Statistics, Global Education Digest (2009). Comparing education statistics across the world. Montreal: UNESCO Institute for Statistics.

4 The multi-model approach to privatization

Questions of sustainability

Introduction

1993 marks the beginning of private higher education experimentation in the GCC, and, not surprisingly, the first innovations occurred in Dubai. During this year, the Australian University of Wollongong established a campus that offered English language courses and later undergraduate degree programs in business and information technology. Two years later, the American University of Dubai (AUD) opened its doors. Although now independent, the AUD was originally a branch campus of little-known American College in Atlanta, Georgia. The establishment of these relatively small, business and technology-oriented universities had four important characteristics that served as benchmarks for many of the private colleges and universities that would soon emerge in the region.

1   The University of Wollongong of Dubai (UOWD) and the AUD were originally connected to home universities in Western countries.
2   Instruction was wholly in English, rather than Arabic.
3   The UOWD and the AUD both offered gender-integrated classes and developed small campuses that (whether planned or not) encouraged the social intermingling of men and women, a first in the region.
4   Expatriate students (primarily from South Asia or other Arab countries) could earn a Western-recognized degree within Dubai, and this could be used to obtain professional employment either within or outside the region.

From these small beginnings in Western-oriented experimentation, the private higher education system has boomed since the 1990s. In the seven emirates of the UAE alone, there were 113 colleges and universities in 2013 (Bhanyani, 2013). Some of these private institutions are branch campuses and others are stand-alone establishments. While the UAE has led the way in the quantitative expansion of the higher education sector, every GCC state (including Saudi Arabia) has experienced a significant explosion and radical structural transformations in its tertiary education sector (Swan, 2013b).

Why have these radical developments occurred in societies that the rest of the world often considers "traditional" and "conservative"? The phenomenal economic

DOI: 10.4324/9780203796139-4

and social transformation of the region, characterized by the importation of advanced technology, sharp increases in living standards, and a population boom of expatriate workers and investors,[1] created a demand for alternative colleges and universities – particularly for the youth of expatriate professional families, since national universities were reserved for citizens. These national universities established during the early decades of independence (1960s, 1970s and 1980s) were also judged by many to be inadequate for the educational needs of GCC societies (see Chapter 5). The growing anxiety about the quality of higher education provided in the public universities led some rulers to attempt to offer alternative institutions of higher education (in the public as well as private sectors) so that talented national students could benefit as well.

This chapter provides an overview of the revolutionary steps taken in privatizing higher education throughout the GCC. To make sense of this flowering of educational alternatives, we develop a typology of the different institutions that now exist in the region. This will allow us to develop both a clearer historical narrative and a framework for assessing the educational viability of the very different colleges and university models that now operate within the GCC.

Classifying the new universities and colleges of the GCC

The new GCC higher educational systems that have emerged are difficult to categorize, and any effort to classify them risks oversimplification. Attempts to distinguish them as private and public colleges or for-profit and non-profit universities or even branch and independent campuses fail to capture the realities on the ground (Heath, 2012).[2] For example, the branch campuses of American universities are often heavily subsidized by local governments but governed from the home campus. Other branch campuses may have a local board of trustees and yet remain loosely connected to their home campus. Independent private institutions may be owned privately or by rulers and, in any event, are often indirectly subsidized by the government. For-profit institutions sometimes behave more like non-profits, and both non-profit and for-profit colleges operate under similar economic stress.

Despite these ambiguities, we believe that it is necessary to develop a classification system so that we can take account for the great heterogeneity in higher education that currently exists within the GCC (see Table 4.1). We associate these types of higher educational systems with different governments because the distinctions we do observe are often a reflection of the educational policies pursued by national governments and/or emirates. This does not mean, however, that all the institutions that could be classified as following a particular model are only located in a specific country or emirate.

The elite branch campus model: Qatar and Abu Dhabi (UAE)

The educational innovation that has attracted the most international attention is the elite branch campus model that is prevalent in Qatar and the Emirate of Abu

Table 4.1 Classification of the private universities in the GCC

Model	Type of ownership	Financial status	Prevalent in
Elite branch campus model	Branch campus of Western university	Dependent on government subsidies For-profit	Qatar Abu Dhabi
Education malls model	Branch campus of foreign university, independent	Self-sufficient For-profit	Dubai Educational Free Zones
Regulated privatization model	Independent with external affiliation	Self Sufficient For profit	Oman, Bahrain, Kuwait
Semi-private model Semi-public	Independent	Indirect government subsidies For-profit or non-profit	Sharjah, Abu Dhabi, Northern Emirates, Kuwait, Dubai

Dhabi in the UAE. These are branch campuses invited by the government to offer specific academic programs. The government offers generous subsidies in terms of capital expenditures by paying for the construction of the campus, its maintenance (Lane and Kinser, 2011) and generous scholarship grants to admitted students. We will argue that it is difficult to assess the educational and economic benefits that this model bestows on the subsidizing country, as few national students are admitted to these branch campuses. Nevertheless, the worldwide reputation of the home universities adds prestige and enhances the image of the host country/emirate.

Qatar's Education City: home of the elite branch campuses in the state of Qatar

Like its GCC neighbors, Qatari higher education is a fairly recent development. Before 1973 Qatar had no higher education institutions and Qataris who wanted and could pursue their education beyond high school had to travel abroad. Qatar's first modern university was its national public university, Qatar University (QU). QU opened in 1973 in order to train nationals to lead their country's development projects. By the mid-1990s, but particularly after the events of 9/11, Qatar embarked on major reforms of its educational landscape by encouraging the establishment of private institutions and initiating reforms of the public ones.

When former Emir Hamad took over from his father as ruler of Qatar in 1995, he implemented major reforms in the sectors of health and education to prepare future Qatari generations to take over the development of their country (Moini *et al.*, 2009). As outlined in Qatar's National Vision 2030 (World Data on Education: Qatar, 2010), the reforms have included human, economic, social and environmental development. However, human development is undoubtedly the major priority in this vision as it is considered the fuel for progress in the other three sectors. This prioritization is manifested in the heavy investment in the educational system and the implementation of a series of reforms from the elementary to the university sectors.

The reforms were a response to both educational and political considerations as well as external pressures. It was believed that the traditional approach to learning in the Arab/Muslim world had failed to develop the analytical and critical thinking skills needed for the twenty-first century economies. In the post 9/11 United States, there were claims that traditional Muslim schooling tended to foster "terrorist tendencies and intolerance" among its graduates (Blanchard, 2008). The US Congress even passed a law that "requires the Administration to submit an annual report to Congress on the efforts of Arab and Muslim countries to increase the availability of modern basic education and to close educational institutions that promote religious extremism and terrorism" (Blanchard, 2008: 6).

To modernize its educational system, the Qatari ruling family invited the RAND Corporation to lead its reforms and overhaul the whole educational system, from its content, methodology and administration, to outcomes. As part of the reforms, QU, still the only national university in the country, adopted a US system of liberal arts education but the more significant step was the establishment of "Education City," housing branch campuses of select foreign universities in Qatar (Lewin, 2008). This resulted in dramatic diversification of the educational landscape. Education City, located in Qatar's capital city, Doha, was established in 2000 by the Qatar Foundation for Education, Science, and Community Development (founded in 1995). Education City is a not-for-profit, semi-governmental body headed by the former Emir's wife, Sheikha Moza Al Misnad.[3] It hosts several research centers, administrative organizations and branch campuses of foreign universities that were carefully selected from leading US universities and invited to offer one of their prestigious, specialized degree programs in Doha. Education City also houses other institutes that offer vocational and technical training even though they are not formally part of the Education City structure. The first branch campuses to open were: Virginia Commonwealth University (1998), Weill Cornell Medical College (2001), and Texas A&M University (2003). Carnegie Mellon University followed in 2004, Georgetown University in 2005 and Northwestern University in 2008 (see Table 4.2). The European branch campuses of HEC Paris and UCL Qatar opened branches in 2011.[4]

Each of the branch campuses was selected to offer its "best programs" and is expected to maintain the same admission, academic and graduation standards as in the home campus. Degrees conferred in Qatar by these branches are supposed to be equivalent to the ones conferred at home. Instruction is in English and is co-educational. To increase the chances of the best qualified Qatari students to access these branch campuses, Qatar Foundation also opened an Academic Bridge Program aimed at improving high school graduates skills in English, mathematics, computer literacy, and study skills.

In addition to the foreign campuses, one Qatari institution, the Qatar Faculty of Islamic Studies (QFIS), is also housed in Education City since 2007 and offers a master's degree in Islamic studies. Additionally, there are other foreign campuses that have opened in Doha since 2002, such as the Canadian Technical College, the College of the North Atlantic (replacing a state-run vocational college), CHN University of the Netherlands offering bachelor's degree programs in hospitality-related fields and in business administration and the University of Calgary which offers a four-year degree program in nursing.

As part of its 2030 vision, Qatar Foundation launched graduate programs and research centers by inviting its branch universities to offer interdisciplinary masters' and PhDs under the new Hammad Bin Khalifa University (HBKU) (Mathews, 2013). According to the new university's provost Dr. David B. Prior, the Western branch campuses will be able "to build graduate programs all the way to PhD in some areas and ... to step beyond what they are doing now and do things they couldn't do on their own." The plan is to build on the strengths of the undergraduate programs offered by each of the branch campuses to create something new under HBKU's leadership. However, this remains a work in

Table 4.2 List of private higher education institutions in Doha, Qatar

Name of institution	Date of establishment	Number of students (2013)
Hamad Bin Khalifa University (HBKU)	1995	2,300
Virginia Commonwealth University in Qatar	1998	259
Stenden University Qatar	2000	58 graduates in Spring 2013 (http://marhaba.com.qa/58-graduate-from-stenden-university-qatar/)
Weill Cornell Medical College in Qatar (WCMCQ)	2001	265
College of North Atlantic Qatar (vocational)	2002	4,600
Texas A&M University-Qatar (TAMUQ)	2003	543
Carnegie Mellon University in Qatar	2004	370
Georgetown University School of Foreign Service in Qatar	2005	230
University of Calgary Qatar	2007	400
Northwestern University in Qatar	2008	400
HEC Paris	2011	44 graduates in Spring 2013 (www.gulf-times.com/qatar/178/details/351771/hec-paris-in-qatar%E2%80%99s-newest-batch-graduates)
University College London Qatar (UCL)	2011	32 students accepted in 2012 (www.zawya.com/story/UCL_Qatar_Welcomes_its_First_Intake_of_32_Students-ZAWYA20120828131143/)

Sources: www.hbku.edu.qa/; www.qatar.vcu.edu/at-a-glance; www.qatar.tamu.edu/; www.stenden.com/en/locations/qatar/Pages/default.aspx; http://qatar-weill.cornell.edu/aboutUs/purposeMission.html; http://qatar.sfs.georgetown.edu/; www.cna-qatar.com/AboutCNAQ/Pages/facts.aspx; www.qatar.cmu.edu/; www.qatar.ucalgary.ca/; www.qatar.northwestern.edu/; www.ucl.ac.uk/qatar; www.hec.edu/.

progress as the branch campuses seem to focus on establishing robust BA programs. As a result, while the response to the proposed integration is generally positive, few steps have been implemented toward this goal. In 2013, Sheikh Abdulla bin Ali al-Thani, President of HBKU and Vice President of the Qatar Foundation, announced that University College London Qatar (UCL Qatar) is the first partner university with HBKU offering a Master of Arts in Library and Information Studies. He also confirmed that another planned master's on energy resources is planned with three of the Education City campuses (Varghese, 2013) where each would cover particular aspects of the program. The three branch campuses to be involved in these graduate programs are Texas A&M which would cover technical subjects, Georgetown University would provide political subjects, and HEC Paris would cover the business field. It is hoped that HBKU will integrate the different branch campuses into new units of graduate instruction, where each will function as an independent department of the new university. Presently, HBKU's website lists five graduate colleges without specific mention of partnerships with the existing branch campuses. These colleges include the College of Sciences, Engineering and Technology, the College of Humanities and Social Sciences, the College of Law and Public Policy, the College of Public Health, the College of Business and the Qatar Faculty of Islamic Studies (QFIS).

The difficulty of establishing these MA and PhD programs is indicative of the limited cooperation between the elite branch campuses even at the undergraduate level. In principle, cross-registration in some select courses is possible to fulfill home degree requirements. For example, it is possible for a Texas A&M University, Qatar (TAMUQ) engineering student to register for an art class at Virginia Commonwealth or a political science course at Georgetown University (Tamar, 2008). However, in practice this cross-registration is problematic due to scheduling conflicts and heavy requirements by each home university (Texas A&M University at Qatar).

In terms of numbers, Education City seems to have already exceeded expectations by 2013. The number of students enrolled in the various campuses reached the 2,500 student population targeted for 2015 and expects to go beyond 4,500 by 2020 (Mathews, 2013). But as Table 4.2 shows, the overall number of students in each branch campus remains relatively low except for vocational institutions such as the College of North Atlantic. Even more significant is the percentage of Qataris, which is publicly unknown, but is not likely to exceed a third of total enrollments (Mathews, 2013). Such low numbers raise questions about the long-term sustainability of these branch campuses independently of the heavy government subsidization. Many Qatari students choose to benefit from the availability of the Hamad Bin Khalifa and Tamim Bin Hamad scholarships for study abroad in pre-designated disciplines selected by the Supreme Educational Council (SEC) instead of studying at home.

Even though Education City sets minimum quotas of Qatari nationals to be admitted to the branch campuses, the quotas cannot be enforced in all campuses because of variations in the demand for the discipline being offered and the skill set required for entry. For example, TAMUQ has the highest proportion of Qatari students because of the high demand for engineers in local companies and a better preparation in math in Qatari high schools. This compares to WCMCQ (Weill-Cornell Medical College-Qatar) which has the lowest proportion of Qatari students, given the skills required and the length of study in medicine. The majority of the students in the six campuses are children of expatriate residents and around 10 percent come as foreign students specifically to join these universities.

While one of the major goals of Education City is to offer quality education to Qatari students, improving high school graduates' competencies to meet admission requirements remains a major challenge that limits their access. In addition to major reforms going on at the pre-university level to raise students' competencies, some branch campuses such as Georgetown University, Qatar are offering pre-college summer programs (Georgetown Pre-College Summer (GPS)) for high school graduates to improve their reading, writing and research skills in order to prepare them for university study. The program also covers mathematics and economics and provides a practical preparation for Scholastic Assessment Test (SAT) exams (School students in Qatar prepared for university life by Georgetown, 2013).

Other challenges relate to cultural norms and political culture differences between the branch campuses and the Qatari context. So far, the foreign universities have been able to evade many questions such as cultural taboos, governance, university autonomy, and pay inequality based on origin of expatriates. They usually justify some of the concessions they have had to make in terms of academic freedom by pointing out that universities are "subject to the laws of the land, and the laws here are somewhat different in some areas," as stated by David Prior, HBKU provost when he was asked about the extent to which universities can criticize the government. In fact, lack of freedom is often mentioned by academics in the home campuses as a costly compromise in return for important financial backing from the Qatari government. Provost Prior explained that: "One has to be sensitive to the political and social environment in which one lives," and that "Academic freedom is in the eye of the beholder. There are different political contexts in which universities have to work" (Mathews, 2013).

A major achievement worth pointing out is the apparent success of providing gender-integrated university instruction. In all GCC countries gender segregation in education is the norm, but each of the six branch campuses is able to offer co-educational education. This constitutes a major break with tradition. Male and female students attend mixed classes and collaborate in all subjects except in the physical education classes that remain segregated.

In the area of governance, all branch campuses follow the US home campus but some have local boards where local members from Qatar Foundation and business leaders participate. For example, Texas A&M University at Qatar established its Joint Advisory Board (JAB) in 2003. The board provides advice regarding the management and operation of Texas A&M at Qatar to the dean and to the Qatar Foundation. The JAB represents an attempt to build a prestigious local body that "is responsible for the ongoing review and evaluation of the success of Texas A&M at Qatar" (Texas A&M University at Qatar website).

The private universities that have opened in Education City and elsewhere in Doha, Qatar, have undeniably brought choice and increased opportunities in higher education for Qatari students. The Qatar Foundation, the sponsor of the Education City project, sought to not only provide quantity but quality in higher education by inviting leading Western universities. The foundation offered these institutions generous financial incentives and a great degree of autonomy relative to the national institutions. Despite this support, it is not clear that the elite branch campuses have sustainable local backing. A survey commissioned by Booz & Co. in the GCC countries found that 40 percent of students surveyed in Qatar felt that they had no input in the decision-making process relating to their education. This exclusion tended to make many of them (21 percent) mistrust their education leaders (Missing link in GCC's education reform strategy, 2013).

One issue, as Mounira Jamjoom, a senior research associate, noted, is the poor output of the rest of the educational system in Qatar and the GCC. Despite great strides in education, the national population still suffers from a high rate of youth unemployment. The Booz & Co. study attributes the educational shortcomings to:

> lack of well-trained teachers, outdated teaching methods, curricula that are neither relevant nor innovative, limited use of technology in the classroom, and little in the way of academic advice or career counseling [that] are contributing to the mismatch between the outputs of the GCC's education system and the needs of the employment market.
>
> (Missing link in GCC's education reform strategy, 2013)

We will explore the linkages between higher education reforms and labor market failings for the national population in Chapter 9.

Abu Dhabi's prestige branch campuses

Five years after Qatar began Education City and seven years after the first elite branch campus was established in Doha, Abu Dhabi Educational Council (ADEC) was formed by the emirate's government "to develop education and educational institutions in the Emirate of Abu Dhabi, implement innovative educational policies ... support educational institutions and staff to achieve the objectives of national development in accordance with the highest international standards" (About ADEC). As a result of the decisions of ADEC, which enjoyed the important backing of Crown Prince Mohammed bin Zayed al Nahyan, the government of Abu Dhabi announced that New York University and Paris-Sorbonne University would open campuses that would offer degree programs that are equivalent to those of their home campuses. Paris-Sorbonne opened in 2006, while New York University began its undergraduate program in the Fall 2010 semester. Each branch campus offers specialized degrees in specific disciplines.

Abu Dhabi's approach to higher education is similar to the Qatari model described above. Both governments offer important financial incentives to high profile universities. ADEC has granted full scholarships to most students joining New York University Abu Dhabi (NYUAD), has built modern state-of-the-art educational facilities, and provides substantial subsidies toward campus operating expenses. But, unlike the Qatar Foundation's policy of requiring that a specified percentage of the student body (40 percent) of the branch campus' student population be nationals, neither NYUAD nor Paris-Sorbonne University at Abu Dhabi (PSUAD) are under such a restriction. As a result, the otherwise diverse student body is almost completely non-national. Indeed, although the NYUAD website and promotional materials highlight the diversity of their student body, very few Emirati youth are part of this experience.[5]

Branch universities position themselves as centers of excellence in education and research in the region. They highlight their ties with the home university to emphasize the Western brand of education generally associated with prestige and status. They also highlight their contribution to the regional economic development and their respect of local cultural norms. Both NYUAD and PSUAD sponsor annual lecture series that attract large national and non-national audiences from Abu Dhabi. In addition, NYUAD runs a small, intensive annual seminar on American politics for approximately 12 students from the three federal universities (University of the United Arab Emirates, Zayed University, and the Higher Colleges of Technology) that includes a trip to New York City and Washington, DC.[6]

Despite these outreach efforts, the overwhelming impression one gets from reading NYU-Abu Dhabi's own publicity is that this is an elite undergraduate university that exists inside a protected Western bubble that separates it from the rest of Abu Dhabi and the UAE. The recent move to the newly built campus on Saadiyat Island outside of the city center further accentuates this separation (Dight, 2014). Students are recruited in large part from outside the UAE and top students are drawn to joining NYUAD by offering them all-expenses-paid education and generous international exchange programs. It is true that this separate world's reality is not unique to the education sector. Abu Dhabi and Dubai in particular are UAE cities that are known for their vibrant expatriate communities and associated entertainment events with little interaction or productive contact with Emirati society in general. Still, the creation of a heavily subsidized institution of higher education which provides hardly any education services to the national population raises the question about the benefits that Abu Dhabi receives from this high profile project.

The other elite university to set up in Abu Dhabi was even more of a gamble. The prestigious French Sorbonne University opened a branch campus in 2006 with 100 students. It offered undergraduate degree programs in arts, social sciences and sciences with French as a medium of instruction (Swan, 2011). Today, the Sorbonne has over 600 students, is opening a research center and with the collaboration of ADEC is encouraging its graduates to enroll in PhD programs in France. It also has had to adapt to the English dominance in the region and started offering its degree program in physics in English. Sorbonne leaders explain this shift to meeting the needs of the job market for physics teachers and the expansion of the aeronautics industry in the Emirate of Abu Dhabi. The Sorbonne AD campus director, Eric Fouache, explained this move by stating that "Although students will study physics in English, they will also have to study French as their secondary language, keeping them rooted to the French way of thinking, culture and language" (Swan, 2013a). INSEAD is another branch campus of a French institution. It opened in 2010 and only offers specialized graduate education in business.

One of the major challenges that the elite branch campuses have to face is aligning learning outcomes of the branch campus to those in the home university. Indeed degree equivalence is one of the attractive features and marketing tools branch campuses use to enroll international students. However, there are many obstacles that stand in the way of achieving this commitment. The obstacles are both at the level of the students' academic backgrounds and study skill sets they bring with them (see Chapter 5) as well as the faculty. While some faculty are on temporary loan from the home campus to the branch campus, most are locally hired or specifically hired for the branch campus. These faculty work under different employment regulations that offer less security and fewer financial benefits for those faculty who are recruited locally. In addition, every faculty member must teach and do research in a different cultural and political environment than their colleagues' experience at the home campus. Finally, locally recruited faculty members receive significantly lower financial benefits than those who are recruited internationally. All these factors make it difficult to really provide an equivalent academic experience. Faculty grievances center on inadequate access to research funds, problems of inadequate local governance and job security.[7] The home campus administrators could not reasonably promise to the faculty in Doha the same employment conditions, and this inevitably led to tension. None of this suggests that the students of the elite branch campuses receive an inferior education when compared to those of the home campus but the education is clearly not identical. The data suggest that the students are highly qualified, and our interviews indicate that the faculty and administrators of these academic outposts are highly motivated as well. Nevertheless, it is also the case that the education experience in Doha and Abu Dhabi is different, and this might make it difficult to maintain the separate but equal commitments of the home institutions and host governments that have sponsored these ambitious endeavors. Despite the achievements of the elite branch campuses, it is not clear that this model is either sustainable or replicable.

Education malls model: Dubai

We noted in the introductory paragraph of this chapter that Dubai played a leading role in the introduction of private universities and colleges into the region. However, its approach to educational innovation is quite distinct from the more famous innovations of Qatar and Abu Dhabi discussed above. Rather than focusing on inviting a few branch campuses from prestigious American or European universities and colleges, the Dubai government offers a neo-liberal or relatively laissez-faire space for producing higher education and has been a fertile ground for experimenting in the selling and marketing of educational services. The emirate provides infrastructure in designated free trade zones and then invites universities and colleges to offer their academic programs. This approach represents a more deregulated branch campus model that creates a much larger number of less prestigious educational products. This is why we call this an educational mall approach which fits in the overall economic development plans of Dubai.[8]

Table 4.3a gives a list of both locally owned campuses and branch campuses in Dubai. Private universities vary in terms of which curriculum they choose to follow – American, British, UAE/Arab, Russian, Iranian or Indian, to name some. There are over 57 branch campuses located in Dubai free zones, Dubai Knowledge Village (DKV) and Dubai International Academic City (DIAC). The phenomenal increase in the number of private higher education institutions in Dubai was encouraged by attractive incentives offered by the TECOM Investments Company for those industries that establish branches in the ten free zones business parks which specialize in five industry clusters (education, information and communication technology, media, sciences, and manufacturing and logistics) (TECOM Investments, 2013). The Education Cluster (EDC) oversees both DIAC and DKV. DKV was the first to open in 2003, followed by DIAC in 2005 where most branch campuses are located today. DKV presently has 450 Human Resource and Training Institutes and DIAC houses 21 of the UAE's 37 international branch universities in addition to other private and public universities. These are relatively self-contained educational zones spread over 18 million square feet. In addition to these two free zones specialized in education enterprises, Dubai also encouraged medical schools and finance institutions to open up educational branches in corresponding industry free zones such as Dubai Healthcare City (DHC) and Dubai International Financial Center (DIFC) in 2004.

The Dubai branch campuses in the free zones (66 percent of the total institutions offering tertiary education) are set up as private for-profit businesses that depend on their revenues for survival. The city of Dubai and TECOM Investments are also in this business for profit, and several of the educational leaders we interviewed stated that the Dubai authorities are primarily interested in their rental income. This approach has meant that even well-established educational institutions are allowed to fail in Dubai. The 2008 economic downturn, for example, led to the closure of an ambitious undergraduate program sponsored by Michigan State University. On the other hand, with the new upturn of the economy there is an increased demand for education. In its 2011 annual report, the Knowledge and Human Development Authority (KHDA) boasts a 10 percent increase in student enrollment from October 2010 in 52 tertiary education institutions. It also notes that the number of Emirati nationals studying in Dubai private institutions rose by 11 percent. It is worth stressing that the institutions defined by KHDA as tertiary institutions include those only offering post-secondary credentials (one year and above) which are physically present in

Table 4.3a Dubai's colleges and universities

Institution	Location	Date of establishment	Number of students (2013)
American University in the Emirates	DIAC	2007	2,500
Amity University	DIAC	2011	700
Birla Institute of Technology and Science (BITS Pilani)	DIAC	2000	1,800
Boston University Institute for Dental Research and Education	DHCC	2008	50
British University in Dubai	DIAC	2004	125 students graduated in Spring 2013 (www. diacedu.com/media-center/success-stories/547-the-british-university-in-dubai-buid-8th-graduation-ceremony-sees-the-first-doctoral-graduates-amongst-125-new-postgraduates)
Cambridge College International	DKV	2007	200
CASS Business School (City University)	DIFC	2007	60
ESMOD	DIAC	2006	150
European University College	DHCC	2006	27 students in 2012 (http://dubaipostgraduate.com/content/about-us)
Exeter University	DKV	2007	5 students graduated in Spring 2013 (http://socialsciences.exeter.ac.uk/education/graduatestudies/professionaldoctorates/eddtesoldubai/)
Heriot-Watt University	DIAC	2006	1,300
Hult International Business School	DIAC	2008	400 students in Fall 2012 (www.thenational.ae/news/uae-news/education/hult-business-school-opens-dedicated-campus-in-dubai-internet-city)
Imam Malik College	DIAC	2011	N/A
Institute of Management Technology – Dubai	DIAC	2006	45
Islamic Azad University	DKV	2004	N/A
London Business School	DIFC	2006	78
Manipal University	DIAC	2000	1,600

Institution	Authority	Year	Number
Manchester Business School	DKV	2006	1,000
Michigan State University Dubai	DKV	2008	200
National Institute for Vocational Education	DIAC	2006	100
Rochester Institute of Technology Dubai	DSO	2008	350
Royal College of Surgeons in Ireland	DHCC	2005	70
S.P. Jain Centre of Management	DIAC	2004	2,500
SAE Institute	DKV	2005	200
Saint Petersburg State University of Engineering and Economics (ENGECON)	DKV	2005	100
Shaheed Zulfikar Ali Bhutto Institute of Science and Technology (SZABIST)	DIAC	2003	185 graduates Spring 2013 (http://gulfnews.com/news/gulf/uae/education/bring-progressive-change-to-society-szabist-dubai-graduates-told-1.1206244)
University of Bradford in Dubai	DKV	2009	N/A
University of St. Josephs (USJ)	DIAC	2008	N/A
University of Wollongong in Dubai	DKV	1993	3,500

Dubai, but sometimes have full-time faculty flown in to teach in the Dubai campus. Eighteen higher education institutions in Dubai (34 percent) are located outside the free zones. All are for-profit institutions and are owned by local businesses except for the Strathclyde campus (housed in HCT) which is a branch campus of Strathclyde UK and offers an MBA in Dubai and Abu Dhabi (KHDA Report, 2012).

Given the rapid change and instability characteristic of the Dubai model, it is difficult to report the exact number of private universities nor access precise statistics on their student body. The size of the student body and the variety of programs offered by these institutions vary a great deal. About half have fewer than 300 enrolled students. In October 2011, there were 52 colleges or universities in Dubai serving 43,212 students (KDHA Report). In addition to the educational mall concept, Dubai also has institutions which are privately owned and generally affiliated to external institutions such as the University of Jazeera (UOJ),[9] the largest private university in Dubai with 3,130 students (see Table 4.3b). The UOJ offers bachelor's degrees in four colleges (law and economics, business administration, information technology and design, and media sciences and communication). The medium of instruction is English in most of its programs.

Regulated privatization model: Oman, Bahrain and Kuwait

The other national governments of the GCC have not followed the Qatar/Abu Dhabi elite branch campus approach or the Dubai educational mall model. Oman, Bahrain and Kuwait have instead chosen to permit the establishment of new private universities and colleges under a new regime of enhanced governmental regulation. This has led to a considerable number of private higher educational institutions that are sponsored by local elites and business groups. In most cases, these colleges and universities have also established ties with foreign counterparts.

We begin this account with Oman. This is because the government of Sultan Qaboos was the first GCC government to launch policies that permitted the establishment of a large number of private colleges and universities to respond to greater demand than public universities could accommodate.[10] Oman's approach encouraged local entrepreneurs to create independent higher educational institutions that would be obligated to subject themselves to new forms of national regulations. One of the key rules was the requirement that external institutions had to play a major role in constructing the degree programs that the new colleges and universities were offering (Donn and Al Manthri, 2010). This ambitious regulatory initiative attempted to ensure that the new institutions being created would follow rigorous rules and procedures developed by Western accreditation authorities. Through these reforms, Oman created a market-based system of higher education that was designed to increase the ability of the state to oversee the academic quality and economic sustainability of the rapidly emerging private network of tertiary educational establishments.

Table 4.3b Dubai's HEIs outside the free zones

Institution	Date of establishment	Number of students
Al Ghurair University	1999	1,000
American College of Dubai	1990	75 graduates in Spring 2013 (www.acd.ac.ae/74-american-college-of-dubai-graduation-2013.html)
American University in Dubai	1995	3,000
Canadian University in Dubai	2006	500 graduates in Spring 2013 (www.cud.ac.ae/news/canadian-university-dubai-celebrates-its-third-graduation-ceremony)
Computer College	1993	468
Dubai Medical College for Girls	1985	N/A
Dubai Pharmacy College	1992	N/A
Dubai Police Academy	1987	N/A
Dubai School of Government	2005	Over 1,500 since 2006
Emirates Academy of Hospitality Management	2001	60 in 2014
Emirates Aviation College	1991	N/A
Emirates College for Management and Information Technology	1998 (renamed in 2004)	263 in Spring 2014
Hamdan bin Mohamed e-University	2002	N/A
Islamic and Arabic Studies College	1986	N/A
University of Dubai	1997	790 in 2013
University of Jazeera		3,000
University of Modern Sciences	2010	N/A

Sources: TECOM investments (2013, July 9). Educational cluster, Annual Review for 2012; Dubai Medical College for Girls: www.dmcg.edu/home.php?navmenu=1; Dubai Pharmacy College; Dubai Police Academy: www.dubaipolice.gov.ae/dp/jsps/content/flat_content.do? contentCode= orgn16&switchLanguage=en&noCache=1 40943098304 1; Emirates College for Management and Information Technology: www.ecmit.ac.ae/detail.php?topmenu=2⊂ Hamdan bin Mohamed e-University: www.hbmsu.ac.ae/about-us/overview; Dubai School of Government: www.mbrsg.ae/HOME/ABOUT-US/The-Fact-Sheet.aspx; Emirates Academy of Hospitality Management: www.emiratesacademy.edu/en/Your-Academy/Managing-Directors-Message/; Emirates Aviation College: www.eau.ac.ae/english/about/default.aspx; Islamic and Arabic Studies College: www.islamic-college.ae/ara.html; University of Dubai: www.ud.ac.ae/en/about-ud/vision/history; www.ud.ac.ae/en/about-ud/ facts-and-figures; University of Jazeera: www.uoj.ac.ae/; University of Modern Sciences: http://ums.ae/en/about-ums/historical-background

The growth of this new sector of private education was surprisingly rapid. During the first few years of the late 1990s, four colleges were initially established in Oman. By 2008–9, however, there were 24 private colleges that provided education services to more than 30,000 students (Donn and Al Manthri, 2010). Many of the degree programs that have been created are vouched for by the external universities with which they are associated. The universities are located in the Commonwealth countries, the United States and non-Western universities such as Jordan, Lebanon and India. The curricula are designed to serve the country's 2020 labor market vision by offering diplomas and degree programs in computer sciences, engineering, commerce, business, health sciences and English language (Donn and Issan, 2007). Most of the institutions listed in Table 4.4 are relatively small with less than 2,000 students, and many are limited to providing specialized degrees in one field of study such as business or information technology. On the other hand, some of the new entrants are universities or colleges which grant both master's and bachelor degrees with more varied curricula in terms of subjects covered and in terms of rigor. In addition, these educational reforms have led to the establishment of a series of medically oriented specialized schools that were formed to train doctors, nurses and pharmacists.

Like the early non-state institutions in other GCC countries, instruction is largely in English. Classes are open to national citizens and non-citizens alike. All classes are sex-segregated, and thus, many of the institutions specialize in providing educational services to a male or female student body (Donn and Issan, 2007). Unlike Qatar and Abu Dhabi, the British, Jordanian and Indian tertiary institutions tend to have a higher involvement with their partner Omani institutions than American institutions.

An examination of private higher education audits reveals that half of the Omani institutions grant degrees that are actually conferred by other institutions. However, British institutions are more likely to have this arrangement than Jordanian and Indian institutions which also confer degrees in Oman. In some cases, only a subset of the total degrees granted by an Omani college is conferred by another institution. In other cases that often involve American universities, degrees are granted by the Omani institution itself, but state on the degree document that the academic program has been partially developed and monitored by a non-Omani institution. For example, Mazoon College states on many of its degrees that the college is affiliated with the Missouri University of Science and Technology.

The nature of external affiliations

A review of the audit panel reports on the academic arrangements that Omani institutions have with non-Omani colleges and universities reveals a variety of different relationships (Government of Oman, Oman Academic Accreditation Authority, 2014). The most intensive affiliation agreements create a type of franchise arrangement, in which the Omani institution agrees to provide a curriculum and course of study that allows the non-Omani higher education institution to grant its own degree. This should imply a very close coordination of the courses of study, supervision of examinations and other assessment instruments, and the external evaluation of the academic accomplishments of Omani students. One would also expect to observe frequent visits of academic personnel between campuses as well as the development of student and faculty exchange programs. Other looser arrangements are agreements in which the external partner agrees to provide advice as a consultant so that the Omani institutions can develop their own academic programs. In this case, an external institution will make frequent visits to Oman, but the involvement of the rest of the campus in such a program is more limited and the time and resource costs are considerably lower. It is less likely that the students and faculty will come to know each other or even, in some cases, be aware of the affiliation agreement itself.

The fact that external institutions are closely involved with the academic programs of the Omani institutions does not mean that each institution in Oman has affiliation arrangements of similar quality.[11] In general, it appears that the British institutions that are involved with Oman devote more time and resources to fulfill the requirements of their affiliation agreements. More of the degree programs are actually conferred by the British partner, and sometimes Omani students spend summers of their final year studying in the UK. Such an arrangement is not without risks. Several auditing panels mentioned that it was difficult to ensure that the Omani students could do the required academic work in English. (See Chapter 6 for further discussion on this issue.) Moreover, universities or colleges can rarely serve as turnkey institutions, in which an identical curriculum is imported into the institutions and taught in exactly the same manner. External academic programs need to be given an Omani context, and if they are not, the academic capabilities of the institution can suffer.[12]

As discussed above in the case of the elite branch model, creating academic programs to meet the needs of students in different countries and guaranteeing equivalent quality at the same time can be challenging. And, it is clear that in some cases, external institutions do not effectively accomplish both of these tasks.

It is clear that not all of the external partnerships have worked well. The international partner might not devote enough resources to fulfill their part of the agreement and the Omani institutions might use this agreement to avoid the hard work necessary to build and maintain academic quality and relevance for the Omani community around it. There is also some indication that some of the more successful institutions are beginning to use these relationships to develop their own academic programs. This type of academic Omanization could lead to the establishment of more independent, reasonably high quality institutions.

The burst of experimentation in the United Arab Emirates, Qatar and Oman did not go unnoticed by the other GCC states. Bahrain's recent higher education experience shares many features with Oman's. Like Dubai, both countries have encouraged the formation of small, for-profit colleges and universities. Also, Oman and Bahrain have attempted to ensure quality by implementing a rigorous regulatory regime inspired by Western accreditation practices. Bahrain aggressively

Table 4.4 Private universities and colleges in the Sultanate of Oman

Name	Date of establishment	Affiliations with external institutions	Degree programs
Majan College	1995	University of Bedfordshire and University of Leeds	Business, Management, Information Technology, and English Language Studies
Muscat College	1996	Scottish Qualification Authority and University of Stirling	Business and Accounting, Computing, and Built Environment Engineering
International College of Engineering and Management	1997	University of Central Lancashire	Health, Safety and Environmental Management; Mechanical Engineering; Fire Safety in Management; Facilities Management
Modern College of Business and Science	1997	University of Missouri, St. Louis	Business and Computer Science
Caledonian College of Engineering	1998	Glasgow Caledonian University; Vellore Institute of Technology (India)	Engineering and Technological Subjects
Al Zahra College of Women	1999	Ahliyya Amman University (Jordan)	Information Technology; English Language and Literature; Graphic Design; and Management and Financial Services
Mazoon College	1999	Missouri University of Science and Technolgy; Banasthali Vidyapeth University	Business and Economics; Computer Science and Information Technology; English; Psychology
Oman Medical College	2001	School of Medicine, West Virginia University	MD and BPharm
Sohar College	2001	Originally University of Lincolnshire and Humberside; presently University of Queensland	Business; Computing and Information Technology; Engineering; Social Sciences; Humanities
Sur University College	2001	Bond University (Australia)	Business; Information Systems and Technology

Institution	Year	Affiliation/Partner	Colleges/Programs
Waljat College of Applied Sciences	2001	Birla Institute of Technlogy (India)	
Middle East College of Information Technology	2002	Originally Manipal Academy of Higher Education; now Coventry University and National Records and Archive Authority, Sultanate of Oman	Business; Information Technology; and Archives and Records Management
Al Buraimi University College	2003	California State University, Northridge; Ain Shams University (Egypt)	English Translation; Accounting; Human Resources; Marketing; Business Administration; Finance and Banking; Information Systems; Computer Science; Law (Arabic)
Dhofar University	2004	American University of Beirut (Expired?)	College of Arts and Sciences; College of Commerce and Business Administration; and College of Engineering
Gulf College	2004	Staffordshire University; University of Reading; and University of Hull	Business; Computing; International Security Studies
Oman College of Management and Technology	2004	Yarmouk University (Jordan); Philadelphia University	Business; Information Systems; and Interior Design
Scientific College of Design	2004	Lebanese American University (Lebanon); Arab Community College (Jordan)	Graphic Design, Interior Design, Fine Arts, Fashion Design and Clothes Manufacturing
University of Nizwa	2004	Fourteen Memoranda of Understanding with universities or companies. Sultan Qaboos plays important advisory role	College of Arts and Sciences, College of Economics, Management and Information Systems, College of Engineering and Architecture, and College of Pharmacy and Nursing
Oman Dental College	2006	Affiliated with A.B. Shetty Memorial Institute of Dental Sciences, Mangalore, India	Bachelor of Dental Services

Source: Adapted from Audits by Oman Accreditation Council.

entered into the private higher education arena in the late 1990s after the University of Bahrain reached its capacity and otherwise qualified students were not admitted. In addition, the 9/11 attacks increased the demand for higher education in Bahrain as Saudi students who might otherwise have gone to the United States looked for alternatives. Students from the Eastern provinces of KSA and Kuwait saw Bahrain as an attractive destination.

The decision in 2001 by King Hamad to permit the accreditation of a private university, Ahlia University, marks the beginning of the effort to launch the private tertiary sector. Planning authorities eventually decided to create an educational hub that would lay the basis for a more technologically dynamic economy. In 2006, Bahrain announced its intention to create a $1 billion world class higher education complex through the Bahrain Economic Development Board.[13] This initiative was to be jointly financed with the Kuwait Finance and Investment Company and led by the reformist Crown Prince, Sheikh Salman bin Hamad al Khalifa. It anticipated attracting high quality branch campuses and 25,000 students to Bahrain. Presently, Bahrain has 17 private universities as listed by its embassy in the United States.[14] Some of the colleges were founded by local investors, while others were sponsored by American, British, Indian and Filipino institutions (see Table 4.5).

Jane Knight (2011) points out that Bahrain appears to be following regional rivals like Qatar and the UAE in its effort to create an educational hub, which she defines as an effort "to build a critical mass of local and foreign actors – including students, education institutions, companies, knowledge industries, science and technology centers – who ... engage in education, training, knowledge production, and innovation initiatives" (Knight, 2011: 211). Knight notes that this goal would, in the best of circumstances, have been hard to attain, given the fact that Bahrain was entering into the higher education innovation business relatively late.

Although the University of Bahrain remains the predominant higher education establishment in the country and the dream of creating a dynamic educational hub remains elusive, the new private sector that has largely emerged in the last decade has significantly reshaped university and college education. In the first place, it is clear that these relatively small institutions have provided expanded openings for students who are primarily interested in business and IT degree programs. These students are less likely to be Bahraini nationals, since a number of students from Saudi Arabia and Kuwait have joined some of these colleges. Institutions such as the Birla Institute of Technology, on the other hand, mainly attract expatriate South Asian students. Finally, some institutions, such as the Royal College of Women or the Arab Open University, recruit students who otherwise might be hesitant to join an institution that permits men and women to mingle together on campus.

Like Oman, many of the new Bahraini institutions are for-profit institutions that have links to higher education institutions outside the country (Karolak, 2012). Unlike Oman, there is a higher proportion of branch campuses within Bahrain. Five of the 12 institutions listed in Table 4.5 are branch campuses, and nine campuses are privately owned by Bahraini entrepreneurs or business groups.[15] Despite these differences, the structure of higher education that has emerged in Bahrain is thus quite similar to that of Oman's and very few of these colleges and universities could be considered prestigious and their quality has come under question. As such they fall short of the Bahraini government's 2006 vision of a dynamic educational hub that integrates higher learning with the construction of a dynamic, technologically sophisticated knowledge economy.

Kuwait also decided to encourage the creation of private higher educational institutions under a regime of enhanced regulations that is very similar to Oman and Bahrain's. Despite the aggressive challenges to many of the Bahraini private higher education institutions discussed above, the Kuwaiti government issued a Private Universities Decree in 2000 that permitted the establishment of higher education alternatives to the University of Kuwait. The decree also established the Private University Council (PUC) to be in charge of evaluating and licensing the academic programs offered by the new colleges and universities. All private universities, as in the case of Oman, are supposed to provide a credible affiliation of a well-regarded university or college from an OECD nation. Credible and well-regarded means that the external institution should be highly ranked within its own country, be actively involved in the development of academic programs in Kuwait, and provide its own evaluation of any change in academic programs that the private university or college with which it is affiliated is considering.

Two new private universities were established soon after these liberalizing measures were issued. The Gulf University for Science and Technology (GUST) is the first private university in Kuwait. It opened its doors to students during the academic year 2002–3. GUST was founded by an alliance of academics from Kuwait University and prominent regional businessmen. It offers undergraduate degrees through two colleges, the College of Arts and Sciences and the College of Business Administration. It also offers a master's degree in business administration. GUST has affiliation agreements with the University of Missouri-St. Louis (UMSL) and the Missouri University of Science and Technology. These partnerships provide consultancy services on the quality of academic programs, staff recruitment and the development of both academic and non-academic departments of the new university.

At around the same time that GUST was established, Shaikha Dana Nasser Sabah Al-Ahmed Al-Sabah, who is a prominent member of the Al-Sabah ruling family, founded the American University of Kuwait (AUK) based on the Amiri Decree #139 in 2003. The AUK was accredited by the PUC, the arm of the Ministry of Higher Education in Kuwait in 2006. Dartmouth College in Hanover, New Hampshire is the AUK's international partner (PUC Resolution, 5/21–2/2005). Based on the 2003 Memorandum of Understanding between the two institutions, Dartmouth provides a wide range of administrative and academic consulting services to the AUK and the two universities collaborate on joint projects. The initial agreement was recently renewed for a third time in April 2013 to extend through 2018 (AUK catalog 2013–14).

Table 4.5 Private higher education institutions of Bahrain (2000–6)

Name	Date of establishment	Affiliations with external institutions	Degree programs or colleges	Number of students
Birla Institute of Technology International	2000	Branch campus Main campus in Ranchi, India	Bachelor's degrees in Engineering, Business Education, Information Technology, and E-Commerce. Master's degrees in Business Adm.	N/A
Ahlia University	2001	Brunel University (UK)	Colleges of Arts, Sciences and Education, Business and Finance, Engineering, Information Technology, Medical and Health Sciences, Graduate Studies	2,000
AMA International University	2002	Branch campus of AMA Computer University in the Philippines	Bachelor's degrees in Business, IT, International Studies. Master's degree in Business	3,945
Arab Open University	2002	One of several open university branch campuses	Bachelor's degrees in Business and IT. Hosts several master's degrees offered by Open University of Malaysia	1,895
University College of Bahrain	2002	Collaborates with American University of Beirut	Bachelor's degrees in Business, IT and Media and Communication MBA in Islamic Finance	1,500 (30% non-nationals from other GCC nations)
Gulf University	2002		Colleges of Engineering and Science; Administrative and Financial Services; Education; and Law	534 graduated in 2011
New York Institute of Technology	2003	Branch campus of New York Institute of Technology	School of Engineering and Computer Science; Management; Architecture and Design; College of Arts and Sciences	900 students

Institution	Year	Affiliation	Faculties/Programs	Students
Delmon University for Science and Technology	2003		Faculties of Business, IT, Education, Arts and Science; College of Law	600 students graduated in 2011
Applied Science University	2004	Affiliated to Mu'tah University (Jordan); Helwan University (Egypt); Royal Police Academy (Bahrain)	Various bachelor's degrees in Business, Computer Science, Law, Political Science, Design	1,200 students (2009) Majority of students non-Bahraini
Royal College of Surgeons in Ireland	2004	Branch Campus of RCSI (Ireland)	Schools of Medicine, Nursing, and Postgraduate Studies	1,176 students
The Kingdom University	2004		Colleges of Arts; Science; Engineering, Architecture and Design; Law	1,000 (in 2008)
Royal College of Women	2006	Programs designed in collaboration with McGill University (Canada) and Middlesex University (UK)	Bachelor's degrees of Arts, Business, Law and Science; Master's degrees of Design and Fine Arts	N/A

Sources: http://moedu.gov.bh/hec/UploadFiles/Reports/HEC%20Student%20Guide.pdf; www.uniagents.com/en/institutions-bahrain/index.htm; www.mofa.gov.bh/Default.aspx?tabid=7749.

Table 4.6 Private institutions in Kuwait (2002–8)

Name	Date of establishment	Opening date and degrees offered	Enrollment
Gulf University for Science and Technology	2002–3	BSc Computer Science BA in English BA in Mass Communications BSc in Accounting BSc in MIS BSc in Finance Bsc in Bus. Administration	Between 2,000 and 3,000
Kuwait Maastricht Business School	2003–4	MBA for part-time students	Approximately 130 students per year
Arab Open University Kuwait Branch		BA in Business Studies BA in Information Technology and Computing BA in English Language and Literature BA in English and Business Masters in Bus. Adm. (MBA) MSc in Software Development MA in English Literature	
Australian College at Kuwait	2004	Bachelor of Engineering (Technology, Civil, Petroleum, and Electronics) Diploma of Engineering (approximately same sub-fields) Diploma of Aircraft Maintenance Bachelor of Business (Management and Marketing) Diploma (Management, Marketing, Human Resources)	
American University of Kuwait	2003	BA in Communications and Media English Graphic Design Accounting Finance Management Marketing Economics Computer Science Information Systems Computer Engineering International Relations Social and Behavioral Sciences (Anthropology)	

Institution	Year	Programs
American College of Middle East		Two-year programs in Business Administration Information Technology
American University of Middle East	2008	BSc in Accounting Business Administration (Finance, Information Systems, Marketing, Human Resources) Computer BSc in Engineering (Industrial Electrical, Information Systems, Telecommunications and Networking) MBA
Box Hill College Kuwait		Two-year Women's College Diplomas in Graphic Design Interior Design Website Development Management Marketing Business Services Management and IT Human Resource Management
Kuwait International Law School*		LLB (four-year undergraduate law program) Master's degree in Law

Source: www.e.gov.kw/sites/kgoenglish/Portal/Pages/Other/Universties.aspx.

According to its provost,[16] the AUK offers a liberal arts education modeled on the American educational system. Its student body is made up of 70 percent Kuwaitis and 30 percent expatriates. Ten percent of the faculty are Kuwaitis, while 60 percent are Americans and 10 percent come mainly from Australia, Canada, the UK and South Africa. Preference in recruiting faculty is given to holders of American terminal degrees. The AUK is made up of two colleges, the College of Arts and Sciences and the College of Business and Economics, and an English Intensive Program.[17]

Both GUST and AUK are for-profit institutions, although it is not clear that the investors expect the same rate of return as they would from other more traditional commercial projects.[18] The other institutions listed in Table 4.6 are very small. The American University of the Middle East (AUM) is affiliated with Purdue University, which assists it in curriculum development, academic and administrative affairs, and application of accreditation standards. The AUM is also associated with the University of Calgary in Canada to develop the College of Medicine and a university hospital.

The semi-private model: Sharjah and elsewhere

While the founding of the new, private colleges and universities began in Dubai and Oman, the opening of University City in Sharjah established one of the most important education hubs in the UAE and the region both in terms of quality and quantity. Dr. Sheikh Sultan bin Muhammad Al-Qasimi, the ruler of Sharjah, an Arab nationalist and avid supporter of education and cultural initiatives, fulfilled his vision of advancing education opportunities in Sharjah, the UAE and the Arab world by sponsoring two new universities, the gender-integrated American University of Sharjah (AUS), and the gender-segregated University of Sharjah (UoS). Sheikh Sultan's initiative can best be labelled as an attempt to create semi-private institutions since the ruler of the Emirate of Sharjah is the president of the two institutions, but administrative authority is delegated to academic administrators and the Boards of Trustees that in many ways operate along Western educational models. Although the Emirate of Sharjah continues to provide important infrastructure support, both universities are supposed to be financially self-sustaining. Enrollment is open to all qualified students.

The AUS was an attempt to create an institution similar to the American University of Beirut and the American University in Cairo, two reputable institutions in the Arab world. As a result, the sheikh decided to contract with the American University of Beirut as well as the American University in Washington, DC to organize and launch this ambitious new project (French, 2010). Other universities such as Texas A&M were contracted for the development of the college of engineering in AUS. Dr. Sheikh Sultan is the president of the AUS Board of Trustees but the day-to-day administrative and academic decisions are in the hands of administrators to offer an American-style liberal arts undergraduate program and master's degrees delivered in its colleges of Arts and Sciences, Engineering, Business Administration and Architecture and Design. As an

American model institution, English was adopted as its medium of instruction. The AUS has one of the highest admission requirements in the region with a mean Grade Point Average (GPA) entry of around 90 percent and a Test of English as a Foreign Language (TOEFL) score of 550. Its reputation as the preeminent higher education institution in the region is widely accepted and it has been ranked among the top 430 universities worldwide by Quacquarelli Symonds (QS) World Rankings. Its student body is around 6,000 students, 17 percent of whom are Emiratis. The rest of the students are a combination of other GCC nationals, children of expatriate residents and a few international students who do not come from the region (AUS website).

The controversy surrounding the creation of the gender-integrated classroom experience in conservative Sharjah was deflected by opening the gender-segregated institution, the UoS, nearby. The UoS is the largest institution in University City. It had approximately 11,000 students in 2012. Half of the student body are Emiratis, a third are Arab residents and about a third of this group are other GCC nationals. Although the UoS curriculum is also based on the American model, some of its colleges are affiliated with Australian and other institutions. English is the medium of instruction in medicine, pharmacy, health sciences, sciences, technology and engineering, while Arabic is used in social sciences and humanities. The UoS is comprised of separate women's and men's campuses and comprises 13 colleges. Its medical and health science college and university hospital are run in collaboration with Australian and British universities. The UoS also has a separate fine arts college, a community college and campuses in other parts of the Emirate of Sharjah (see Table 4.7).

Both the AUS and UoS are located in University City, which also houses the branches of the federal Higher Colleges of Technology (HCT) Sharjah Men and Women campuses, in addition to many other institutes and the Police Academy. The Emirate of Sharjah also has other private higher education institutions (HEIs) such as the privately owned Skyline College University and other tertiary institutions located outside University City such as Abu Dhabi's Khalifa University Sharjah campus and Troy University. In 2014, the ruler added a new Arabic Islamic university, Al Qassimiya University (also known as the Islamic University), to the University City complex. The university will offer majors in media, Islamic finance, Arabic studies, economics, Sharia law, engineering and Islamic architecture (*Gulf News*, 2013).

The semi-private institutions of Abu Dhabi

In addition to its high profile flagship branch campuses of NYUAD and the Sorbonne AD, the Emirate of Abu Dhabi houses other tertiary institutions that are either completely or partially supported by the government of Abu Dhabi rather than the UAE's Ministry of Higher Education. These semi-private or public institutions have specific industries and foreign partnerships such as the Petroleum Institute (PI) and Masdar Institute of Science and Technology (MIST), which are both specialized in energy sciences. The PI was established in 2001 and offers both graduate and undergraduate degrees in engineering with a focus on oil industry research. It has several collaborative partnerships with companies in the domain, particularly the Abu Dhabi National Oil Company (ADNOC) as well as BP, Japan Oil Development Company, Shell and Total (The Petroleum Institute website). MIST was established in 2009 in collaboration with the Massachusetts Institute of Technology (MIT) as its primary partner and stakeholder. It offers specializations focusing on renewable energies. "The joint partnership [with MIT] extends from collaborative research and development of the Institute's degree programs, to the assessment and recruitment of potential faculty, students and senior administration staff" (Masdar University website). MIST is part of Masdar city in Abu Dhabi, which is a large scale experiment of a green, zero carbon emissions space within this very energy-intensive region. MIST offers graduate programs and has an ambitious R&D focus on alternative energies and ecology.

Other institutions such as Fatima College of Health Sciences and Emirates College for Advanced Education provide training in health care and education professions. Khalifa University of Science, Technology and Research (KUSTAR) was launched by the Abu Dhabi government in 2007. The university has partnerships with foreign universities as well as local industries and offers both graduate and undergraduate degrees in Information and Communication Technologies (ICT), aerospace, transport and logistics, energy and the environment, health care and security (Khalifa University website).

Another category of universities in Abu Dhabi is its six private universities, four of which are locally owned. These are Abu Dhabi University, Al Hosn University, Al Khawarismi International College and Al Ain University of Science and Technology. The other two are the New York Institute of Technology set up in 2005 and University of Strathclyde Business School opened in 1995, which are the only branches of foreign institutions that are not supported by the government. Like Abu Dhabi, the other emirates, Ajman, Ras Al Khaimah, Umm Al Quwayn and Fujairah, have adopted a combination of approaches and offer both private and branch universities as listed in Table 4.8.

The above description of the UAE's private higher education shows that it is difficult to fit all the institutions in clearly defined models. Given its unique federal structure, it is not surprising that the educational models followed (from elite branch campus to educational mall to regulated privatization to semi-private) coexist within this small state. The extraordinary experimentation we observe in Sharjah, Dubai and Abu Dhabi makes this country unlike any other in the region. Indeed as French (2010: 13) argues:

> The major center for education in the Gulf if not the region, will be the UAE. The three leading emirates in this enterprise are Abu Dhabi, Dubai and Sharjah. The hallmark of reforms and expansion in all three cases has been Americanization but the distinct differences in the models adopted by the three governments are in themselves instructive.

Table 4.7 Private universities in the Northern Emirate

Emirate	Name	Date of establishment	Enrollments
Sharjah	American University of Sharjah (http://en.wikipedia.org/wiki/American_University_of_Sharjah)	1997	6,000
	University of Sharjah		
	Al Qassimiya University	1998	11,000
	Khalifa University – Sharjah branch (http://en.wikipedia.org/wiki/Khalifa_University)	2014	No info
	Skyline University College, Sharjah	1989	1,300 at present
	Troy University	1990	No info
		No info about Sharjah campus	No info
Ajman	Ajman University of Science and Technology (http://en.wikipedia.org/wiki/Ajman_University_of_Science_and_Technology)	1998	No info
	City University College of Ajman		
	Gulf Medical College, now Gulf Medical University (http://en.wikipedia.org/wiki/Gulf_Medical_University)		
RAK	Cornerstone College of International Studies	2011	No info
		1998	No info
	American University of Ras Al Khaimah (http://en.wikipedia.org/w/index.php?title=American_University_of_Ras_Al_Khaimah&action=edit&redlink=1)	2011	No info
		No info about it (I checked diff. websites)	No info
	Birla Institute of Technology	No info	
	Bolton University of Ras Al Khaimah	2008	No info
		2006	Over 500 at present (from official website)
	RAK Medical & Health Sciences University – College of Dental Sciences (http://en.wikipedia.org/w/index.php?title=RAK_Medical_%26_Health_Sciences_University_–_College_of_Dental_Sciences&action=edit&redlink=1)		967 (from official website)
Fujairah	Fujairah College	2006	No info

Sources: www.aus.edu/; www.kustar.ac.ae/; www.skylineuniversity.com/Page/Home.aspx; www.ajman.ac.ae/; www.cuca.ae/; www.gmu.ac.ae/; http://cornerstonecollegerak.com/; www.aurak.ac.ae/; bitrak.ae/www.bolton.ac.uk/UAECampus/Home.aspx; http://courses.laimoon.com/uae/schools/university-of-bolton (date of establishment for Bolton university); www.rakmhsu.com/; www.fc.ac.ae/.

Table 4.8 The branch and private universities in the Emirate of Abu Dhabi (UAE)

	Date of establishment	Degrees offered	Number of students
Elite branch campuses			
New York University, Abu Dhabi (NYUAD) http://nyuad.nyu.edu/	2005	**Undergraduate programs** BA in Arab Crossroads BA in Art and Art History BS in Biology BS in Chemistry BS in Civil Engineering BS in Computer Engineering BS in Computer Science BA in Economics BS in Electrical Engineering BA in Film and New Media BS in General Engineering BA in History BA in Literature and Creative Writing BS in Mathematics BS in Mechanical Engineering BA in Music BA in Philosophy BS in Physics BA in Political Science BA in Psychology BA in Social Research and Public Policy BA in Theater BA in Visual Arts **Graduate programs** PhD in Chemistry PhD in Biology PhD in Engineering	450

| Paris Sorbonne University, Abu Dhabi (PSUAD) www.sorbonne.ae/EN/pages/default.aspx | 2006 | **Undergraduate programs**
French and Comparative Literature
Philosophy and Sociology
Geography and Planning
Applied Foreign Languages (LEA)
History
Sociology
Law
Economics and Management
Physics
Archaeology and History of Art
Information and Community

Graduate and postgraduate programs
Muslim and Arab World Studies
Social Research: Consulting, Survey and Evaluation
International Law, International Relation and Diplomacy
International Business Law
Sustainable Development Law
Banking and Finance
Health Economics
Marketing Management Communication and Media
International Business and Languages
Teaching French as a Foreign Language
Publishing, Information and Multimedia
Transports, Logistics, Territories and Environment
Urban and Regional Planning
Environment: Dynamics of Territories and Societies
History of Art and Museum Studies
Performing Arts Management | 700 |

continued

Table 4.8 Continued

	Date of establishment	Degrees offered	Number of students
INSEAD		MBA Executive Education Global Executive MBA Master in Finance Executive Master in Consulting and Coaching for Change PhD	
Other branch campus			
Université Mohammed V-Agdal Abu Dhabi (UM5A-AD)		No information available	
Private HEIs			
Al Khawarizmi International College www.khawarizmi.com/	1985	Associate and bachelor's degrees in Business Administration Information Technology Health Management Computer Graphics and Animation Fashion Designing Medical Records Islamic Banking and Finance	N/A
University of Strathclyde Business School – UAE www.strath.ac.uk/business/internationalcentres/dubaiandabudhabi/	1995	MBA	
NYIT	2005	Undergraduate and graduate degrees in: Business Administration (BS and MBA) Interior Design (BFA) Instructional Technology (MS) Information, Network and Computer Security (MS)	N/A

Abu Dhabi University (ADU) www.adu.ac.ae/	2000		4000

College of Arts and Sciences
Bachelor of Arts in Arts, Culture and Heritage Management
Bachelor of Arts in Mass Communication
Bachelor of Science in Environmental Health and Safety
Bachelor of Science in Public Health (offered for female students only)
Bachelor of Arts in English
Bachelor of Arts in Persian Language
Bachelor of Science in Environmental Science (offered for female students only)
College of Business Administration
Bachelor of Business Administration
Bachelor of Business Administration in Accounting
Bachelor of Business Administration in Finance
Bachelor of Business Administration in Human Resources Management (offered for female students only)
Bachelor of Business Administration in Management
Bachelor of Business Administration in Marketing
College of Engineering
Bachelor of Architecture
Bachelor of Science in Chemical Engineering
Bachelor of Science in Computer Engineering
Bachelor of Science in Interior Design
Bachelor of Science in Mechanical Engineering
Bachelor of Science in Aviation
Bachelor of Science in Civil Engineering
Bachelor of Science in Electrical Engineering
Bachelor of Science in Information Technology

continued

Table 4.8 Continued

	Date of establishment	Degrees offered	Number of students
		Postgraduate programs College of Arts and Sciences Professional Graduate Diploma in Teaching College of Business Administration Master of Business Administration MBA with concentration in Finance Doctor of Business Administration MBA with concentration in Human Resource Management Master of Human Resource Management College of Engineering Master of Science in Civil Engineering (Construction Engineering Management concentration) Master of Science in Civil Engineering (Structural Engineering Concentration) Master of Project Management Master of Science in Civil Engineering (General Civil Engineering) Master of Engineering Management Master of Science in Information Technology	
Al Ain University of Science & Technology	2005	BSc in Computer Engineering BSc in Network and Communications Engineering BSc in Computer Science BSc in Software Engineering BSc in Pharmacy BA in Law BEd – Teacher Education (Arabic Language and Islamic Studies) BEd – English Language Teacher Education Bachelor of Arts in Applied Psychology Bachelor of Arts in Applied Sociology Bachelor of Education in Special Education BBA – Management BBA – Accounting	N/A

BBA – Marketing
BBA – Human Resources Management
BBA – Management Information Systems
Bachelor of Mass Communication – Journalism
Bachelor of Mass Communication – Advertising
Bachelor of Mass Communication – Public Relations
Master in Private Law
Master in Public Law
Master of Art in Teaching English to Speakers of Other Languages
Professional Diploma in Teaching
Master of Business Administration (MBA/General, Accounting,
Finance, Marketing, HRM and MIS)

Al Hosn University	2005	500

Undergraduate programs
Bachelor of Architectural Engineering (BAE)
Bachelor of Business Administration (Finance)
Bachelor of Business Administration (HRM)
Bachelor of Business Administration (Marketing)
Bachelor of Business Administration in Accounting
Bachelor of Business Administration(Intl. Business)
Bachelor of Business Administration (Intl. Economics)
Bachelor of Education
Bachelor of Interior Design (BID)
Bachelor of Management Information Systems
Bachelor of Science in Civil Engineering (BSCE)
Bachelor of Science in Industrial Engineering (BSIE)
Bachelor of Science in Mechanical Engineering (BSME)
Bachelor of Science in Software Engineering (BSSE)
Bachelor of Urban Planning (BUP)

continued

Table 4.8 Continued

Date of establishment	Degrees offered	Number of students
	Graduates Diploma of Education (Arabic) Graduate Certificate in Building Engineering Graduate Certificate in Engineering Management Master in Buildings Engineering (MBE) Master in Engineering Management (MEM) Master of Business Administration (MBA) Master of Education	

Sources: www.nyuad.nyu.edu/; www.fchs.ac.ae/; www.sorbonne.ae/; www.ecae.ac.ae/; www.um5a.ac.ma/; www.kic.ae/; www.strath.ae/; www.adu.ac.ae; www.alainuniversity.ac.ae/; www.alhosnu.ae/; www.nyit.edu/united_arab_emirates/.

Concluding thoughts

The Qatar and Abu Dhabi model of allowing elite branch campuses to set up academic programs in the Gulf may seem to be very successful because it removes the need to impose an extra layer of governmental regulation. The sponsoring university has a stake in maintaining the prestige of its academic product and will therefore ensure that educational quality is protected. After all, such programs must involve the sponsoring Western institution in the direct supervision of the academic program and staff. While attractive as a short cut to academic quality, our earlier analysis of Education City in Qatar and NYU in Abu Dhabi suggest that such turnkey projects are not automatically suitable for the national population (Ross, 2011; Lehman, 2011). In both cases, the academic standards of the imported institutions serve to exclude most national students. Even more serious is the problem of Western cultural hegemony. An aggressive commitment to the superiority of the Georgetown or Texas A&M or NYU way of doing things can prevent or prohibit administrators from both making adjustments in the academic curriculum of the branch campus and providing a welcoming environment to talented students from the GCC. Paradoxically, the demand that the branch campuses provide *structurally identical* degree programs reinforces the tendency to create higher educational institutions that do not engage with the bulk of the national population.

One could argue that these are short-term problems. Eventually, the branch campuses will have to embed themselves in the community. However, the ways in which the branch campuses have been created can lead one to question this optimistic scenario. In the first place, the enormous financial commitment of Qatar or Abu Dhabi to these prestige academic products could lead to an unexpected retrenchment if economic conditions ever deteriorate in the Gulf. It is more likely that more acceptable and less controversial national educational institutions will be rescued if budget cuts have to be implemented. In the second place, the liberal political economic projects of many of the Gulf rulers are not necessarily accepted by all members of the national population or even by all members of the ruling families. As we shall see in our analysis of reform of the national university systems, policies can change rapidly and unexpectedly in the GCC. In such a world, it is important for non-public higher educational institutions to be able to exist relatively autonomously from the state. This requires a sound financial footing and some popular support. For that reason, Qatar's insistence on maintaining a quota for national students within the elite branch campuses may serve these institutions well in the long run.

The final difficulty with the elite branch campuses is that their existence also relies on support in the home campus, and this is often difficult to guarantee. Most of the decisions by educational authorities in New York City or London or Paris or College Station, Texas are made by high level educational officials within the home university with few consultations with the rest of the faculty. Thus, most of the faculty and students of the home universities are disconnected from the globalizing ambitions of the university leaders and may come to resent what seems like an unnecessary diversion of precious academic resources. More-over, since the political environment of the Gulf is very different from that of the United States, France or the United Kingdom, it is not difficult to make the case that establishing a branch campus in a non-democratic society violates principles of academic freedom and integrity (Brooks, 2011).

Whatever the validity of this argument, the important point here is that the sustainability of branch campuses depends on a continued political commitment to this project in both the home and host country. It is not at all inconceivable to imagine a new president of NYU or some other home institution deciding to cut back on international commitments. This will especially be the case if the educa-tional practices of the home and host campuses gradually begin to diverge. In Qatar, the attempt to found integrated graduate programs might signal the weak-ening of ties between home and host institutions. In both the Education City campuses and NYUAD and the Sorbonne, the campuses rely on faculty who would not necessarily be hired to teach by the university in the United States, United Kingdom or France.[19] Our sense is that while the branch campuses cur-rently provide a high quality educational experience for a largely expatriate population, forces will eventually force these campuses to become more inde-pendent. At that point, the problem of ensuring quality and establishing new methods of regulation will reappear.

If the elite branch campus model potentially suffers from its isolation from the national population, the impact of the educational mall, regulated privatiza-tion and semi-private models we have outlined are much more difficult to summarize. The types and quality of the large number of educational institutions that have been created through these educational reforms are heterogeneous. Some institutions (such as the American University of Sharjah, the University of Sharjah, Abu Dhabi University, the British University of Dubai or the Gulf Uni-versity for Science and Technology) have aggressively attempted to create an institution that can offer a diverse number of degree offerings, while others have limited themselves to providing less prestigious degrees in business, information technology, and other professional vocations.

The future of these small institutions remains to be seen as the educational market reaches saturation and experiences increasing competition. As mentioned above, most of these small institutes and colleges have relatively small numbers of enrolled students which casts doubt on their financial long-term viability. In addition, it is just not clear how many training and vocational institutes are needed to serve a relatively small population. There are already signs in Oman, for example, that the local labor market cannot absorb all the graduates from ter-tiary institutes who have started looking for jobs elsewhere in the GCC (Al Barwani *et al.*, 2009).

The difference in academic offerings is reflected in distinct governance and ownership structures. The majority of the new colleges and universities are for-profit institutions, but the less vocationally oriented, multi-disciplinary institu-tions have attempted to create robust boards of trustees that are primarily charged with ensuring the academic quality of the institution. On the other hand, the smaller, more vocationally oriented colleges are often directly managed by owners who have established more hierarchical and less participatory governance structures. We will explore this issue more fully in Chapter 6, when we discuss more systematically what the new regulatory bodies' investigations of the colleges and universities of the GCC reveal about educational quality.

We close by noting that both the prestigious and less prestigious universities of the region do face some common challenges. A major one concerns the academic preparedness of the high school students who are entering the higher educational system. The need to offer academic bridge programs that attempt to improve students' ability to do academic work in English and upgrade basic mathematical and information processing competencies has become a necessary feature of the reconstituted higher educational landscape of the GCC. One result is that the privatization of higher education seems to require the privatization of secondary and primary schools, as more elite parents believe that their children can attain the English linguistic and academic skills necessary for academic success only in private schools. The revolution in higher education we have outlined is part of a broader restructuring of the fundamental educational practices and social arrangements of Gulf society.

Notes

1 To reside in some GCC countries, one has to have an employment contract or have investment in real estate property in freehold areas or have a business with local sponsorship.
2 Indeed many studies have in fact attempted classifications based on these categorizations. See, for example, Peter Heath (2012).
3 Sheikha Moza is the mother of the current Emir of Qatar.
4 HEC Paris (2011) and UCL Qatar (2011) offer graduate programs only.
5 It is very difficult to have access to numbers of local students in the elite branch campuses as they are not published, but colleagues we talked to from these campuses confirm our assessment that very few nationals are enrolled in them.
6 When one of the authors of this book went to Qatar to interview for a position as Assistant Dean that would oversee faculty development and student outcomes, some of the faculty of this Education City campus presented a "manifesto" arguing that they should be accorded increased rights and access to resources that their Georgetown counterparts already enjoyed.
7 Dubai's International Academic City is one of the many industry specific cities which are conglomerations of businesses in a particular domain such as Dubai Media City, Dubai Internet City, Dubai Heath Care City, Dubai International Financial City, etc. Dubai is, of course, famous for its numerous large shopping malls.
8 All numbers are approximate and vary somewhat from one source to the other. For example, the same official KHDA source reports the number of private institutions as 57 and 52 in different places.
9 For example, each year there are about 27,000 potential applicants for tertiary education, but only about 5,000 can join the national university, Sultan Qaboos University (SQU), and the other public technical and vocational colleges.
10 Al Buraimi College, for example, states on every degree that, "This certifies that the curriculum of the Al Buraimi University College was developed with the California State University, Northridge, USA." This certainly implies rather close coordination between the two institutions, but the audit panel also states that "The Panel was

unable to find evidence of how the activities specified in the CSUN agreement explicitly guarantee the quality of education." In contrast, the audit panel of Majan College praises the support and quality assurance activities of the University of Bedfordshire.

11 For example, the audit report of the College of Applied Sciences, Nizwa, argues that the academic arrangements that all of the public Colleges of Applied Sciences in Oman have with the New Zealand Tertiary Education Consortium (NZTEC) led the internal academic leadership of the colleges to pay less attention to the development of its academic programs. This suggests that one danger of external affiliations is that the academic management capabilities of the Omani institutions become stunted.

12 Bahrain's vision 2030: Launched in 2009, the first National Economic Strategy (NES) started the journey toward realizing the aspirations of Bahrain's Economic Vision 2030. The second NES 2011–14 continues the journey, responding to the latest challenges and aligning initiatives with the 2011–12 Budget. During 2011, further progress was made in continuing Bahrain's major reform programmes in education, health and housing. Annual Report 2011 – Bahrain Economic Development Board. Available at: http://45angles.com/clients/edb/aug4/operations_reform.html.

13 The official website (www.mofa.gov.bh/Default.aspx?tabid=7749) lists 17 institutions and Wikipedia lists 18 by including Kent Business School where students spend the foundation year in Bahrain and go to the home campus in the UK to complete their studies (retrieved October 2014).

14 In addition to the institutions listed in the table, one should note that one other private higher education institution of long-standing exists in Bahrain. The Bankers Institute of Banking and Finance (BIBF<HS>) was originally founded as a vocational training center in 1981. Now, BIBF offers a variety of business-oriented degree programs, which include graduate and undergraduate degrees sponsored by the University of Wales, Bangor, DePaul University and Bentley University.

15 Interview with then AUK Interim Provost on 24 November 2013.

16 The relatively high percentage of Kuwaiti nationals in both the student body and faculty is worth noting compared to much lower participation in private universities elsewhere.

17 The Sheikha is Executive of the Al-Futooh Investment Company, which has holdings in the Kuwait Projects Company, the United Education Company, Syria Gulf Bank, and Kuwait Hotels Company. Available at: www.zawya.com/cm/profile.cfm?companyid=284054.

References

About ADEC. Available at: www.adec.ac.ae/en/AboutADEC/Pages/default.aspx.

American University of Sharjah. Available at: www.aus.edu.

Ahlia University home page. Available at: www.ahlia.edu.bh/ahliaweb/about-the-university/ (accessed June 6, 2013).

Al Barwani, T., Chapman, D.W. and Ameen, H. (2009). Strategic brain drain: Implications for higher education in Oman. *Higher Education Policy*, 22: 415–432.

AUK catalog 2013–14. Available at: www.auk.edu.kw/pr/catalog/2013/aukDart.html.

Bhanyani, A. (2013). The market route to higher education in UAE: Its rationales and implications. *International Review on Public and Non-Profit Marketing*, 11(1): 75–87.

Blanchard, C.M. (2008). Islamic religious schools, madrasas: Background. CRS Report for Congress (Order RS21654), January 23.

Brooks, P. (2011). The exported university. *The Chronicle of Higher Education*, December 4. Available at: http://chronicle.com/article/The-Exported-University/129932/ (accessed May 28, 2012).

Dight, C. (2014). Moving home: The brave new world of New York University Abu

Dhabi's new Saadiyat campus. *The National.* Available at: www.thenational.ae/arts-lifestyle/the-review/moving-home-the-brave-new-world-of-new-york-university-abu-dhabis-new-saadiyat-campus.

Donn, G. and Al Manthra, Y. (2010). *Globalisation and Higher Education in the Arab Gulf States.* Oxford: Symposium Books.

Donn, G. and Issan, S. (2007). Higher education in transition: Strategies for change in the Sultanate of Oman. *Scottish Educational Review,* 39(2): 173–185.

French, R. (2010). United Arab Emirates (UAE): Flagship of the Gulf. In *Higher Education and the Middle East: Serving the Knowledge Based Economy.* Middle East Institute.

Government of Oman, Oman Academic Accreditation Authority (2014). Available at: www.oaaa.gov.om/Default.aspx (accessed December 29, 2014).

Gulf News (2013). Sharjah Islamic University to open in 2014. *Gulf News, UAE Education,* April 18. Available at: http://gulfnews.com/news/gulf/uae/education/sharjah-islamic-university-to-open-in-2014-1.1172347.

Heath, P. (2012). Recent trends in higher education in the Arabian Gulf states. Unpublished paper.

HEC Paris (2011). Available at: www.hec.edu/ (accessed December 10, 2014).

Karolak, M. (2012). Bahrain's tertiary education reform: A step towards sustainable economic development. *Juin 2012 REMMM,* 163–181. Available at: http://remmm.Revues.org/7665.

Khalifa University website. About us: Strategic partnerships. Available at: www.ku.ac.ae/aboutus/strategicpartnerships/default.aspx (accessed May 29, 2015).

KHDA report (2012). *The Higher Education Landscape in Dubai 2011.* Dubai: Knowledge & Human Development Authority. Available at: www.khda.gov.ae/CMS/WebParts/TextEditor/Documents/Draft%20HE%20Landscape%202011%20v26.pdf (accessed May 27, 2015).

Knight, J. (2011). Education hubs: A fad, a brand, an innovation? *Journal of Studies in International Education,* 15(3): 221–240.

Lane, J. and Kinser, K. (2011). Reconsidering privatization in cross-border engagements: The sometimes public nature of private activity. *Higher Education Policy,* 24: 255–273.

Lehman, J.S. (2011). Universities in a complex world. Available at: http://chronicle. com/article/Universities-in-a-Complex/129933/.

Lewin, T. (2008). In oil-rich Mideast, shades of the Ivy League. *The New York Times/Education.* Available at: www.nytimes.com/2008/02/11/education/11 global.html?pagewanted=1&_r=1&ref=todayspaper.

Masdar University website. About us: Partnerships. Available at: www.masdar.ac.ae/about-us/mit-partnership.

Mathews, D. (2013). Qatar strives to weave its western branches into one. Available at: www.timeshighereducation.co.uk/news/qatar-strives-to-weave-its-western-branches-into-one/2001980.article.

Missing link in GCC's education reform strategy (2013). *Qatar Today.* Available at: www.qatartodayonline.com/the-missing-link-in-the-gccs-education-reform-strategy (accessed May 30, 2015).

The Petroleum Institute. About PI. Available at: www.pi.ac.ae/aboutPI.php (accessed December 10, 2014).

Qatar University. RAND Corporation. Available at: www.rand.org/content/dam/rand/pubs/monographs/2009/RAND_MG796.sum.pdf.

Ross, A. (2011). Not just another profit-seeking venture. *The Chronicle of Higher Education*. Available at: http://chronicle.com/article/Not-Just-Another/129935/.

School students in Qatar prepared for university life by Georgetown. Qatar (2013). AMEinfo, July 27. Available at: http://ameinfo.com/blog/education/school-students-in-qatar-prepared-for-university-life-by-georgetown.

Swan, M. (2011). Sorbonne to focus on research as it marks five years in capital. *The National*, July 6. Available at: www.thenational.ae/news/uae-news/sorbonne-to-focus-on-research-as-it-marks-five-years-in-capital#ixzz3IAxxTL9i.

Swan, M. (2013a). Paris-Sorbonne UAE offers course in English instead of French. *The National*, March 22. Available at: www.thenational.ae/news/uae-news/education/paris-sorbonne-uae-offers-course-in-english-instead-of-french#ixzz3IAwUeP00.

Swan, M. (2013b). International branch campuses' key role in the UAE. *The National*, September 18. Available at: www.thenational.ae/uae/education/Tinternational-branch-campuses-key-role-in-the-uae#ixzz38vMqiFMP.

Tamar, L. (2008). U.S. universities rush to set up outposts abroad. New York Times, February 10. Available at: www.nytimes.com/2008/02/10/education/10global.html?_r=1& (accessed May 27, 2015).

TECOM Investments: Educational cluster: Annual review for 2012 (2013). Report, July 9. Available at: www.diacedu.com/images/files/Annual-Review-2012.pdf (accessed November 12, 2014).

Texas A&M University at Qatar website. Cross-registration. Available at: www.qatar.tamu.edu/academics/office-of-records/cross-registration/ (accessed December 9, 2014).

Texas A&M University at Qatar. Governance. Available at: www.qatar.tamu.edu/about/governance/ (accessed December 9, 2014).

UCL Qatar (2011). Available at: www.ucl.ac.uk/Qatar (accessed December 20, 2014).

Varghese, J. (2013). HBKU to start master's in energy soon. *Gulf Times*. Available at: www.gulf-times.com/Mobile/Qatar/178/details/365425/HBKU-to-start-master%E2%80%99s-in-energy-soon.

World Data on Education: Qatar (2010). Available at: www.ibe.unesco.org/fileadmin/user_upload/Publications/WDE/2010/pdf-versions/Qatar.pdf.

5 GCC public universities

Growing pains

Introduction

Although the establishment of the GCC national universities preceded the private tertiary revolution discussed in Chapter 4, the transformations undergone by the national institutions must be interpreted mainly as a response to the broader transformations taking place in the GCC and are no less revolutionary than the process of privatization. In the previous chapters we have demonstrated that the global expansion of higher education has had important qualitative and quantitative impacts on the educational landscape in the GCC. Not only are the numbers of university students growing steadily, but global educational institutions are becoming more homogeneous overall. These broad trends are important to acknowledge, but should not be used to obscure the fact that the mechanisms that govern them are still largely determined by local governments and regional market forces. The GCC higher education transformations vary from government to government but are all the result of political decisions that are influenced by the predominantly welfare nature of the oil-rich states, the demographic composition of the GCC societies, their adoption of laissez-faire liberalism and their ambitious goals to join the "knowledge societies." This chapter begins by providing a brief historical background of the birth of public education in the GCC before presenting a general overview of the major GCC national universities. This chapter will analyze the impact of the higher educational reforms that have transformed most of the GCC national universities in recent years. In addition, we ask whether or not these reforms will help governing authorities to achieve their stated goals of integrating national workers into the private sector workforce while strengthening the Arab-Islamic identity of the GCC.

The rise of the national university

The oil discoveries of the 1930s and the exploitation of their revenues by local governments in the 1970s were decisive in transforming the Arabian Gulf region from a relatively obscure region and a minor player in Arab world affairs to a major force, despite their relatively small sizes and populations compared to traditional power players in the region such as Egypt, Iraq or Syria (before the

DOI: 10.4324/9780203796139-5

US invasion of Iraq or the Arab Spring revolutions). In addition to their new-found political and economic influence in the region, the GCC countries have made it clear that they aspire to become leaders amongst the knowledge-producing societies (Al Maktoum, 2006). All GCC governments recognized the important role of an educated citizenry to achieve this goal and have invested heavily in education in the last four decades.

Before the advent of its oil wealth, the GCC region had no schools to speak of where mosques were almost the only institutions that provided any sort of formal literacy and religious education. UNESCO estimates in the 1950s put illiteracy rates at more than 90 percent of the Gulf population (Wiseman, 2011).[1] Those few families who could afford it sent their male children to neighboring Arab countries, mainly to Egypt, to have an education. The 1960s marked the inception of a modern public education system that was developed and implemented by teachers and administrators from other Arab countries, initially from Egypt, and later from Iraq, Palestine and Syria. This dependence on non-citizens in the educational system continues to this day. While an important number of Arabs from across the Arab world still make up the majority of the teaching staff and administration, recently GCC countries have turned to experts from the West as part of reforming their public educational system.

Given the origin of the first planners, early public schools and universities in the GCC followed mainly the Egyptian educational model in terms of its structure, curriculum and use of Arabic as the medium of instruction. Enrollments in free public universities were reserved to national students only, although recently, some foreign students, mainly from Arab nationalities, are being admitted to these public institutions.

Starting in the second half of the twentieth century, each state established its national university. Kuwait University was the first to open its doors in 1966 followed in 1973 by Qatar University and the United Arab Emirates University in Al-Ain in 1976. The Sultan Qaboos University in Oman and the University of Bahrain were established in 1986 (see Table 5.1). Public higher education is free for citizens who also enjoy generous government stipends to cover other expenditures such as books and housing.

Table 5.1 The first state universities in the Gulf

Country	University	Date of establishment
Kuwait	Kuwait University	1966
Qatar	Qatar University	1973
UAE	United Arab Emirates University	1976
Oman	Sultan Qaboos University	1986
Bahrain	University of Bahrain	1986

Sources: Kuwait: www.kuniv.edu/ku/AboutKU/BriefHistory/index.htm; Qatar: www.qu.edu.qa/the-university/history.php; UAE: www.uaeu.ac.ae/en/about/; Oman: www.squ.edu.om/tabid/61/language/en-US/Default.aspx; Bahrain: www.uob.edu.bh/english/pages.aspx?module=pages&id=2990&SID=312.

At their onset, national universities were modeled on their sister Arab institutions and most faculty and administration were also imported from other Arab countries. Up until the 1990s they were the only available higher education institutions in each country. The beginning of the millennium saw a dramatic increase in the number of smaller public colleges and institutes primarily designed to offer vocational and technical education to meet the need of increasingly larger numbers of high school graduates seeking alternative types of free tertiary education. The following sections provide a description of the major national universities in each state starting with the earliest public university in the region.

Kuwait public higher education institutions

Kuwait was the first to construct a higher education system that is today largely controlled by Kuwaitis. Its public university, Kuwait University (KU), was the first and became an important institution for students in the whole region. Presently, KU has 16 undergraduate colleges, from sharia and Islamic studies, to engineering, social sciences and the arts. It also offers approximately 25 graduate programs (see Table 5.2). Courses of study heavily emphasize the sciences with five doctoral programs in mathematics, chemistry, microbiology, physiology and pathology. Most of the instruction is in Arabic, and, as with all of Kuwait colleges and universities, the actual classes are still sex-segregated, even if the common areas in which students congregate and socialize often are not (Calderwood, 2009; Sharaf and Ibrahim, 2013). The number of students attending KU is around 37,225 as of 2013 (Kuwait University). The majority are female students. Depending on the college being applied to, students must have a high school GPA between 75 and 85 percent.

Unlike the rest of the region, a relatively high proportion of professors at KU are Kuwaiti citizens with tenure. In an effort to encourage research among faculty, the government has created incentives and faculty promotion and success depends on successful academic publishing. For example, Kuwaiti academics are able to get two research sabbaticals during their careers, unlike nonnationals who usually can only obtain research funding if they agree to collaborate with Kuwaitis.

A unique feature of KU, compared to others in the region, is the strong tradition of faculty governance. Kuwaiti academics belong to a faculty union, and certain professors are actively involved in monitoring other higher education institutions. Unlike any other state university in the region, KU and its faculty play an important role in the shaping of the nation's higher education policy as will be described below.

KU lost its monopoly over higher education in Kuwait when the Emir of Kuwait, Jaber al-Ahmed al Sabah, promulgated law no. 34 in 2000. The law permitted the Ministry of Higher Education to license private universities as long as the shared capital of the new institutions is more than 50 percent owned by Kuwaiti nationals. This stipulation applied to any non-Kuwaiti institution that

Table 5.2 Degree programs in Kuwait's public HEIs

	Programs offered	Student enrollments
Kuwait University (1966)	College of Law College of Arts College of Science College of Medicine College of Engineering and Petroleum College of Allied Health Science College of Education College of Sharia and Islamic Studies College of Business Administration College of Pharmacy College of Dentistry College of Social Science College of Life Sciences College of Architecture College of Computer Science and Engineering College of General Health	37,225
The Public Authority for Applied Education and Training (PAAET) (1982)	College of Basic Education (http://en.wikipedia.org/wiki/ Basic_Education_College) College of Business Studies College of Technological Studies College of Health Sciences Training Institutes: The Higher Institute of Energy The Higher Institute of Telecommunication and Navigation Industrial Training Institute (Sabah Al-Salem & Shuwaikh) Nursing Institute Constructional Training Institute Vocational Training Institute.	17,459 (in 2005–6)
The Higher Institutes for Theater and Music Arts	Music and Theatre diplomas	765 in 2005–6

Sources: Kuwait University: www.kuniv.edu/ku#; PAAET: www.paaet.edu.kw/mysite/Default.aspx; The Higher Institutes for Theater and Music Arts: http://en.wikipedia.org/wiki/Education_in_Kuwait (Note: just a brief description with the number of students in 2005–6. Maybe not enough to cite this); www.e.gov.kw/sites/kgoEnglish/Portal/Pages/CitizensAndResidences/Education_information.aspx (Note: This is the Kuwait's govt. website with info on the procedure for admission

wished to establish a branch campus. As expected, the introduction of private universities into the higher education landscape, discussed in Chapter 4, deeply affected the public university which had to face this competition by enacting several reforms discussed below.

The State of Kuwait also sponsors other technical and vocational institutions which are governed by the Public Authority for Applied Education and Training (PAAET) under the Ministry of Higher Education. The PAAET was established in 1982 to replace the Technical and Vocational Education Department and institutes under its umbrella are expected to produce a technically trained workforce to respond to the economic and industrial development of the country. They focus on vocational education and training in the areas of business, education, energy, industry, health sciences, technology, telecommunication and navigation leading to certificates for short courses or diplomas at the end of longer two-year study programs.

Qatar University

Qatar's national university (QU), the only national university in Qatar, grew out of the College of Education, which was established in 1973. In 1977, responding to a growing need for higher education, three new colleges were added (social sciences, science and Islamic studies) leading to what is today Qatar University (see Table 5.3). In 1980, QU opened its engineering, business and economics colleges. In 2006 a pharmacy program was added which became the College of Pharmacy in 2008. From 150 students in 1973 the student body has steadily grown to reach over 14,000 students, 65 percent of whom are Qatari nationals, representing around one-sixth of the eligible Qatari population (Qatar University).

QU offers 30 undergraduate programs and 19 master's degrees. It also offers doctoral programs in biological and environmental sciences, engineering and pharmacy. The colleges of engineering, science and business and economics use English as a medium of instruction while the other colleges have recently switched back to Arabic as the medium of instruction.[2] All graduate programs use English as a medium of instruction with the exception of Arabic and Islamic studies master's degrees. Women make up about 70 percent of the student body

Table 5.3 Qatar University

	Colleges	Students enrollments
Qatar University	Arts and Sciences Business and Economics Education Engineering Law Pharmacy Sharia and Islamic Studies	14,000

Source: Qatar University: www.qu.edu.qa/ (no info about the number of students).

and facilities and classrooms are gender segregated. Five research centers are linked to the university: the Scientific Applied Research Center, the Sira and Sunna Research Center, the Educational Research Center, the Documentation and Humanities Research Center, and the National Center for Economic Research. QU is open to Qatari nationals free of charge provided they meet the admission requirements set up by each college and based on their performance on national standardized examinations at the end of high school. Usually high school scores of 70 percent are required in the sciences and 85 percent in pharmacy, while the other colleges accept an overall high school score of 75 percent.

The UAE's public higher education institutions

The UAE has three federal institutions (see Table 5.4): the United Arab Emirates University (UAEU), which is located in Al Ain, is the flagship university. The UAEU was founded by the late Sheikh Zayed in 1976. The Minister of Higher Education is its chancellor and presides over a University Council composed of other ministers and influential business national leaders and university top administrators. The majority of UAEU students are female, with close to 11,000 compared to 3,000 males in 2013–14. Instruction is gender segregated. The UAEU is the highest ranked university in the region. It was ranked 370th in 2012/13 by QS World University Rankings and in the top 50 young universities. The university has nine colleges and offers both undergraduate and graduate degrees including PhDs in a wide range of disciplines.

Two other public institutions were established later by the UAE Ministry of Higher Education, the Higher Colleges of Technology (HCT) which were initially set up as vocational training institutions across the seven emirates making up the UAE. HCT is a system of 17 separate campuses for men and women, serving around 20,000 students throughout the UAE. It was founded by federal decree in 1988. Since then, the mission of the HCT has undergone several changes. The goal of the HCT is to provide technical and professional diplomas to prepare Emirati students for the job market. Instruction is in English, and this requires most students to take one-year foundation in language and math courses to prepare them for college-level work. From primarily a two-year vocational training institution, the HCT system evolved into offering bachelor degrees and some graduate-level classes.

The third public institution is Zayed University (ZU) with two campuses in Abu Dhabi and Dubai. It was established in 1998 based on an American model of education. ZU has a University Council that was established by Federal Decree No. 11 of 1999. The University Council, equivalent to a Board of Trustees, is headed by the President of the University and must include "at least seven UAE citizens well known for their experience, balanced thinking and competence to be elected by the Cabinet of Ministers from various sectors of the UAE upon nomination by the university president"[3] (ZU website, July 16, 2014). Although ZU began admitting male students in recent years, there are rumors suggesting that that decision will be reversed. Instruction is gender segregated

Table 3.4 The UAE federal public universities

UAE federal public universities	Colleges	Accreditation*	Enrollments
UAEU	College of Business and Economics College of Education College of Engineering College of Food and Agriculture College of Humanities and Social Sciences College of Information Technology College of Law College of Medicine and Health Sciences College of Science	Institutional accreditation by CAA (March 31, 2014)	14.000
Zayed University	College of Arts and Creative Enterprises College of Business College of Communication and Media Sciences College of Education College of Sustainability Sciences and Humanities College of Technological Innovation The Institute for Islamic World Studies University College Academic Bridge Program	Middle States Program accreditations	7,000 (in 2011)
HCT (17 Campuses)	Applied Communications Business Computer Information Science Education Engineering Technology and Science Heath Sciences Foundations General Studies	Institutional accreditation by CAA Program accreditation (ACA, USA, Australia and Canada)	20,000

Sources: UAEU: www.uaeu.ac.ae/en/about/ (www.uaeu.ac.ae/en/colleges.shtml); Zayed University: www.zu.ac.ae/main/en/explore_zu/index.aspx; HCT: www.hct.ac.ae/(www.hct.ac.ae/programs/accreditation/for accreditation).

Note
* Starting in 2013, the CAA is charged with institutional accreditation of the federal institutions (www.uaeu.ac.ae/en/about/accreditation.shtml, accessed July 16, 2014).

and the medium of instruction is English in most disciplines. Today, the ZU student body (around 7,000) remains almost exclusively female on both campuses.

The three federal institutions offer a variety of undergraduate degree programs and a limited number of graduate programs some of which are open to international students. Starting in 2014 all federal institutions are required to obtain institutional accreditation by the Commission on Academic Accreditation established by the Ministry of Higher Education (CAA) which until then was only required from private institutions (CAA website). The establishment of ZU and HCT is part of the grand plan of reforming the public sector of higher education to provide public alternative systems of education to national students. In fact, ZU's establishment coincided with the burgeoning of the private universities across the GCC and the university's system mirrors that of many private universities in the country. UAE nationals can also obtain scholarships for study at local institutions as well as abroad. Recently, there has been an increase of over 7 percent of UAE students choosing to study in the United States (Sabry, 2014).

In addition to the federal national universities, other institutions are funded by the government of the Emirate of Abu Dhabi and open to all UAE citizens (ADEC website). These include Khalifa University, which is the largest and has two campuses, one in Abu Dhabi and one in Sharjah. Others listed in Table 5.5 are relatively small institutions each specializing in a particular discipline in science, medical health sciences, IT, engineering or technology. These institutions are financed by the government of Abu Dhabi either directly or indirectly through different government agencies such as ADEC (Abu Dhabi Educational Council) or ADNOC (Abu Dhabi National Oil Company). The number of students in each of these institutions is relatively small from 600–1,300, although not all of these colleges have published enrollment numbers. It is worth noting that the ADEC list (see Table 5.5) includes the branch campuses of NYU Abu Dhabi, the Sorbonne and INSEAD discussed in Chapter 4. University Mohammed V-Agdal Abu Dhabi (UM5A-AD) is also a branch campus of a Moroccan public university but very little information is available publicly on this arrangement. The other institutions also have partnerships with foreign universities and industries in their fields of specialization.

Oman's public university system

When it opened in 1986, Sultan Qaboos University had five colleges: Medicine, engineering, agriculture, education and science. One year later the College of Arts was added and since then three more colleges have been established: The colleges of commerce and economics in 1993, law (replacing the former college of sharia and law) in 2006 and nursing in 2008. The university is designed to maintain gender segregation with separate access for females and males and separate seating arrangements. In addition to its national university, Oman opened several institutes listed in Table 5.6. There are five technical industrial colleges, one institute of banking and 14 health institutes. Higher education in the public sector is free of charge to all Omani students. Furthermore, the Ministry awards scholarships to study abroad to both undergraduate and graduate students. For example in the academic year 2011–12, the ministry granted more than 2,700 scholarships for study abroad (Al Sarmi, 2014).[4]

A particularity of Omani higher education lies in its controlling mechanisms. In addition to the Ministry of Higher Education, the ministries of health, social affairs, labor and vocational training, and the Central Bank of Oman are directly responsible for specific institutions as illustrated in Table 5.7 (Al Lamki, 2002). The Council of Higher Education established by decree in 1999 oversees all tertiary education institutions and is in charge of developing education policies and strategies.

There are many challenges facing public tertiary education in Oman. The duplication of administration, inefficient management and the lack of accountability due to the fact that higher education institutions are controlled by three ministries, the central bank and two councils is often blamed for unnecessary competition over resources and the difficulty to agree on strategies. In addition, the decline in revenues from oil has led the Omani government to stress the importance of developing well trained citizens to create an alternative economy that is less reliant on oil export revenues. However, the expansion has resulted in more graduates than the white-collar local job market can absorb. Specialists are predicting that the Omani labor market will be unable to absorb all higher education graduates and that emigration toward neighboring countries in the GCC will increase (Al Lamki, 2002; Al Barwani *et al.*, 2009).

Bahrain's higher education institutions

The contemporary structure of Bahrain's higher education system has taken shape relatively recently (see Table 5.8). The country's major public university, the University of Bahrain (UoB), was formed in 1986 through the merger of the University College of Arts, Science and Education and the Gulf Polytechnic. These two institutions were originally founded in the late 1960s as the Higher Institute for Teachers and the Gulf Technical College. By 2010, the University of Bahrain had nine colleges and one professional college (Bahrain Teachers College).[5] The student body numbered approximately 18,000 with two-thirds female to one-third male. More than 90 percent of the students are Bahraini citizens, and, unlike most other Gulf countries, more than 60 percent of the faculty members are nationals as well (Higher Education Review Unit, 2010). The dominant position of the UoB has been further reinforced by the 2011 decision to merge the independent College of Health Sciences with the UoB. The UoB is now directly involved in the training of nurses and other health care professionals (College of Health Sciences, University of Bahrain, 2011).

In addition to sponsoring the aggressive expansion of the UoB, the Bahraini government established the more vocationally oriented Bahrain Polytechnic in 2008. It offers bachelor's and associate degrees in business, engineering

Table 5.5 Abu Dhabi's public, non-federal HEI

Institution	Date established	Programs offered	Student enrollments
Petroleum Institute (PI)	2001	Bachelor of Science in Chemical Engineering Bachelor of Science in Electrical Engineering Bachelor of Science in Mechanical Engineering Bachelor of Science in Petroleum Engineering Bachelor of Science in Petroleum Geosciences **Master of Engineering degrees are offered in the following areas:** Chemical Engineering; Electrical Engineering; Health, Safety & Environment Engineering; Mechanical Engineering; Petroleum Engineering **Master of Science degrees are offered in the following areas:** Applied Chemistry; Chemical Engineering; Electrical Engineering; Mechanical Engineering; Petroleum Engineering; Petroleum Geosciences	1,200
Fatima College of Health Science	2006	Nursing Pharmacy Physiotherapy Radiology & Medical Imaging Health Emergency (Paramedics)	500 graduates since 2006 (from the official website)
Emirates College for Advanced Education (ECAE)	2007	**Bachelor of Education (BEd) in:** Special Needs Education Art and Music Early Childhood Education Counselling in Education Information Technology Education Health and Physical Education Applied Behavior Analysis **Master of Education (MEd) in** Special Education Mathematics Education Science Education Social Studies Educational Technology Educational Leadership Early Childhood TESOL	N/A

Institution	Year	Number	Programs
Khalifa University of Science, Technology & Research (KUSTAR)	2007	1300	**Undergraduate programs** BSc in Aerospace Engineering BSc in Civil Engineering BSc in Computer Engineering (optional concentration in Software Systems) BSc in Industrial and Systems Engineering BSc in Biomedical Engineering BSc in Communication Engineering BSc in Electrical and Electronic Engineering (optional concentration in Power Systems) BSc in Mechanical Engineering **Graduate programs** MA in International and Civil Security MSc in Information Security MSc in Electrical and Computer Engineering PhD in Engineering MSc in Nuclear Engineering MSc by Research in Engineering MSc in Mechanical Engineering
Masdar Institute of Science and Technology (MIST)	2007	600–800	MSc in Chemical Engineering MSc in Computing and Information Science MSc in Electrical Power Engineering MSc in Engineering Systems and Management MSc in Materials Science and Engineering MSc in Mechanical Engineering MSc in Microsystems Engineering MSc in Water and Environmental Engineering MSc in Sustainable Critical Infrastructure PhD in Interdisciplinary Engineering **Outreach program** YFEL Summer Research Internships Ektashif Student Internships

Sources: from ADEC's website and the institutions' websites: PI institute: www.pi.ac.ae/admissions.php; Fatima College: www.fchs.ac.ae/En/Programs/Pages/default.aspx; Emirates College for Advanced Education (ECAE): www.ecae.ac.ae; Khalifa University: www.kustar.ac.ae/pages/undergraduate-programs, www.kustar.ac.ae/pages/graduate-programs; Masdar Institute of Science and Technology (MIST): www.masdar.ac.ae/programs/masters-program

Table 5.6 Colleges in the public institutions in Oman

Institution and date of establishment	Colleges of:	Controlled by:
Sultan Qaboos University (SQU) (1986)	Arts and Social Sciences Commerce and Economics Education Law Nursing Agriculture and Marine Sciences Medicine and Health Sciences Engineering Science	Ministry of Higher Education
Colleges of Applied Sciences (2005)	International Business Administration Communication Design Engineering IT	Ministry of Higher Education
Higher Colleges of Technology	Information Technology Business Science Pharmacy Engineering Photography Fashion Design	Ministry of Manpower
Institute of Sharia Sciences College of Banking and Financial Studies. (1983)	BSc Accounting and Finance BSc Business and Management Diplomas in Business and Computing MBA	The Ministry of Awqaf and Religious Affairs Central Bank of Oman
Health Institutes Institute of Health Sciences (1982)	Oman Assistant Pharmacy Institute (1991) Oman Institute of Public Health (1991) Muscat Nursing Institute (1993) Oman Nursing Institute (2000)	Ministry of Health

Sources: SQU: www.squ.edu.om/; CAS: www.cas.edu.om/; HCT: www.hct.edu.om/; Institute of Sharia Sciences: http://international-relations.auth.gr/en/Oman_

Table 5.7 Oman's higher education governing bodies

Council of Higher Education	All institutes of higher education
University Council	Sultan Qaboos University
Ministry of Higher Education	Colleges of education and private colleges
Ministry of Health	Health institutes
Ministry of Social Affairs, Labor	Technical industrial colleges and vocational training
Central Bank of Oman	Institute of Banking

Source: Sultan Qaboos University, Ministry of Higher Education, Ministry of Health and Ministry of Social Affairs, Labor and Vocational Training (1999). From Al Lamki (2002).

technology, information and communications technology, visual design, and web media. The number of students who attend the polytechnic is approximately 1,000. Sixty percent of the students are female (Bahrain Polytechnic home page).

Another institution located in Bahrain but sponsored by all the GCC Ministers of Higher Education is the Arabian Gulf University. It was founded in Bahrain in 1981 shortly after the creation of the GCC itself. The original purpose of this project was to establish a medical school that would train GCC citizens. Since then, the university has modestly expanded to include a College of Graduate Studies that focuses on environmental issues and a French Arabian Business School in partnership with the well-known French Ecole Superieure des Sciences Economiques et Commerciales (ESSEC). Altogether, the Arabian Gulf University graduates approximately 250 students every year (Arabian Gulf University home page). The university has several chairs endowed by GCC Emirs. Given the greater emphasis on formal education in Bahrain during its mid-twentieth-century history, it was not surprising that the GCC states would choose to locate a regional university in Bahrain rather than in the less educationally developed countries at that time. By the first decade of this century, however, it would be hard to argue that Bahrain is a leading higher education innovator in the GCC.

This overview shows that in most GCC countries the public tertiary system has dramatically grown in the last 50 years. The majority female student body in all the national universities previewed above may partly be explained by the fact the local institutions are not the only option available for students who want to pursue higher education. Male students had more opportunities to study abroad. GCC citizens could often obtain generous state funding to send their children to Western universities as well as other Arab universities abroad. Studying abroad, preferably in the United States or the United Kingdom, is generally perceived to be a status symbol and more impressive on one's CV, by students, parents and employers (Sabry, 2014). The result is that the well-connected and those with higher GPA averages obtained scholarships to pursue university education outside the country. This tendency has generally resulted in a two-tier output of university graduates in which the national universities products are considered less prestigious. Another reason could be that male students opt to work in

Table 5.8 Bahrain public HEIs

Institutions	Colleges	Enrollments
University of Bahrain (1986)	College of Arts College of Business Administration College of Engineering College of Information Technology College of Law College of Science College of Applied Studies Bahrain Teachers College College of Physical Education and Physiotherapy College of Health Sciences	18,137 (2013)
Bahrain Polytechnic (2008)	Business (www.polytechnic.bh/default.asp?action=category&id=38) Engineering Technology (www.polytechnic.bh/default.asp?action=category&id=49) Engineering Technology (Associate Degree) (www.polytechnic.bh/default.asp?action=category&id=361) Information and Communications Technology (www.polytechnic.bh/default.asp?action=category&id=51) International Logistics Management (www.polytechnic.bh/default.asp?action=category&id=53) Visual Design (www.polytechnic.bh/default.asp?action=category&id=54) Web Media (www.polytechnic.bh/default.asp?action=category&id=55) Certificate in Academic Preparation (Foundation)	1,000
Arabian Gulf University (1980)	College of Medicine and Medical Sciences College of Graduate Studies French Arabian Business School	
College of Health Sciences (1976) (merged with university of Bahrain in October 2011)	Nursing (http://en.wikipedia.org/wiki/Nursing) Dental Hygiene (http://en.wikipedia.org/wiki/Dental_Hygiene) Pharmacy Public Health Medical Laboratory Technology Radiography (http://en.wikipedia.org/wiki/Radiography)	2,000

Sources: www.uob.edu.bh/english/pages.aspx?module=pages&id=2990&SID=312; www.agu.edu.bh/Default_en.aspx; www.chs.edu.bh/History.aspx.

family businesses after high school graduation and the less wealthy ones join the military or police training academies.

The national universities enjoyed a monopoly in the GCC until the end of the twentieth century when higher education opened its doors to privatization. Competition with the newcomers exposed major weaknesses and chipped away at the prestige of the national universities. In addition, the transformations of the GCC economies, the import of large numbers of expatriate workers to lead a rather aggressive integration into the global market exposed national universities graduates' inadequate skill sets to join the private sector job market. Governments reacted by adopting several reforms to raise their profile and improve their competitiveness.

Reforming the GCC public university

In the 1980s, increasing criticisms were levelled at the national universities as being an anachronism, providing education that was inappropriate for a new epoch of economic globalization (Ghabra, 2010). Ghabra was one the first voices to call for Western-inspired reform of Kuwait's and the GCC's higher education systems. He complained about the bureaucracy and lack of innovation within Kuwait's higher education system. Ghabra and Arnold (2007, 3) observed that: "Many Arab state-owned universities have been reforming their methods of instruction, but this reform has been slow because of the size of the bureaucracy." They claimed that the education provided by Kuwait University did not encourage the creation of well-rounded students who could be critical and innovative thinkers and called for the creation of a private co-educational institution that would be founded on American liberal arts principles, thus suggesting that the creation of a more competitive higher education environment was needed to challenge Kuwait University's monopoly position. In Qatar, Sheikha Mozah, the Qatari Emir's wife (present Emir's mother) and president of Qatar Foundation (QF), was even more critical in her assessment of Qatar University in 2009. She observed that:

> In its earlier years, Qatar University had been regarded by many observers – both inside and outside Qatar – as one of the better universities in the Middle East. By a number of measures, however, the University's performance had been deteriorating for several years before the reforms were launched. Among the most prominent problems were the lengthening time that students required to complete their degree programs and the growing fraction of graduating students who did so with very poor grades. Qualitative indicators of student engagement also suggested problems – particularly among male students.... At the beginning of the reform effort, students, faculty, and administrators agreed that no university community existed in any meaningful sense.
>
> (Moini *et al.*, 2009)

Calls for reforming the public education system were coming from all corners. International organizations looking into the obstacles facing economic development in the Arab world pinpointed serious shortcomings of the educational system and its inability to produce human resources capable of leading their societies' development (UNDP, 2003; Galal, 2008; World Bank, 2009). GCC governments responded by launching major reforms of the entire educational landscape. In addition to opening the higher education landscape to privatization, the reforms ranged from establishing additional public universities and colleges that offer special market-driven programs, to major curricular, structural and administrative changes in the national universities. The reforms share common features which include the following:

1   Reforms of national universities through the adoption of American models of higher education.
2   Adoption of imported curricula that are not aligned with secondary schools outcomes in terms of students' competencies and socio-cultural backgrounds.
3   A top-down approach based on short-term politico-economic considerations.
4   Implementation of education policies and practices that create universities as teaching institutions rather than centers of research.
5   Use of foreign experts who are not organically committed to national agendas to lead the reform drive.
6   Utilization of a human capital model approach emphasizing professional education at the cost of a more general higher education (see Chapter 3).
7   Adoption of English as a medium of instruction with consequences on socio-cultural and economic development (see Chapter 8).

The following sections focus on the first five features of the reforms in the "education revolution" outlined above while the other features are discussed elsewhere.

Reforms of national universities through the importation of Western models

By the beginning of the twenty-first century GCC governments invited international experts to conduct reforms of public universities that radically transformed them. A "Westernization" wave swept the public universities which initially had been established by Arab academics from neighboring countries largely based on European models. The reforms implemented across the five GCC countries share the following key characteristics. First, Arab (non-national) administrators were replaced by Westerners and Western trained staff and faculty to transform the public universities into American model institutions. Former US university administrators held top positions at the Ministry of Higher Education and were in charge of running public universities (Mills, 2008a, 2008b). They oversaw the design, content and implementation of the reforms. The Western experts' involvement took place through several arrangements, from establishing partnerships with universities from the United States and the Commonwealth countries to inviting consulting groups and think-tanks to design the reforms.[6]

Second, program offerings were aimed at professionalizing higher education to prepare graduates for the labor market with a strong focus on business, IT, engineering, health sciences and communication programs. To achieve this goal the curriculum was modeled on the American system and American and British textbooks were adopted. Western trained faculty with experience in teaching "the American way" were hired and English became the medium of instruction for all subjects that had value in the labor market (see Chapter 8). The UAE and Qatar went further by adopting hiring policies that expressed preference for American and other Western administrators to lead the reforms. Finally, the reforms also introduced a number of steps to ensure quality assurance by creating national accreditation bodies and applying for external program accreditation (discussed in Chapter 6).

Many of the reforms were motivated by the belief that importing Western curricula is expedient given the pressures of globalization and its fast-paced challenges. Stakeholders felt that they were in a race against time to join the globalized world and that the most efficacious way to reach development was to import the knowledge available from the West. The mission of the university was defined as providing professional training to young citizens to serve their countries' fast-paced economic development. It was believed that university education should align and link everything it does with national needs by "supporting the business community and the economic development of the country" (personal communication, March 2009).

Another reason often cited as justifying this "Westernization" was the serious criticisms levelled against the Arab educational system in the Arab world. Drzeniek-Hanouz and Yousef (2007: 8) argued that "aside from quantitative targets, the quality of outcomes in tertiary schooling needs to be enhanced to reverse the low valuation of educational credentials by the private sector." As we noted in Chapter 3, the Arab Human Development Report identified three key areas where progress is lacking. These are "freedom, empowerment of women and knowledge" (2002: vii). The World Bank Report on Education in the MENA region leveled similar criticisms. To participate in knowledge acquisition and production, higher education should enable its graduates to develop critical thinking, problem solving and lifelong learning skills required in the twenty-first century global knowledge society through the transplantation of Western educational models. Education in the Arab world has often been equated with rote learning, outdated teaching methods and a teacher-centered approach (Boyle, 2006) that do not enhance citizens' productive capacities as researchers, innovators and producers of knowledge (Bollag, 2006; Mazawi, 2007).

The story of QU is particularly instructive. The creation of elite branch campuses open to academically talented national citizens and expatriates did raise important questions about the status of QU. Even if the degrees offered by QU would be less prestigious, authorities realized that QU needed to offer a credible university educational experience for its students. Government officials recognized that the new branch campuses were too small and their admissions standards too high to replace QU which must remain as the main educational establishment providing university-level education to most national citizens. As Sheikha Mozah Al Misnad, President of QF (Moini *et al.*, 2009: xviii) recognized:

> The Education City branch campuses cannot accommodate – and were never intended to accommodate – the large majority of Qatari secondary school graduates who sought academically oriented higher education but did not qualify for or chose not to attend foreign universities. For these graduates, Qatar University was the traditional and still most appropriate option.

The rigorous admission criteria of the Education City elite branch campuses further exposed the poor quality of education in Qatar and led the government to initiate reforms at all levels of the public education system. To reform QU, Sheikha Mozah, who heads Education City, commissioned the RAND–Qatar Policy Institute (RQPI) "to conduct an in-depth examination of the conditions and resources needed to turn Qatar University in a model national university" (Moini *et al.*, 2009: xiv). The criticisms levelled at QU were many and were levelled at both its administrative structure and its educational outcomes. The RAND assessment found that the university administration was overly bureaucratic and failed to provide academic units and faculty with the autonomy necessary to create and operate high quality academic programs. At the same time, the university itself was too dependent on budgetary and personnel decisions by the Ministry of Finance and the Ministry of Civil Service Affairs and Housing. The result was the worst of both worlds: Excessive centralization of authority combined with arbitrary and chaotic decision-making that was rarely guided by a consideration of the university's needs. With respect to educational outcomes, Sheikha Mozah pointed to evidence that QU was failing to graduate students with the skills needed in the twenty-first century. To tackle the problem, Qatar's ruler decided to create a Senior Reform Committee (SRC) comprised of American and British experts recruited by the RQPI and selected senior faculty and administrators from QU. The SRC was chaired by the president of the university and the head of the RQPI project team (Moini *et al.*, 2009: 21).

The RQPI[7] and the Office of Institutional Research and Planning set up by the government, with input from other constituencies, performed an evaluation of QU, resulting in far-reaching reforms and the formulation of its 2010–13 Strategic Plan. The SRC (not a decision-making body) submitted its recommendations to the ruler in June 2004. The plan was to have QU function mainly as an undergraduate university focused on teaching. Its objectives were to improve the quality of education, the effectiveness of its administration and services and to expand its scholarly capacities and service to the community (Qatar University website, History). This entailed revising personnel practices that would increase salaries in return for more rigorous faculty evaluation. The report also recommended the establishment of an autonomous Board of Regents that would oversee a university administration that granted more autonomy and power to academic units. In addition, it advised QU to submit its academic programs to Western accreditation. The RAND-led reforms also called for the change of the language of instruction from Arabic to English in all social sciences and humanities in addition to the other scientific disciplines already using English. Such a change had serious repercussions as the majority of Qatari students could not meet the language admission requirements and even those who did were having problems in their courses taught in English.

In order to implement some of the recommendations, supportive faculty were selected to create courses of study that would emphasize instruction in English and introduce a new assessment process. The reforms required the hiring of senior scholars that would increase the visibility and prestige of the university but also meant potential loss of job security for Qatari nationals and took away substantial budgetary and personnel powers from the Ministry of Finance and the Ministry of Civil Service Affairs and Housing. At the academic level, the reforms were put in place with little preparation or advance notice of affected faculty. The result was considerable confusion. Heads of academic departments were generally not prepared to assume their new responsibilities for personnel management and budget planning, and the university did not initially have resources in place to support the department heads with these responsibilities. Some department heads resisted the changes, and personnel policies and budget planning were in some disarray during the first academic year of reform implementation. Qatari faculty who could not teach in English and senior faculty who opposed the changes were marginalized. Parents and students protested the new standards of GPAs, complaining that these had been imposed without adequate warning. And the Faculty Performance Appraisal System had to be revamped significantly after pilot testing.

It seems that resistance to the reforms led to an even speedier attempt to introduce them even if the change came with significant short-term costs. Those who wanted to reform QU were clearly aware of the difficulties inherent in moving rapidly, but they also saw advantages in doing so. The most significant of these was that the rapid pace left little time for opposition to the reforms – within the university itself or within the larger community – to become entrenched. These "shock and awe" tactics were successful in the sense that almost the entire new faculty recruited to QU came with advanced degrees from Western institutions. In addition, seeking accreditation of academic programs from British and American organizations has become a feature of QU's approach to quality control.

The UAE tertiary public system reforms, although on the surface may appear not as profound as QU's, also went in the same direction. The three federal institutions had as their president the long-serving Minister of Higher Education for the United Arab Emirates – Sheikh Nahyan bin Mubarek al Nahyan – until 2013. During his tenure, there was a clear preference for Western-oriented reforms and use of English as a medium of instruction. For example, the UAEU, the flagship university of the nation, embarked on changes to its academic programs and started using English as a medium of instruction for many of its disciplines by the early 2000s. To achieve this end, the minister replaced the university's Arab leadership with American administrators to oversee the transformations of the university (Mills, 2008a).

In addition the federal government added two new tertiary institutions, the HCT system and Zayed University for women. The decision to create a vocationally oriented tertiary institution such as the HCT was innovative at the time. The HCT opted for English in the delivery of all of its programs and emphasized its link to the UAE labor market. The HCT website states that its programs "are developed in consultation with leading UAE corporate and governmental employers." Moreover, the establishment of Zayed University (ZU) in 1998 was partly in response to criticisms of the UAEU's educational outcomes and their falling short of preparing nationals with the skills needed in the labor market. ZU was from its start modeled on the American system and run by American leadership. It also adopted English as its medium of instruction in most of its colleges. One of its published goals on its website in 2011 clearly stated that it will "continue to appoint Western educated and experienced faculty, most of whom are native English speakers."

While ZU and the HCT campuses were designed to offer programs that were complementary rather than directly competitive with the UAEU, the implications for the UAEU were clear. It would have been difficult for the first and largest federal university to maintain its traditional academic programs and policies while the others offered a more "attractive" Western-style education and promoted their adoption of English and use of the latest technologies in teaching. The UAEU soon followed the same reforms of Westernization.

The other three public universities in Kuwait, Bahrain and Oman also took similar steps toward the Westernization of the curriculum, quality assurance and pedagogy and the use of English to replace Arabic as the language of instruction for all scientific subjects. One could speculate as to why the Westernization of the administration was not as pronounced in these three nations as it was in the UAE or Qatar. Historical factors as well as political considerations may explain some of these differences. Bahrain and Kuwait had the oldest educational systems in the region and could rely on their own educated citizens to a greater extent to administer the university. In Kuwait, there is the further established tradition of the greater political and parliamentary participation of academics who have a say in decisions regarding the university.

Backlash against extensive Westernization

The changes in higher education outlined above did not end there. Higher education in the GCC has been highly dynamic and in a state of constant flux particularly since the beginning of the second decade of this century. The eroding position of public universities in the face of private ones, the reliance on outside consultants, administrators, and the marginalization of national academics in the decision-making process of the reforms raised existential questions. A significant number of GCC observers, including academics, politicians, education and language defenders, and parents, began to worry about the impact of the reforms on achieving stated visions for the future direction of their nations and the preservation of national identity.

The reforms adopted by public universities to make them into the image of American institutions had significant impact on national students' access to higher education. An important percentage of national students saw their chances of being admitted to national universities diminished given new admission requirements including English proficiency prerequisites. Their chances of obtaining scholarships were also jeopardized because of these new requirements. Some governments allocated scholarships only to students choosing specific majors such as engineering and technology. The reforms also impacted national faculties by limiting their participation in the leadership and decision-making process of their national educational system. In the society at large, the reforms generated mixed feelings and ambivalence about the outcome of the Westernization of education on cultural preservation, language and identity.

On January 24, 2012, the SEC in Qatar reversed a major reform policy and decreed that Arabic would return as the medium of instruction in several colleges which included the College of Arts and Sciences, the School of Business, Law and Sharia and Islamic Studies, International Affairs, Media and Mass Communication. It however, maintained English as the medium of instruction in the natural sciences, pharmacy and engineering (Lindsey, 2012; Qatar University opts for Arabic teaching medium, 2012). Engineering and pharmacy majors with low proficiencies in English and/or mathematics must first complete a foundation program (QU Undergraduate Catalog, 2013–14) before they can join their college.

This abrupt shift back to Arabic came with its own challenges in terms of requiring new textbooks, curricular changes and faculty reorientations. Faculty members that were not competent Arabic speakers in the Arabized disciplines had to be shifted to new positions or let go.[8] It should be pointed out that these reform reversals did not affect the pre-university levels where the use of English continues to be expanded and the teaching in and of Arabic has not undergone any serious revamping. It would not be surprising if this misalignment between policies in pre-university and tertiary education resulted in more mayhem in the future and led to new, abruptly implemented reforms (Qatar University opts for Arabic teaching medium, 2012).

Similar misgivings about the Westernization policies in education have been expressed across the GCC. In the UAE, the appointment of a new Minister of Higher Education by the end of the academic year 2012–13, led to seismic shifts in federal higher education institutions. The first move was to abruptly replace foreign presidents and provosts with Emiratis. The change in top leaderships also brought about change in middle tier administration and administrative processes. Within a period of less than a year, ZU has had two presidents, the latest one adding the ZU presidency portfolio to her position of Minister of Development and International Cooperation in the federal government. As of the 2014–15 academic year, ZU's president and provost are UAE citizens while most of the administrative and academic leadership remain Western expatriates. The university's future direction remains unclear at this stage and faculty are uncertain about their future. The university has charged its Arabic Language Center with Arabizing the curriculum. Although this is still work in progress, its prospects of success remain uncertain.[9] As part of the 2013 changes, there are rumors that the HCT may be returning to its original mission as a technical and vocational college. However, the HCT website accessed in July 2014 still affirms that the "HCT confers degrees at the Master's, Bachelor and Applied Diploma levels."[10] The UAEU has also experienced changes in its American leadership which was replaced by UAE academics.

These erratic changes in Qatar and the UAE are the outcome of reforms that are motivated by political considerations, short-term economic outlooks and a top-down approach. It is difficult to see how they can fulfill the national goals expressed in every country's vision. However, an important factor remains the lack of academic preparedness of students being admitted to higher education.

Secondary education outputs and university expectations

Misalignment of high school outputs with university requirements

There is a general acknowledgment that primary and secondary education systems suffer from many problems. International agencies have repeatedly pointed to the low quality of pre-university education in the Arab region as a major obstacle standing in the way of Arabs' competiveness on the global stage (UNDP, 2003; World Bank, 2009; World Economic Forum, 2013). One of the major reasons behind universities' weak outputs is attributed to the weak inputs in their student intake. A general observation about freshmen entering universities in the GCC is that they are generally not well prepared for university study. Instructors complain about students' language proficiencies (both in Arabic and English), their study skills, time management, critical thinking and analytical skills. Most tertiary institutions have had to set up foundation years to improve weak learning skills. And in many cases this compensatory step has not been enough to prepare students for the academic programs they join. Furthermore, the financial and time costs of remedial programs have often driven the direction taken by pre-university public schooling reforms.

This low quality of high school education outcomes is well documented by low rankings on most international standardized tests. Even in the UAE, which has made the most progress in improving the quality of its education, students' scores remain below international averages in PISA (Program for International Student Assessment) and TIMMS (Trends in International Mathematics and Science Study) results. For example, in the 2012 PISA scores, the UAE was forty-eighth in math, forty-fourth in reading and forty-sixth in science out of 65 participating OECD members (Pennington, 2014). All the other GCC (and Arab) countries that participated in these tests scored even lower than the UAE.

Reforming pre-university education

In the UAE it was the "Vision 2020" launched in 1999 that initiated a series of reforms. Several types of schools have been implemented by the Ministry of Education such as "Model Schools," "Schools of Tomorrow (MAG)," and "Partnership Schools," alongside regular public schools based on various recommendations from successive external consultants (Singapore, the United Kingdom, the United States, New Zealand, Australia, Finland, the Parthenon group, McKinsey, and others) (ADEC, 2010; Ahmed, 2012, 2013). Many of these reforms have focused on improving English language skills, math, science and the use of technology to better prepare students for university. Several initiatives by the government were centered on providing iPads to every student. For example, the Sheikh Mohammed Bin Rashed Al Maktoum IT Education Project (ITEP) was launched in 2000 in Dubai and included a professional development program to enable teachers to use ICT to improve teaching practice and acquire the needed skills to use ICT in ways that promote learning (Lightfoot, 2011). However, these reforms of the public primary and secondary educational sectors have not stopped the majority of UAE parents who now send their children to private schools.

The RAND Corporation overhaul of the Qatari educational system from elementary schools to universities had the "the mission of upgrading the nation's human capital as quickly as possible" (Rubin, 2012: para. 3). In a report based on the RAND Corporation intervention Gonzalez *et al.* (2008: 30) remark that in Qatar:

> the Ministry of Education, the Supreme Educational Council, Qatar University and Qatar labor force survey show that graduates of Qatar's K-12 public education system score far below international standards in core subjects and that there are too few graduates in the science, engineering and technology fields, which are the fields particularly in demand in the private sector.

The Qatari reforms began at the K-12 levels with the introduction of state-funded 'independent schools' designed to decentralize the system, increase autonomy and accountability and offer more choice for Qatari parents and students (RAND–Qatar Policy Institute). The reforms emphasized the development of critical thinking skills and instruction in English to better prepare graduates for university study.

Like its neighbors in the GCC, Oman embarked on a series of reforms of its pre-university system. The Ministry of Education adopted what it called a Basic Education Curriculum (BEC) aimed at providing its youth with "life skills" to help them participate in the global economy. The BEC is designed to meet both global pressures and local goals of building on its heritage as an Islamic Arab society and Omanization of its workforce (Donn and Issan, 2007). These educational reforms are part of strategic five-year plans adopted by the Omani government, following UNESCO and other international recommendations. They are based on the objectives of diversifying the country's economy by encouraging other sectors outside of oil industries and Omanization of the labor force to lessen Oman's dependence on foreign expatriates. To improve the quality of education the reforms implemented in 1998 included the 12 aspects discussed in a UNESCO publication spanning from structural changes and procedures, outlining clear objectives, teacher training assessment, curriculum and materials, encouraging privatization, and enhanced financial resources. In his assessment of education reforms outcomes, Rassekh (2004: 33) outlines several achievements of the reforms, which include:

> equalizing opportunities among its citizens, particularly between men and women. The quality of education has improved dramatically and the initiation of students to new information technology has advanced at a rapid pace. Better-trained teachers have been employed and the mechanism of professional development and upgrading of teachers and other educational personnel has proceeded satisfactorily. Vocational training and technical education have expanded rapidly, though not to the degree required in order to respond adequately to the Omanization objectives.

In 2008, the Kuwait Ministry of Education announced its strategy of general education 2005–25. The strategy revolved around the creation of a national authority for standards and quality control, a review of curricula and teaching methods, use of information and communication technology and the set-up of programs of pre-service teacher preparation. However, in 2009, the World Bank had warned Kuwait that its educational practices must change if its high school diplomas are to be recognized by the international community. In particular, the World Bank pointed to the short number of contact hours and warned that Kuwaiti high school graduates were running the risk of not receiving equivalencies in major international universities (Gangal, 2009). In November of 2013 the Minister of Education announced plans for a national curriculum, outsourcing certain administrative functions to the private sector, to alleviate teachers' heavy loads, and regulating the private sector. It was expected that the new national curriculum would serve as a framework for both the public and private systems in the country and would allow it to assess the quality of delivery of education (Oxford Business Group, 2013a).

The government of Bahrain launched its "schools of the future" project in 2003 to transform its public education from a traditional to a modern system by emphasizing e-learning and "an IT based system that prepares future generations to establish an advanced information society and build a knowledge-based economy" (King Hamad's schools of the future project, 2003). Eleven pilot schools were chosen to start the program to be expanded progressively to cover all schools in Bahrain. The National Education Review Initiative launched in 2006 (NERI) which is part of the Vision 2030, claims that educational reforms have helped Bahrainis make substantial progress in achieving their goals of transforming the educational outcomes to match the needs of their economic goals (Oxford Business Report, 2013b). However, the review carried out in 2010 by the Quality Assurance Authority for Education and Training (QAAET) found extensive discrepancies in the implementation of the project. Lightfoot (2011: 5) reports:

> On the whole, the reports [on Bahrain's and the UAE's ICT initiatives] indicate that: many of the far-reaching "knowledge economy" skills, which the education reform policies were seeking to promote, are underdeveloped. On the contrary, in many, or most, cases, ICT implementations have seldom moved far beyond teachers using data projectors and interactive whiteboards.

There are many factors that can explain the identified inadequate secondary school outcomes. These include the instability of education policies, pedagogical and methodological approaches, teacher qualifications and lack of parents' involvement with their children's schools experiences (Badry, 2015; Al Sumaiti, 2012). Moreover, it is possible that students' motivation is affected negatively by questions of identity as a result of the fast-paced impact of globalization (Badry, 2012). In addition, students are imbued with a sense of entitlement that leads them to exert little effort to learn. The welfare state nature of these countries and the consumerist approach to education increase the sense of entitlement and decreases students' motivation and engagement in the learning process. University education is for some students a holding pen, a rite of passage but not necessarily a gateway to knowledge. The goal is more to get a degree than to get knowledge. Many young nationals know that they can easily access employment in the public sector or join their family business, which often consists of the passive supervision of expatriate-run establishments.

Assessing the reforms

The GCC countries recognize the deficiencies in their pre-university education and are investing heavily to revamp it based on recommendations from international consultants. It is important to recognize, however, that the youth bulge that characterizes GCC societies constitutes a real challenge in the face of governments' development plans (Al Munajjed and Sabbagh, 2011). Despite all the efforts, results have not matched expectations and are not commensurate with investments in education so far. Sakr (2008: 1) remarked that:

> when it comes to education reform, the striking shared aspect ... has been the frankness with which ministers of education have acknowledged poor performance to date. In fact, they sometimes seem to be competing to outdo one another in self-criticism, while agreeing on the need for development and launching various initiatives.

An area that the reforms have emphasized is the introduction of IT in schools; this is based on the assumption that providing young learners with iPads will lead to improved learning experiences in schools. "The promotion of education reforms that relate to the development of 21st-century learning skills has become synonymous with the investment in ICT infrastructure in schools" (Lightfoot, 2011: 4). However, the key is to have investments directed to where quality matters as Faryal Khan, UNESCO's program specialist for education, pointed out. It is not possible to unequivocally evaluate whether these investments are in areas that make "a difference in key drivers of quality" (Pennington, 2014) because of lack of data and transparency. Based on long personal experience in the region, it is clear that areas such as teachers' qualifications and training do not receive the investments needed to improve learning in pre-university education (Badry, 2015). In addition, another problem with the reforms is that they are not grounded in the socio-cultural, economic and political contexts (especially in the wealthier countries such as Qatar, the UAE and Kuwait). Little effort is made to engage with parents in order to buttress the legitimacy of these reform efforts.

Gulf policy-makers are aware of some of these issues. For example, given the heavy reliance on expatriates in the economy of all GCC states, one of the major expectations from educational reforms is to help reduce the reliance on foreign labor by replacing them with educated and skilled nationals. Nationalization or Gulficization (Hertog, 2014) is one of the major goals driving educational reforms at all levels.

The above review of the pre-university educational reforms across the GCC countries suggests that despite substantial investments and multiple initiatives, they have fallen short of their two major objectives: preparing their graduates with the appropriate skills to join the private sector of the economy in order to advance nationalization and reduce the heavy reliance on expatriates, and developing the necessary competencies in those students who pursue higher education to enable them to become "knowledge workers" and contribute to a national knowledge-based economy.

The public university: teaching and research missions

The role of the university as a research center in addition to its teaching function is usually what distinguishes high ranking universities from the rest. Research output of higher education is an indicator of socio-economic and technological progress and is credited with the transformation of societies into knowledge hubs. Research is also central to the reputation and standing of the university itself and is important in the professional advancement of its faculty. Spending on research is usually taken as an indicator of development and varies greatly between the developed and developing worlds as Table 5.9 reveals. Common to all vision statements of the GCC countries is the goal of transforming GCC societies into knowledge-producing communities by encouraging research. In order to achieve this goal one would expect GCC public universities which are under government control to reflect these national aspirations. It is therefore surprising to see a low percentage of expenditure on research and development that is less than 1 percent.

Table 5.9 Scientific and technological capacities in world regions (percentage of world total, 1995)

	Expenditure on R&D	Scientific publications	European patents	US patents
Arab States	0.4	0.7	0.0	0.0
North America	37.9	38.4	33.4	51.5
Western Europe	28.0	35.8	47.4	19.9
Latin America	1.9	1.6	0.2	0.2
Sub-Saharan Africa	0.5	0.8	0.2	0.1
Japan and NICs	18.6	10.1	16.6	27.3
China	4.9	1.6	0.1	0.2
India and Central Asia	2.2	2.1	0.0	0.0
Others	2.2	2.9	1.3	0.6
World	100	100	100	100

Source: UNESCO (1998) (data for 1994).

This number has led many, including the UNDP and other international agencies and academics, to criticize the quality of higher education and research so far achieved in the Arab world (UNDP 2002, 2003; McGlennon, 2006). The fact that this includes the rich GCC countries is surprising. McGlennon (2006: i) observes that: "The Gulf Cooperation Council (GCC) countries have developed world levels of GDP per capita and yet investment in R&D remains at developing world levels." According to the government-controlled Emirates Industrial Bank (EIB), "average GCC allocations for scientific research stood at around 0.03 per cent of the gross domestic product in 2009 compared with nearly 2.6 per cent in Switzerland and 2.7 per cent in the United States" (Edarabia, 2014). The report goes on to assert that "the region's economic development with all its elements depend almost entirely on imported technology at a time when member states possess sufficient human and financial resources needed for the creation of major research institutions."

The GCC countries have made much greater progress in many economic measures compared to other Arab countries as Table 5.10 shows. The global competiveness index rankings show that all the GCC countries are ranked within the top 40 countries out of 144 countries listed. The next closest Arab countries, Jordan and Morocco, come in at sixty-fourth and seventieth of the countries included in the rankings. However, their low public funding earmarked for R&D shown is comparable to other poorer Arab countries (see Table 5.11) and their achievement in developing a knowledge economy are relatively similar to that of the rest of the Arab world.

There are additional factors within and outside the university that stand in the way of transforming the university into research centers. These include the prioritization of undergraduate studies, the focus on skills to meet immediate labor market needs, the lack of adequate facilities to conduct research and factors related to faculty. Although universities claim that they value research they

Table 5.10 Global Competitiveness rankings (2012–13)

Country	Rank/144	Score
Qatar	11	5.38
KSA	18	5.19
UAE	24	5.07
Oman	32	4.65
Bahrain	35	4.63
Kuwait	37	4.56
Jordan	64	4.23
Morocco	70	4.15
Lebanon	91	3.88
Egypt	107	3.73
Algeria	110	3.72
Libya	113	3.68

Source: Adapted from the Arab World Forum p. 10: www3weforum.org/docs/WEF_AWCR_ Report_2013.pdf.

Table 5.11 Public expenditure on education as a percentage of GDP

Country	HDI rank	Percentage of GDP spent on R&D (2011)	Percentage of GDP dpending on education in 2012 (very high human development 5.3; high human development 4.6; medium human development 3.7; low human development 3.8)
Qatar	31	–	2.5
KSA	34	–	5.6
UAE	40	0.49	–
Oman	56	0.13	4.3
Bahrain	44	–	2.9
Kuwait	46	0.09	3.8

Source: Adapted from Human Development Report, 2013 and the World Bank report, http://data. worldbank.org/indicator/GB.XPD.RSDV.GD.ZS/countries/1W-IL-US-EU-SG?display=graph.

remain primarily teaching universities as reflected in faculty teaching loads and research funding policies (Al Enezi, 2007). The fact that few universities offer doctoral degree programs limits the availability of research assistants and faculty are expected to teach at least 9–12 credits hours per semester. In addition, teaching obligations are the same regardless of rank or research portfolio. Since most of the universities are relatively new and undergo constant reforms, faculty are expected to spend an important amount of their time in service committees. As a result, those who are interested in research must devote their summer breaks to it.[11]

Azad and Seyyed (2007) studied several factors influencing faculty research productivity among the faculty of business schools at three GCC public universities, the

UAEU in the UAE, KU in Kuwait and King Fahad University of Petroleum and Minerals in Saudi Arabia. They found "that the university's expectations for time allocation for the two activities of scholarship/professional growth and research are significantly lower than those of the faculty's preferences; and the opposite is true for teaching and service" (2007: 101). The second factor investigated was what the authors referred to as two areas of "self-knowledge and individual competencies," which included faculty perceptions relating to their satisfaction with their personal academic achievements and performance. Results suggest that faculty feel that their potential and competencies for research in their fields are good but this potential is underutilized by their institutions. The third cluster of factors were classified under work environment as represented in Table 5.12. Table 5.12 presents statistical analysis of the significance of these factors in faculty perception of their role in research productivity and their level of satisfaction with each factor. Findings show that faculty consider all the factors listed to be significant in encouraging research but that they were not satisfied with most of them. The only factors deemed satisfactory were availability of data and journal resources, IT support and travel support to attend conferences. Surprisingly, access to external grants was not considered significant in influencing faculty research productivity. The authors attributed this finding to university rules that tend to limit the financial benefits to the faculty, department or college. The last cluster of factors was social contingencies, which included:

1 family responsibilities;
2 health related considerations;
3 financial pressures and constraints;
4 social demands and expectations;
5 external professional commitments.

Among these factors family responsibilities and financials pressures were the most significant, which supports earlier studies about the negative influence of social contingencies on faculty research productivity in the region.

In another study, Chapman *et al.* (2014) examined the degree of identification and commitment of faculty to their institutions through interviewing faculty in five universities across the UAE. "Findings suggest that the extensive use of expatriate staff on short-term contracts can work against the development of institutional loyalty or commitment." Although employees felt that their work was valued by their institutions and were dedicated to quality teaching, their "high professional instability" and the feeling of being disposable does not encourage them to become "national builders" (Swan, 2014).

Others have attributed poor research outputs to perceived lack of academic freedom engendered by the political environment in the Arab world. Romanowski and Ramzi (2010), in their article "Faculty perceptions of academic freedom at a GCC university," quoted from a speech by Her Highness Sheikha Mozah Bint Nasser Al Misnad, when she stated:

Table 5.12 Comparative analysis of perceived significance versus satisfaction

Description of factors	Number of observations	Mean values		Paired mean difference	t-value	2-tailed probability
		Perceived significance*	Perceived satisfaction**			
Clarity of institution's research expectations	115	3.60	2.49	1.21	4.49	0.0001
Availability of research assistance	115	3.99	1.58	2.40	9.25	0.0000
Availability of secretarial support	112	3.55	1.59	1.92	7.13	0.0000
Financial incentives for doing research	112	4.10	1.87	1.96	6.23	0.0000
Other research incentives such as reduced teaching	115	4.45	1.99	2.12	9.60	0.0000
Favorable research culture	115	4.15	1.91	2.49	10.86	0.0000
Time spent on teaching related commitments	115	4.22	1.91	2.39	10.99	0.0000
Time consumed by non-teaching responsibilities	115	3.91	2.23	1.91	6.49	0.0000
Other research support	115	4.19	2.16	1.88	7.99	0.0000
Availability of information technology support	112	4.11	3.29	0.89	5.90	0.0000
Access to internal research grants	115	3.78	2.69	1.10	4.79	0.0000
Access to external research grants	115	2.49	1.91	0.99	4.41	0.0000
Procedural simplicity for receiving research grants	115	3.80	2.22	1.64	6.91	0.0000
Access to databases and academic journals	115	4.23	3.13	1.10	5.23	0.0000
Travel support for participating in conferences	114	4.11	3.18	0.99	4.00	0.0004
Availability of course release time	114	4.18	2.17	2.11	9.19	0.0000
Collegial relationship among faculty	115	3.73	2.09	1.45	7.99	0.0000
Establishing a research support office	115	4.13	1.78	2.41	9.99	0.0000
Support by unit's chair/dean for research efforts	115	3.67	2.14	1.99	8.89	0.0000
Annual performance evaluation	115	3.62	2.92	0.99	3.88	0.0000
Existence of formal mentorship programs	115	3.61	2.11	1.69	6.91	0.0000

Source: Adapted from Azad and Seyyed (2007).

Notes
* 1 – Slightly insignificant; 5 – Most significant
** 1 – Very dissatisfied; 5 = Very satisfied

We cannot talk about a culture of quality without talking about massive political and social reforms throughout the Arab world, and indeed the world in general. It is useless to "play" at being free in schools while society squelches this freedom. Actually, it can even lead to more instability. Recent studies have shown, internationally, that extremist and violent organizations are heavily populated with educated, politically disenfranchised youth, whose education taught them to expect the right to participate politically, but their environments refuted this expectation.

(Opening speech at the conference on Arab Women Past and Present: Participation and Democratization, Doha, Qatar, March 3–5, 2006)

The Sheikha's speech follows one of the recommendations of the Arab Human Development Report (2003: 76) stating that Arab governments should be persuaded that "restricting intellectual freedom is tantamount to depriving society of its capacity to generate the meaningful, innovative and productive knowledge that is a precondition for survival and success in the 21st century."

In much of the advanced world, industry plays an important role in research funding. This is not the case in the GCC. The nature of industry in the GCC does not offer research opportunities. Companies such as the giant oil companies, which totally depend on foreign companies for equipment and servicing, are contractually expected to limit their engineers to being executors of functions, thus curtailing creativity and innovation.

An additional challenge is a competitive attitude between Gulf countries and even between emirates within the UAE. This competition limits collaborative research across borders or even inter-institutions. It must be noted, however, that recently many efforts have been launched by the Qatar Foundation in particular to encourage collaborative research, but these are still in their infancy.

There are some exceptions however (see Table 5.13). In Abu Dhabi, the Masdar Institute is focused on research related to creating a sustainable environment. Collaboration between industries and research institutes and universities is beginning. Oil companies and banks are beginning to award research grants, particularly to local universities (emirate rather than federal in the UAE). In Abu Dhabi, the Petroleum Institute and the Masdar Institute have many partnerships which are also governmental. In Qatar, the Qatar Foundation has also been actively engaged in funding research that pertains to Qatar. Every year several calls for research in the areas of science, social science, technology and humanities are launched.

After a decade of reforms and serious investments, results remain below expectations.

The urgency of creating a tertiary education system that prepares GCC citizens and residents to enter a fast developing economy understandably led to a focus on the role of universities as teaching institutions. The GCC countries needed citizens with professional and vocational training to respond to economic and business development plans.

However, promoting research in order to achieve all GCC nations' future visions of transforming their societies into knowledge-producing societies is yet

Table 5.13 Main research centers in the GCC

Qatar	Qatar Foundation Office of Institutional Research and Planning RAND-Qatar Policy Institute Qatar National Research Fund Qatar Computing Research Institute Qatar Environment and Energy Research Institute Qatar Biomedical Research Institute The Social and Economic Survey Research Institute (SESRI) – established by Qatar University
UAE	National Research Foundation (NRF) Emirates Center for Strategic Studies and Research (ECSSR) Centre of Excellence for Applied Research and Training (CERT) Gulf Research Center (GCR) Masdar Institute of Science and Technology Ras Al Khaimah Center for Advanced Materials (RAK CAM) Mohammed bin Rashid School of Government
Oman	The Research Council International Research Foundation
Kuwait	Kuwait Institute for Scientific Research – KISR The Center for Research and Studies on Kuwait Kuwait University
Bahrain	Bahrain Centre for Studies and Research (BCSR) Gulf Research Center Bahrain Research Center Shaikh Ebrahim Bin Mohammed Al Khalifa Center For Culture And Research CBRE Bahrain Royal College of Surgeons in Ireland – Medical University of Bahrain

Sources: Qatar: www.qu.edu.qa/offices/research/academic/; http://qnl.qa/find-answers/research-insti-tute-directory/research-institute-directory; UAE: www.masdar.ac.ae/; www.ecssr.com/ECSSR/app-manager/portal/ecssr; www.certonline.com; www.indexuae.com/Top/Education/Research_Institutes (this website has the list of almost all the research institutes); Oman: home.trc.gov.om/tabid/40/lan-guage/en-US/Default.aspx; www.omanirf.org; Kuwait: www.kisr.edu.kw/; gckuwait.com/institu-tional/center-for-research-and-studies-on-kuwait; Bahrain: www.cirs-tm.org/org-eng.php?pays=Bahr ein&matiere=techno; www.eldis.org/go/home&id=4442&type=Organisation; www.rcsi-mub.c; www.shaikhebrahimcenter.org/.

to receive the support it needs to become a reality. Governments are beginning to recognize the importance of research support. Across the region, they are creating research institutes and foundations with a wide variety of research agendas as illustrated in Table 5.13.

Conclusion

There is little evidence in both educational policies and practices that show that the GCC public institutions have succeeded in combining the acquisition of instrumental/professional knowledge with reflexive knowledge grounded in local culture. Reforms so far have focused on an education that prepares students to enter the entrepreneurial global economy. But they seem to have fallen short of achieving even this goal when the actual participation and productivity of GCC graduates in the development of their countries is measured. In pursuing the goal of education as a major engine of development, educational choices and practices have tended to isolate social development from economic integration which has so far missed the mark of drawing the national population into the global economy. The very low participation of nationals in the private sector raises serious doubts about the effectiveness of these policies and suggests that changes in the incentive system that structures the labor market needs to accompany educational reforms (see Chapter 9).

Substantial investments have helped expand educational opportunities for GCC nationals and residents but they have done little to sow the seeds for a future knowledge society. The transplantation of top-down reforms are motivated by short-term economic constraints that are not likely to achieve the two long-term goals of nationalization of the labor force and the creation of a knowledge society, as stated in the national visions of each GCC member state and restated in mission statements of all public higher universities.

Notes

1 Today literacy rates are comparable to rates in Europe and range between 90 and 98 percent.
2 The switch back and forth between Arabic and English is discussed in more detail later in this chapter.
3 Zayed University website, available at: www.zu.ac.ae.
4 Abdullah bin Mohammed Al-Sarmi (Undersecretary of the Ministry of Higher Education, Sultanate of Oman). "From one university to 54 higher education institutions: The experience of Oman in higher education." Posted on QS Showcase Asia, Middle East and Africa, February 11, 2014, http://qsshowcase.com/main/category/showcase-middle-east/ (accessed June 4, 2015).
5 The nine non-professional colleges are information technology, business administration, law, arts, engineering, science, applied studies, physical education and physiotherapy, and health sciences. See University of Bahrain website, available at: www.uob.edu.bh/english/ (accessed June 17, 2013).
6 This is the case for the entire educational system from K-12 to tertiary levels.
7 The RAND Qatar Policy Institute (RQPI) and RAND Education is a partnership of the RAND Corporation and the Qatar Foundation for Education, Science, and Community Development.
8 On the other hand, Qatar's community colleges, North Atlantic Qatar and the Community College of Qatar, are allowed to maintain English as the medium of instruction.
9 There have been so many changes to the goals of this institute as well as its leadership in the last year that make it impossible to describe what it stands for. At one point its goal was to work on Arabizing the curriculum by asking faculty to create their own textbooks. The steps to implement such a project are to say the least very questionable as its conceptualization and implementation started with English teachers leading the project. This seems to have changed again. It is very hard to keep up with the reforms. No sooner are they announced than they are changed.

10
    HCT mission: The Higher Colleges of Technology is dedicated to the delivery of applied and vocationally focused programmes that achieve national and international standards at the Diploma, Bachelor's and Master's levels. Delivered through excellent instruction based on "learning by doing" and in a technology-rich environment, supported by applied research, our programmes are designed to meet the employment needs of the UAE and support Emirati students in becoming innovative and work-ready.
             (Available at: www.hct.ac.ae/about/overview/ (accessed July 16, 2014))

11 One of the authors received a research grant to carry out the research for this book but was unable to use some of the funds to buy out time because of the rules governing research funds. When she asked the dean for a course release in 2012, he responded that she, like everyone else, has to find time to do her research and teaching loads should not be reduced "just because one has research plans."

References

ADEC (2010). ADEC Signs agreement to implement Finnish education system model in two public schools. June 15. Available at: http://gsec.abudhabi.ae/Sites/GSEC/Navigation/EN/MediaCentre/government-news,did=225712,render=renderPrint.html.

Ahmed, A. (2012). Pupils prepare for a new curriculum in Abu Dhabi. *The National* online, August 1. Available at: www.thenational.ae/news/uae-news/education/pupils-prepare-for-a-new-curriculum-in-abu-dhabi (accessed January 14, 2013).

Ahmed, A. (2013). Bell rings as UAE schools re-open for new term. *The National* online, January 7. Available at: www.thenational.ae/news/uae-news/education/bell-rings-as-uae-schools-re-open-for-new-term (accessed March 2, 2013).

Al Barwani, T., Chapman, D.W. and Ameen, H. (2009). Strategic brain drain: Implications for higher education in Oman. *Higher Education Policy*: 415–432. Available at: http://search.proquest.com.ezproxy.aus.edu/docview/203161366.

Al Enezi, A. (2007). Why academics fail to utilize academic-funded research opportunities? An empirical study. *International Journal of Management*, 24(4): 712–726.

Al Lamki, S.M. (2002). Higher education in the Sultanate of Oman: The challenge of access, equity and privatization. *Journal of Higher Education Policy and Management*, 24(1): 75–86.

Al Maktoum, S.M. (2006). *My Vision: Challenges in the Race for Excellence*. Dubai: Motivate.

Al Munajjed, M. and Sabbagh, K. (2011). *Youth in GCC Countries: Meeting the Challenge*. Booz & Co., Inc. Ideation Center Insight. Available at: www.youthpolicy.org/library/wp-content/uploads/library/2011_Youth_GCC_Countries_Meeting_Challenge_Eng.pdf.

Al Sarmi, A. (2014). From one university to 54 higher education institutions: The experience of Oman in higher education [Showcase Middle East web post], February 11. Available at: http://qsshowcase.com/main/from-one-university-to-54-higher-education-institutions-the-experience-of-oman-in-higher-education/.

Al Sumaiti, R. (2012). *Parental Involvement in the Education of their Children in Dubai (Policy Brief No. 30)*. Dubai School of Government. Available at: www.khda.gov.ae/CMS/WebParts/TextEditor/Documents/Parental_Involvement_in_the_Education.pdf.

Arabian Gulf University home page. Available at: www.agu.edu.bh/Default_en.aspx (accessed June 6, 2013).

Azad, A.N. and Seyyed, F.J. (2007). Factors influencing faculty research productivity: Evidence from AACSB accredited schools in the GCC countries. *Journal of International Business Research*, 6(1): 91–112. Available at: www.alliedacademies.org/Publications/Papers/JIBR%20Vol%206%20No%201%202007%20p%2091-112.pdf.

Badry, F. (2012). Education in the UAE: Local identity and global development. In *Essentials of School Education in the UAE*. Abu Dhabi: ECSSR Publications, 85–106.

Badry, F. (2015). UAE bilingual education: Searching for an elusive balance. In Mehisto, P. and Genesee, F. (eds.). *Building Bilingual Education Systems: Forces, Mechanisms and Counterweights*. Cambridge: Cambridge University Press, 197–214.

Bahrain Polytechnic home page. Available at: www.polytechnic.bh/default.asp?action=category&id=58 (accessed June 6, 2013).

Bollag, B. (2006). America's hot new export: Higher education. *The Chronicle of Higher Education International*. Available at: http://heglobal.international.gbtesting.net/media/7038/chronicledunnettintlprograms.pdf.

Boyle, H.N. (2006). Memorization and learning in Islamic schools. *Comparative Education Review*, 50(3): 478–495.

Calderwood, J. (2009). Kuwaiti politicians invited to see mixed gender classes. *The National*, October 16. Available at: www.thenational.ae/news/world/middle-east/kuwaiti-politicians-invited-to-see-mixed-gender-classes.

Chapman, D., Austin, A., Farah, S., Wilson, E. and Ridge, N. (2014). Academic staff in the UAE: Unsettled journey. *Higher Education Policy*, 27(1): 131–151.

College of Health Sciences, University of Bahrain (2011). Dean's welcome. Available at: www.uob.edu.bh/english/pages.aspx?module=pages&id=2681&SID=644 (accessed June 6, 2013).

Commission for Academic Accreditation. Available at: www.caa.ae/caa/.

Donn, G. and Issan, S. (2007). Higher education in transition: Gender and change in the Sultanate of Oman. *Scottish Educational Review*, 39: 173–185. Available at: www.scotedreview.org.uk/pdf/180.pdf (accessed December 20, 2014).

Drzeniek-Hanouz, D.M. and Yousef, T. (2007). Assessing competitiveness in the Arab world: Strategies for sustaining the growth momentum. Available at: www.weforum.org/pdf/Global_Competitiveness_Reports/Reports/chapters/1_1.pdf.

Edarabia (2014). GCC urged to boost spending on research. Available at: www.edarabia.com/12886/gcc-urged-to-boost-spending-on-research/ (accessed August 15, 2014).

Galal, A. (2008). *The Road Not Traveled: Education Reform in the Middle East and North Africa*. Washington, DC: World Bank. Available at: http://siteresources.worldbank.org/INTMENA/Resources/EDU_Flagship_Full_ENG.pdf.

Gangal, N. (2009). World Bank warns Kuwait about education system. *Arabian Business*. Available at: www.arabianbusiness.com/world-bank-warns-kuwait-about-education-system-15825.html.

Ghabra, S. (2010). Student-centered education and American style universities in the Arab world. In *Higher Education and the Middle East: Empowering Underserved and Vulnerable Populations*. Washington, DC: Middle East Institute, 21–26.

Ghabra, S. and Arnold, M. (2007). Studying the American way: An assessment of American-style higher education in Arab countries. Policy Focus #71. The Washington Institute for Near East Policy.

Gonzalez, G.C., Karoly, L., Constant, L., Salem, H. and Goldman, C. (2008). *Facing Human Capital Challenges of the 21st Century. Education and Labor Market Initiatives in Lebanon, Oman, Qatar, and the United Arab Emirates*. Doha: RAND. Available at: www.rand.org/pubs/monographs/MG786z1.html (accessed June 3, 2015).

Hertog, S. (2014). Arab Gulf states: An assessment of nationalization policies. Gulf Labor Markets and Migration (GLMM). GLMM research paper. N.1/2014.

Higher Colleges of Technology. HCT overview. Available at: www.hct.ac.ae/about/overview/ (accessed July 16, 2014).

Higher Education Review Unit (2010). Institutional review report. University of Bahrain. Kingdom of Bahrain, 21–25.

King Hamad's schools of the future project (2003). Available at: www.moe.gov.bh/khsfp/khsfpdoc/future-eng.pdf.

Lightfoot, M. (2011). Promoting the knowledge economy in the Arab world. Sage Open. Available at: http://sgo.sagepub.com/content/1/2/2158244011417457.

Lindsey, U. (2012). Debate arises at Qatar U. over decision to teach mainly in Arabic. *The Chronicle of Higher Education*. Available at: http://chronicle.com/article/Debate-Arises-at-Qatar-U-Over/130695/ (accessed August 2, 2012).

McGlennon, D. (2006). *Building Research Capacity in the Gulf Cooperation Council Countries: Strategy, Funding and Engagement*. Available at: http://portal.unesco.org/pv_obj_cache/pv_obj_id_02DCDD543BD8930F0C0A68F80DC77E24AAB70100/filename/McGlennon-EN.pdf.

Mazawi, A.E. (2007). "Knowledge society" or work as "spectacle": Education for work and the prospects of social transformation in Arab societies. In Farrell, L. and Fenwick, T. (eds.). *Educating the Global Workforce: Knowledge, Knowledge Work and Knowledge Workers*. London: Routlege, 251–267.

Mills, A. (2008a). Emirates look to the west for prestige. *The Chronicle of Higher Education International*, 55(5): A1.

Mills, A. (2008b). U.S. universities negotiate tricky terrain in the Middle East. *Chronicle of Higher Education*, 54(46): A1.

Moini, J.S., Bikson, T.K., Neu, C.R. and DeSisto, L. (2009). *The Reform of Qatar University*. RAND Corporation. Available at: www.rand.org/content/dam/rand/pubs/monographs/2009/RAND_MG796.sum.pdf.

Oxford Business Group (2013a). Economic update: Kuwait steps up pace of education reform. Available at: www.Oxfordbusinessgroup.com/economic_updates/kuwait-steps-pace-education-reform.

Oxford Business Group (2013b). The report: Bahrain. Available at: http://books.google.ae/books?id=10yGU0GRnjEC&pg=PA172&lpg=PA172&dq=reforms+of+public+education+in+Bahrain&source=bl&ots=-ZhN8iaLK8&sig=YXT6X2OCZ6vYCSgy1WiNRV67M8Y&hl=en&sa=X&ei=CSfrU9HuOYWi0QWcyIHoCQ&redir_esc=y#v=onepage&q=reforms%20of%20public%20education%20in%20Bahrain&f=false.

Pennington, R. (2014). Quality is the biggest challenge facing UAE's education. *The National*, January 6. Available at: www.thenational.ae/uae/education/quality-is-the-biggest-challenge-facing-uaes-education#ixzz3A42ZIGum.

Qatar University. History. Available at: www.qu.edu.qa/theuniversity/history.php (accessed November 28, 2014).

Qatar University. Programs. Available at: www.qu.edu.qa/students/programs.php (accessed November 28, 2014).

Qatar University. Students. Available at: www.qu.edu.qa/theuniversity/student.php (accessed November 28, 2014).

Qatar University opts for Arabic teaching medium (2012). AMEinfo.com, January 26. Available at: www.ameinfocom/288061.html (accessed August 1, 2012).

QU Undergraduate Catalog 2013–2014. Available at: www.qu.edu.qa/students/documents/catalog/undergraduate-catalog-2013-2014.pdfp (accessed December 6, 2014).

Rassekh, S. (2004). Education as a motor for development: Recent education reforms in Oman with particular reference to the status of women and girls. Innodata. Monographs 15. Educational innovations in action. International Bureau of Education. Geneva, Switzerland. Available at: www.ibe.unesco.org.

Romanowski, M.H. and Ramzi, N. (2010). Faculty perceptions of academic freedom at a GCC university. *UNESCO IBE Prospects*, 40: 481–497.

Rubin, A. (2012). Higher education reform in the Arab world: The model of Qatar. Middle East Institute.

Sabry, S. (2014). Emiratis continue to choose US for higher education. *Gulf News. Nation*, A10.

Sakr, A. (2008). Gulf states: Competing in educational reform. *Arab Reform Bulletin*, 5(4): 7–8.

Sharaf, N. and Ibrahim, A. (2013). Move to end gender segregation: In-class separation stays. *Arab Times*, June 2.

Swan, M. (2014). UAE universities are under threat from job insecurity, research suggests. *The National* online, August 13. Available at: www.thenational.ae/uae/education/uae-universities-are-under-threat-from-job-insecurity-research-suggests (accessed October 26, 2014).

UNDP (United Nations Development Programme) (2003). Arab Human Development Report: Building an Arab knowledge society. New York: UNDP.

Wiseman, A.W. (2011). Impact of science education on the GCC labor market. *The Emirates Occasional Papers*, 1–71, 73–78.

World Bank (2009). The World Bank annual report. Available at: http://siteresourcesworldbank.org/EXTANNREP2K8/Resources/YR00_Year_in_Review_English.pdf.

World Economic Forum (2013). *The Arab World Competiveness Report 2013*. Insight Report. Geneva: World Economic Forum and the European Bank for Reconstruction and Development (EBRD).

6 Assessing quality
Adopting Western standards of accreditation

Introduction

Within the first few weeks of an introductory economics course students usually learn that a healthy economic system requires market competition. The struggle against other enterprises for consumer expenditures forces firms to provide cheaper and/or higher quality products and services as well as to design new commodities to meet consumer needs. This sort of competition is supposed to make consumers sovereign and raise economic welfare by promoting efficiency and economic dynamism. Producers will certainly benefit from a less competitive regime in the form of higher profits, but the total society (represented by large numbers of consumers) will suffer. This simple model relies on premises that do not apply to the case of higher education. In this case, intensified competition might not be associated with a higher quality product that is delivered efficiently.

One key argument of the standard model is that consumers have good knowledge of the product or service they are consuming. A buyer of an apple usually has an understanding of what a high quality apple provides him or her. The consumer knows what an apple will normally cost and can judge the apple's characteristics through sensory inspection. Armed with this information, a consumer can then make decisions about which and how many apples to buy and at what price. A potential consumer of higher education, however, is likely to have much less information about the quality of the educational service than the seller does. This information asymmetry can prevent the consumer from making an informed decision, while allowing the supplier to capture unwarranted economic rents. Without some extra-market intervention, it will be difficult for the market system to produce the economic benefits that are meant to accrue to the public (Stiglitz 2001).[1]

An additional consideration for parents and students attempting to choose the appropriate higher education institution is that purchasing a service that will be delivered to the student for four or more years requires one to trust the provider. As soon as a specific decision is made to send a student to an existing higher education system, the bargaining power of the buyer is reduced. Parents and governmental authorities have to hope that the university or college is both

DOI: 10.4324/9780203796139-6

financially viable and can provide a suitable educational experience. The longer a student pursues her or his course of study, the more difficult it is for that student to decide to leave the educational institution if it proves to be unsatisfactory. The costs of restarting education become increasingly onerous, and this can allow a higher education institution to pay less attention to educational quality for its captive group of consumers. This is a key factor that differentiates higher education as a commodity from products like apples. If one does not like the apple, it is possible to learn from that experience and "exit" that particular market for apples. Market competition encourages consumers to use this negative power to discipline suppliers. But in the education market the cost of exiting can be very high. Thus, a key process that allows consumers to exercise power and assert their sovereignty is much weaker.

Why regulation and accreditation?

As Albert Hirschmann noted in his book, *Exit, Voice and Loyalty*, the inability to discipline an organization by threatening to cut one's relationship with it means that the only other key mechanism available to a group of individuals dissatisfied with the good or service they are consuming is to use the political process or the society's social "voice" (Hirschmann, 1970). The particular institutions in the regulation and governance of higher education should be seen as a response to the dual problems of information asymmetry and the lack of credibility of an exit threat. The parents and high school students considering higher education might be able to make tentative judgments about the quality of a possible university or college by discussing this issue with friends and colleagues or by examining media reports. However, it is difficult for them to assess the benefits of alternative educational opportunities particularly if the parents themselves have not experienced college education as they are less likely to have independent knowledge of the actual educational process that their child will be experiencing.

The issue of getting appropriate information about the functioning of higher educational institutions also concerns future employers. While most businesses and public agencies understand they will have to provide training to teach new employees the idiosyncratic technical and social skills specific to a workplace, employers expect higher education to supply a stream of qualified job applicants who possess high-level analytical and organizational skills as well as an appropriate work ethic that will make it relatively easy for them to learn how to do the professional jobs into which they are entering. Employers are generally not able to spend the time to evaluate the individual educational experience of each job applicant. Instead, they rely on the credential or the degree which the job applicant has earned to begin the assessment of the candidate's suitability. In other words, a college degree is supposed to provide an accurate signal to employers about the quality of the potential employee.

These information problems facing the direct consumers (parents and students) or indirect consumers (potential employers) of higher education suggest that it would be unreasonable to expect that market competition alone could ensure educational quality because consumers have difficulty both assessing the quality of the commodity and exiting the educational relationship if they are dissatisfied. Beyond these information issues, there is also the issue of the particular type of market structure that the privatization of higher education has created in the GCC. In the countries we have studied, one important tendency we have noted needs to be highlighted. The privatization of universities and colleges has created a series of relatively small colleges that offer business and information technology degrees. Intensified competition in this sub-sector of the educational universe can be unstable. Because of low financial barriers to entry, it is relatively easy to set up a college or university. On the other hand, this factor also means that it can be difficult for these institutions to maintain market share. The threat of bankruptcy or economic failure is real, and standard economic theory would predict that such monopolistically competitive market structures will be characterized by excess capacity and organizational churning as a result of the birth and death of a noticeable proportion of higher educational institutions (Chamberlin, 1933).

We are used to such instability when we consider restaurants, small clothing boutiques, or other retail outlets that operate within monopolistically competitive market structures, and while economic failure can be a catastrophe for the business owners and workers involved in such business breakdowns, these bankruptcies usually have few significant social repercussions. On the other hand, a similar collapse of a higher educational institution has far greater ramifications because of the central role that attaining higher education plays in the lives and career plans of families. Given this reality, ruling authorities will be reluctant to allow colleges and universities to emerge and disappear in a completely unregulated fashion. Governments find that they have to ensure that universities and colleges operating within their territory are financially stable and can provide a satisfactory educational experience for students, parents and employers. One of the ironies of introducing more competition in the higher educational sector is that the government is placed under increasing pressure to create more robust systems of educational regulation. In other words, market competition often results in the enhancement of the "voice" or power of governmental regulatory institutions.

The Westernization of regulation and accreditation in the GCC

The decision in the 1990s and early 2000s by GCC governing authorities to create a more competitive higher education system produced a variety of educational models that we have outlined in Chapter 3. One key finding is that the establishment of elite branch campuses in Qatar and Abu Dhabi, despite their visibility, do not represent the majority of higher educational innovations that the GCC governments promoted. Likewise, the Dubai neo-liberal educational mall approach avoids the problem of devoting considerable governmental resources to regulation by insisting that all the foreign institutions established within Dubai Knowledge Village and the Dubai International Academic City be branch campuses under the control of a host institution. Most other governments have not followed this path, and the result is the emergence of a complex network of small colleges and larger universities that must submit to conditions set both by the government in terms of their academic program offerings as well as by their partnerships with external universities.

The growth of cross-border collaborative arrangements and the establishment of institutions, that claim to use American higher educational principles, have led to the adoption of common methods of assessment and accreditation. Institutions which offer joint degree programs must guarantee that all students receiving the degree are subject to similar curricula and evaluated in similar ways even if, for example, an MBA from a Western university is granted to students who never set foot on the home university campus. Any attempt to do otherwise risks undermining the credibility of the degree-granting institutions. Similarly, home campuses must vigilantly monitor and regulate their far-flung branch campus if they are to ensure that the quality of the academic programs being offered is broadly similar.

Quality control mechanisms are different for those institutions that attempt to replicate Western higher educational practices, but are not directly linked to a foreign university or college. In these cases, the higher education institutions themselves and governments have created accreditation policies and evaluative procedures that attempt to ensure that each college or university follows generally recognized international standards. These standards are articulated by the International Network for Quality Assurance Agencies in Higher Education (INQAAHE). The goal of this body is to promote a rigorous process of assessment that requires administrators and faculty to evaluate their own work practices.

The INQAAHE believes that it is crucial for the faculty, administrators and indeed students to participate in this quality control process through the writing of a self-study report that assesses the institution's governance, finances and academics. An outside body of experts then visits the campus and uses the self-study report to identify strengths and weaknesses of the college or university under investigation. The ultimate goal is to accredit both specific degree programs and the institution as a whole. In addition, all universities and colleges undergo periodic evaluations in order to continue to be licensed by the government agency charged with certifying the quality of their education quality (see Table 6.1). All countries in the GCC with the exception of Qatar have government accreditation agencies that are full members of the INQAAHE. (Qatar is probably an exception because of its reliance on a branch campus model to ensure academic quality.) The significance of these affiliations is that the GCC have embraced global standards of higher education that are closely linked to the practices of Western academia (INQAAHE, 2014).

Free-standing institutions that are not branch campuses also have the option of pursuing additional institutional accreditation by an American accreditation

Table 6.1 Government higher education accreditation and assessment agencies: IQAAHE
members

Country	Name of agency
Bahrain	National Authority for Qualification and Quality Assurance for Education and Training
Kuwait	Private universities – Ministry of Higher Education
Oman	Oman Academic Accreditation Authority
Saudi Arabia	National Commission for Academic Accreditation and Assessment
Qatar	No agency is a member of the INQAAHE.
United Arab Emirates – Abu Dhabi	UAE Commission for Academic Accreditation
United Arab Emirates – Dubai	University Quality Assurance International Board

Note
INQAAHE – Members. Available at: www.inqaahe.org/members/list.php (accessed June 17, 2014).

authority (all educational institutions must be certified by the national government). Within the Gulf itself, the American University of Sharjah, Zayed University and the American University of Dubai have received accreditation from either the Middle States Commission on Higher Education (MSCHE) or the Southern Association of Colleges and Schools (SACS).[2] Zayed University's (a public university) successful accreditation represents the culmination of efforts by the previous Minister of Higher Education of the UAE (Sheikh Nahyan al Nahyan) to begin to subject public institutions of the UAE which are funded by the federal government to American educational standards.

More common than this non-governmental institutional accreditation, which is largely linked to free-standing institutions that present themselves as American universities, liberal arts institutions also seek the Western accreditation of particular degrees. The Gulf has participated actively in the drive to receive American recognition of its engineering and business programs. With respect to engineering, the chief accrediting body, Baltimore-based ABET, has certified a large number of degree programs in applied science, computing, engineering and engineering technology outside the United States. Saudi Arabia and the UAE have used this service most extensively, but of the 68 non-American institutions whose four-year undergraduate degree programs have been accredited by ABET, 24 have come from the Gulf (see Table 6.2), 31 have come from the Arab world, and if we include Turkey as part of the broader Middle East, 36 institutions have had programs accredited by this American institution.

With respect to the accreditation of business school degree programs, the UAE has the most institutions that have received accreditation from the Association to Advance Collegiate Schools of Businesses (AACSB) (see Table 6.3). This finding corresponds with our general conclusion that the universities and colleges of the emirates are consistently attempting to obtain Western recognition for their academic programs.

Table 6.2 ABET accreditation of engineering, computer science and information systems programs in the GCC

Country	Institution	Number of programs accredited	Dates of accreditation
Bahrain	AMA International University	1	2013
Bahrain	University of Bahrain	8	2007 and 2009
Kuwait	Kuwait University	7	2006
Oman	Sultan Qaboos University	4	2007
Qatar	Qatar University	7	2009
Qatar	Texas A&M at Qatar	7	2007
Saudi Arabia	King Abdulaziz University	15	2007 and 2011
Saudi Arabia	King Fahd University of Petroleum and Minerals	16	2008
Saudi Arabia	King Saud University	12	2008, 2010 and 2011
Saudi Arabia	Qassim University KSA	3	2008
Saudi Arabia	Taif University	2	2013
Saudi Arabia	Umm Al-Qusa University	2	2010
Saudi Arabia	Yanbu Industrial College	10	2008, 2009 and 2010
Saudi Arabia	King Faisal University	2	2009
United Arab Emirates	American University in Dubai	4	2006 and 2007
United Arab Emirates	American University of Sharjah	6	2004
United Arab Emirates	Higher Colleges of Technology	11	2008 and 2010
United Arab Emirates	The Petroleum Institute	5	2010
United Arab Emirates	UAEU University	8	2008 and 2009
United Arab Emirates	University of Dubai	1	2006
United Arab Emirates	University of Sharjah	4	2009, 2010 and 2011
United Arab Emirates	Zayed University	2	2010

Source: ABET website. Available at: http://main.abet.org/aps/Accreditedprogramsearch.aspx (accessed November 21, 2013).

Table 6.3 Gulf institutions with AACSB accreditation

Country	Institution
Kuwait	Kuwait University
Qatar	Qatar University
Saudi Arabia	King Fahd University of Petroleum and Minerals
United Arab Emirates	American University of Sharjah
	United Arab Emirates University
	University of Dubai
	Zayed University

Source: AACSB International. Available at: www.aacsb.net/eweb/DynamicPage.aspx?Site=AACSB &WebCode=AccredSchlCountry (accessed February 13, 2015).

The new regulatory institutions of the GCC: a recent history

When the national universities were first established in the GCC, the ministries of higher education of the respective national governments were responsible for overseeing their functioning and education quality. As discussed in Chapter 5, GCC governments initially relied on expatriate Arab experts both to operate the national universities and to assess their quality and control their finances. The major focus of this control was to make sure that the appropriate rules and procedures were followed rather than to evaluate the quality of the educational experience. The ease with which nationals were able to join lucrative government jobs after graduation may have further contributed to reducing the pressure on national universities to adopt comprehensive quality assurance processes and regulations.

The move to adopt the new regulatory approach began with the introduction of private institutions in the GCC. Four of the five smaller GCC countries[3] adopted similar approaches by creating regulatory bodies that are directly or indirectly linked to their respective ministries of higher education. The steps followed have generally been modeled on UK and US accrediting practices that include the development of standards to be followed in preparing self-study reports by the institution seeking program accreditation. The self-study report is then submitted to external visiting teams of experts who evaluate the institution's meeting of the standards. This section describes the organization and process of accreditation in each of the GCC countries.

The UAE Ministry of Higher Education and Scientific Research was the first to establish an accreditation body, the Commission for Academic Accreditation (CAA), in August/September 2000. The CAA is responsible for granting licensures and program accreditation to all non-federal tertiary institutions in the UAE. As of 2011, it has licensed 70 institutions and accredited 560 programs. The CAA states that one of its major goals is to "maintain and implement a quality framework which assures that institutions of higher education in the UAE operate in line with international academic, administrative, managerial, and operational standards" (Government of the United Arab Emirates, Commission for Academic Accreditation, 2010: 6). On its tenth anniversary, the CAA conducted its own self-study of its standards and functioning which were assessed by external reviewers from the United States and Ireland. The CAA has also been recognized by the INQAAHE as "one of the 6 institutions in the world to meet their 'guidelines for good practice'" (Government of United Arab Emirates, Commission for Higher Education, 2011: 15).

All UAE private institutions are required to be licensed and have their major programs accredited by the CAA in order for their degrees to be recognized by the Ministry of Higher Education and Scientific Research. In addition, they need to apply for reaccreditation every five years. The process of accreditation begins with a self-study report submitted by the program being accredited and the university to the CAA. The self-study must respond to 11 standards, each with its own stipulations. The next step in the accreditation process is a site visit of a team led by the CAA commissioner and between two and four external reviewers (usually from the United States, the United Kingdom, and other Arab countries) who are deemed experts in the disciplines being accredited. During their visit, the reviewers check the self-study report against the actual documentation of all aspects of the educational program. These include institutional effectiveness, governance, students' facilities, financial resources, research and scholarly activities, faculty and staff resources, physical facilities, learning resources, quality assurance, public disclosures and community engagement. During its site visit, the visiting team conducts interviews with administrators, faculty and staff, students, alumni and employers before writing a report to the CAA commissioner. The commission review culminates in a decision to approve, delay, put on probation or deny accreditation (Government of United Arab Emirates, Commission for Higher Education, 2011a).

In addition to the CAA, which is a federal agency, the Emirates of Dubai and Abu Dhabi have additional bodies involved in quality assurance control. Dubai's Knowledge and Human Development Authority's (KHDA)

> role in higher education is to provide academic authorization and support quality assurance for all Free Zone universities in Dubai. Students who graduate from these higher education institutions can have their degrees certified by KHDA for employment and other purposes in Dubai.
> (Government of Dubai, Knowledge Human Development Authority, 2014)

In order to carry out this role the KHDA set up the University Quality Assurance International Board (UQAIB). All higher education providers operating in Dubai free zones are required to renew their authorizations annually. The UQAIB relies on quality assurance processes in existence in those institutions or CAA assessments in its own certification. However, the UQAIB reserves the right to undertake its own audit in cases where existing assessments warrant it (Government of Dubai, Knowledge and Human Development Authority, 2014).[4]

Oman established its accreditation procedures soon after the UAE implemented its policies. Starting in 2001, the Ministry of Higher Education established an

Oman Accreditation Council, which four years later became the Oman Academic Accreditation Authority (OAAA). This body attempts to follow the procedures regulated by the INQAAHE. Thus, not only are Western institutions playing a very important role in the formation of individual colleges and universities, but the methods of assessment and review are heavily influenced by the regulatory cultures of Europe and the United States (Government of Oman, Oman Academic Accreditation Authority, 2014).

A chief goal of this system has been to establish practices of self-study and assessment within each higher education institution. The evidence suggests that the Omani authorities have taken this charge very seriously. The OAAA has introduced a certification process that is similar to that implemented by the federal government of the UAE.

After receiving the initial approval to establish a higher education institution, the institutions must undergo a quality audit, which uses an internally generated self-study by the college or university as a framework to guide the work of an external audit committee. (Normally, each panel or audit committee has five members.) This body, three-fifths of which are made up of higher education experts who do not work in Oman, visit the campus and issue a report that identifies strengths and weaknesses of the institution. The college or university then has four years to respond to the report before a second visit culminates in a standards assessment that lead to the issuing of a higher education certificate. An institution can appeal a negative evaluation at any point and use the time that is purchased by this objection to persuade the regulators that the evaluation was incorrect or that further improvements have been made in the institution so that the negative assessment is no longer relevant. In any event, the goal of the assessment process is not to create a high number of failed higher education institutions, but to pressure these colleges and universities to conform to international standards.

This regulatory approach ensures that there will nearly always be a body of non-Omani experts actively involved in evaluating an Omani university or college. (The public institutions are also required to undergo the same assessment process.) Between 2008 and December 2014, for example, there were 41 published audit reports. The Oman authorities post many of their reports on their website. Thus, the evaluative practices are unusually transparent.

Bahrain has largely replicated the Omani system and also makes its assessment reports electronically available. The regulatory framework to supervise the expansion of private higher education started changing in 2005. At that time, the Higher Education Council was formed under the auspices of the Ministry of Education. This body became responsible for licensing and accrediting all higher education institutions in the Kingdom of Bahrain. In addition, Bahrain established an independent agency responsible for evaluating the institutions and academic programs by using standard Western techniques of quality assurance. In 2008, King Hamad issued a royal decree that created the Quality Assurance Authority for Education and Training (QAAET). This new organization is meant to evaluate all of Bahrain's educational efforts, including primary and secondary education, vocational training, Bahrain's system of national examinations, and higher education. With respect to the latter, the main body responsible for evaluating colleges and universities is the Higher Education Review Unit (HERU) within the QAAET (Government of Bahrain, National Authority for Qualifications and Quality Assurance of Education and Training 2014).

Like the Oman Academic Accreditation Authority, the HERU performs both institutional and program reviews. It follows standard international practice by asking the higher education institution to do an exhaustive self-study which is then submitted to a panel of experts who review the material within the self-study and then visit the campus to reach their own independent assessment. Since its establishment, the HERU has pursued an aggressive schedule of reviews and assessments. Between 2008 and March 2013, for example, 15 institutions had been rigorously evaluated and 12 of these have also been subject to a follow-up report. These evaluations have been quite stringent as have separate assessments of degree programs. Since 2008, at least 37 specific degree programs have been reviewed and assigned an evaluation of "confidence," "limited confidence," or "no confidence."

The institution that supervises the licensing and accreditation of private universities in Kuwait is the Private University Council (PUC), which was created by the Emir's 2000 decree referred to earlier. Eight experts comprise the membership of the PUC. They are appointed to three-year terms and must have no institutional relationship with any private university. The powers of the PUC are broad and, in many ways, go beyond those of the governmental accreditation agencies in other GCC countries (Government of Kuwait, Ministry of Higher Education, Private University Council, 2014).

The eight-member board of the PUC oversees a process that includes institutional self-studies and site visits by a panel of academic peers. Unlike Oman, Kuwait mainly relies on academics who are working within Kuwait. Only 30 percent of the outside peer reviewers are not based in the country. In this sense, Kuwait and Bahrain are very similar. On the other hand, unlike Bahrain, the evaluation of universities within Kuwait is much less transparent, since none of the reports are publicly available. Although detailed documentation is absent from the public record, it is clear that the PUC does not automatically grant licenses to institutions that want to set up operations in Kuwait. Up until 2011, only half of the applicants received licenses to open, and as of December 2014, only eight private universities or colleges have received accreditation.

Another factor that distinguishes the PUC from other accreditation agencies is its more direct involvement in the day-to-day running of private universities. This is partly a reflection of the more participatory political structure available to Kuwaiti nationals, who can use parliament and government agencies to complain directly about the services provided by the state. In the case of the PUC, this means that it more aggressively gets involved in creating and enforcing regulations that might in other countries not exist or, if they exist, not be enforced. In addition, the PUC has powers to limit enrollment as well as to communicate to the higher education institution any problems or criticisms coming from well-placed members of the Kuwaiti polity. Professor Marjorie Kelly of the American University of Kuwait summarizes the PUC's power particularly well:

The PUC has wide-ranging powers in that it (1) licenses institutions, programs, majors and minors, (2) accredits institutions, and (3) provides students with scholarships – which then entitles the PUC to select their majors for them. Further, the PUC specifies the number of students who may attend an institution and can withhold scholarships from those over the limit when the maximum number is exceeded. It even has a say in campus construction projects that could facilitate a larger enrolment. Lastly, the PUC is the communications channel between the government (whether the Ministry of Higher Education or Parliament) and Kuwait's private universities. If a Member of Parliament has a complaint or the Ministry wishes to implement new regulations, it is communicated to campus officials via the PUC.

(Kelly, 2011: 203)

Kelly notes in her article that this power is in fact exercised, at least with respect to the American University of Kuwait. For example, the PUC has ruled that students cannot specialize in minor fields that are not also available as majors. The enforcement of this regulation meant that AUK was forced to cancel eight unlicensed minors in Arabic, business administration, Gulf studies, mathematics, natural sciences, public relations and advertising, psychology, and visual and performing arts. This micro-meddling can clearly reduce the academic flexibility of an institution. On the other hand, the PUC has insisted that at least 85 percent of all faculty members have PhDs, and one could certainly argue that this intervention is important for the maintenance of quality when the attempt to maximize net revenue by private owners of universities could lead to a search for cheaper, less qualified teachers. Perhaps, most ominously, the PUC has occasionally used complaints from members of the public to attack liberal arts education itself. Still, it must be said that this "traditionalist" critique of Western education has not yet found much traction.

Assessing the quality of new higher educational institutions

In all of the GCC countries, the purpose of the many layers of this assessment system described above, is to separate the evaluation of the institution from those administrators who directly manage it. This, in principle, should allow governmental authorities who might be concerned about the quality of a particular university or college to acquire more accurate information.

What are the assessment teams looking for? What constitutes a good university?

Given their association with the INQAAHE, it is not surprising that the evaluative standards are relatively similar for all of the GCC countries and fall under two major categories, institutional effectiveness and academic quality. Most external reports begin with an evaluation of an institution's system of governance. Review boards expect each higher education institutions to have a clear system of administration that separates academic management from the ownership group. In practice, this means that the Board of Directors (which represents the owners) should be distinct from the Board of Trustees (that is responsible for the overall quality of the university or college). The direct management of the institution by an owner is normally taken as a sign that the educational mission of the college is subordinated to the financial, political or idiosyncratic demands of the owner. For this reason, review boards also focus on the organizational structure of the institution so that it is clear which academic administrator is responsible for which parts of the university mission. In addition, the assessment bodies want to be sure that affiliations with non-national higher educational institutions are meaningful and productive. Overall, the audit review wishes to ensure that the management systems of the institution's finances and operations are clear, stable and responsive to the Board of Trustees – which is seen as the entity that has final responsibility for the quality and stability of the higher educational institution.

In investigating the academic quality of the institution, the review panels check whether or not the institution is able to deliver a high-quality curriculum that produces effective learning. This involves implementing assessment systems that can evaluate student learning and teacher quality. For students, entry requirements are supposed to be clear and transparent; they are advised appropriately so that a high proportion successfully complete their degree program in a reasonable period of time; course and program outcomes are clearly stated and well aligned with assessment tools; academic integrity is enforced and students are able to find employment after graduation.

For faculty, the expectation is that they are directly involved in developing curriculum as well as in student evaluation. Moreover, depending on the category of the college and university, professors and instructors are expected to be active researchers or attract consultancy funding. With respect to teaching, the expectation is that an audited university or college will be able to demonstrate that the institution has implemented measures that allow administrators to effectively evaluate teaching quality through student assessment as well as through the development of portfolios that can document student achievement. As with assessment procedures in the United States, the emphasis is on generating data that can be evaluated by outside bodies. Such information can obviously be of use to governmental authorities as well when they are attempting to ensure that these new colleges and universities are fulfilling the goal of providing high quality educational alternatives to the national population.

One result of the drive to create new regulatory measures to assess the performance of the new universities is that researchers now possess a considerable amount of information on the new higher education institutions of these countries. Bahrain and Oman have not only embarked on an aggressive assessment of all the new colleges and universities, but they have also chosen to allow the public to read many of their reports. The CAA in the UAE publishes on its portal the results of the accreditation process but the audit reports are not public. This provides researchers with an abundance of information which has not yet been tapped. Our review of these reports reveals several issues which suggest that the drive to create more private colleges and universities has not necessarily upgraded the quality of higher education. The first issue concerns the difficulties many of these new institutions face in establishing the appropriate governance procedures that can ensure academic quality. A second problem relates to heavy teaching loads that generally affect both their teaching quality and potential for serious high-level research. Finally, these challenges are compounded by the inadequate academic preparation of high school students, even with the provision of foundation programs to improve students' competence in English, mathematics and IT to enable them to perform university-level academic work.

The issue of governance

Established Western academic institutions have governance systems that are quite different from most workplaces. The professoriate is more intimately involved in the governance of their own institutions than most other professionals – even if formal power resides with university administrators who are normally recruited from the ranks of senior academic workers. Academic workers are largely responsible for the development and management of the curricula. Senior professors often play a major role in deciding on the future composition of the academic faculty. Tenured faculty have both job security and time to pursue research projects which interest them. Despite trends of convergence and homogenization in higher education curricula, it is less clear that the transplantation of Western education models have carried these institutionalized governance practices with them. With the increasing trend of corporatization of higher education, it is worth noting, however, that this model is under some threat, even in the West where alleged cost pressures are leading to the hiring of a more contingent adjunct faculty and academic workers with temporary contracts. Nevertheless, the question is worth asking: does the attempt to create high quality Westernized degree programs or academic institutions imply the adoption of the participatory system of governance just outlined?

The Bahraini and Omani auditing panels flag the issue of governance as a major problem in their reports. They begin by assessing evidence showing that the academic policy-making decisions and the management procedures are often dictated by an owner or a Board of Directors. The panels recommend the creation of an independent Board of Trustees and academic governance procedures that include academic officers and the faculty. The premise behind this approach is that if the Board of Trustees operates effectively and contains respected members of the business community and civil society who have an independent voice, the university is more likely to be managed in a way that protects the academic integrity of the college and university. Moreover, it is assumed by the accreditation authority that investors or members of the Board of Directors will normally not have the expertise to manage an educational institution appropriately. As the audit panel of the Al Zahra College for Women said in its report, "The separation of ownership, governance, and management is essential to avoid potential conflicts of interest and to ensure that the contribution of each is made within the sphere of its own expertise" (Government of Oman, Oman Academic Accreditation Authority, 2010: 11).

In Oman, it is clear from the reports that many of the private higher educational institutions fail to meet these governance accreditation standards. According to the 18 accreditation reports submitted for private colleges up until 2013, nine institutions failed to have a functioning Board of Trustees. Moreover, of the remaining nine, five of the Boards of Trustees did not seem to be able to assert oversight responsibilities for the educational mission of the institution. The most common problems cited in these sections of the report are excessive control by the Chair of the Board of Directors (who is often, one can assume, the principal owner), a failure of the Board of Trustees or Academic Councils to meet regularly and keep minutes, and an insufficient delineation of responsibilities between the Board of Directors and other governing bodies.

In Bahrain, the reports of the HERU reveal similar governance problems. On the one hand, most of the branch campuses are controlled by their parent institutions in such a way that the institution cannot respond to the particular problems associated with running an effective higher education program in Bahrain. On the other hand, many of the other private, for-profit colleges are excessively controlled by the owner of the institution. In both cases, the academic staff's ability to have some influence in the design of degree programs is limited. In addition, there is strong evidence that the colleges and universities organized in this way are more concerned about the cash generated by tuition fees than the ability of students to do the required academic work.

The private institutions which seem to be more successful in meeting the criteria of the accreditation authorities are moving toward a model of governance that most closely resembles that of a non-profit Western institution. For example, as an extreme case, the Board of Directors of Dhofar University in Oman has dissolved itself and transferred all authority to a Board of Trustees. On the other hand, it is clear that a relatively large proportion of the smaller IT and business colleges are having difficulty making this transition. The Omani auditing reports do not give enough institutional detail, but it is apparent that many of the owners do not wish to cede authority that could negatively affect financial returns. In other words, some of the ownership groups probably fail to recognize either explicitly or implicitly that a higher educational institution cannot be run as a normal business if it hopes to gain national or international recognition.

It is important to note that there is insufficient evidence relating to issues associated with governance. Gathering complete data would require more detailed, institution-specific studies followed by the aggregation of information that could be extracted from these ethnographies. On a more general, impressionistic level, however, the accreditation reports give us reason to question whether the transplantation of academic programs will automatically carry with them the participatory practices of academic governance. The creation of effective faculty senates and related regulations that promote academic administrative autonomy depend on the political culture of the host society and the potential for academic staff to use their voice to force changes in their own universities and colleges. This is particularly difficult given that in most cases the majority of the faculty are expatriates whose residency requirements limit their freedom of action or simply do not feel engaged enough in meaningful long-term change. Moreover, the decision to privatize higher education and subject universities and colleges to international influences has been, more often than not, a top-down process driven by shifts in state policy and financial constraints.

Faculty working conditions and student preparation

The second problem addressed by the reports concerns teaching loads. A teaching load of four to five courses per semester seems to be the norm for most institutions, and in some cases, there have been reports of faculty having to teach seven classes in a single semester. Given this teaching load, it is impossible to expect faculty to develop creative, engaging courses, and in a few cases, this issue is "resolved" by providing faculty members with PowerPoint slides and syllabi that they are then expected to follow. Some reports also suggest that faculty members are teaching courses outside their field of expertise. It is clear in these cases that it would be impossible to expect the academic staff to produce and disseminate research, and indeed, many reports note that pledges to enhance the research capabilities of the new universities and colleges are often not persuasive. For such institutions, we seem a long way from the idea that reforming higher education will lead to a dynamic "knowledge economy."

These difficulties are compounded by the issue that many of the students entering higher education are unprepared to do tertiary level academic work. The reports frequently mention the lack of academic preparation of many of the students enrolling in these private universities. Often the problem centers on the inability to pursue higher education studies in English. Nearly all private higher educational institutions, for example, require students to pass standardized tests to demonstrate their competence in English, the medium of instruction in most subjects, mathematics and information technology. Low test results lead to a large number of students needing to spend between one to four semesters in foundation programs. But even this is not enough to raise proficiency levels. For example, all Omani audit panels' reports express concern that students are passed through the foundation programs too quickly. More than half of the higher institutions were passing students onto degree programs even though they had not obtained the minimum TOEFL score (500) set by Omani national authorities. In addition, the audit report on Oman's public Sultan Qaboos University noted that the requirement that incoming students only had one year to pass through the foundation program often placed pressure on the program to pass students through too quickly.

These difficulties inevitably lead to negative academic evaluations by many of the external review panels. Bahrain's HERU, for example, evaluated the majority of the degree programs negatively. Only 11 of the degree offerings of the 37 degree programs that were reviewed received the "confidence" grade; 11

other degree programs obtained the "limited confidence" evaluation; while the program review team stated that they had "no confidence" in the final 15 degree programs they assessed. Nine follow-up reviews led to improvement in six cases, but this still leaves a rather large number of programs being offered in Bahrain that do not meet minimal accreditation standards (Government of Bahrain, 2013).

Although accreditation reports from the rest of the GCC countries are not publicly available, other sources of information such as the RAND reports from Qatar, reports from ADEC and KHDA in the UAE as well as media reports in all GCC countries point to similar conditions everywhere. The poor preparation of high school graduates for university study is well attested and, as we indicated in Chapter 5, has led to significant reforms everywhere in the GCC primary and secondary educational sectors.

Repercussions of poor quality higher education: the case of Bahrain

The problem of inadequate quality of higher education has had at least one highly publicized regional repercussion. On September 27, 2007, the Bahraini *Al Wasat* newspaper reported on rumors that the Kuwait Minister of Education had decided not to recognize or accredit the degrees of a series of private universities in Bahrain (Awadh, 2007). This rumor was confirmed on May 29, 2009, when newspapers reported that the Kuwaiti authorities had announced that the degrees of 40 universities around the world would not be recognized by the Ministry of Education. Such a decision obviously is of great import for those Kuwaiti students and their parents who have decided to get college degrees in Bahrain and elsewhere.[5] Within Bahrain, six of the new private universities were on the list. Kuwaiti students who had already received degrees from these institutions would not be punished, but all other Kuwaiti students were directed to suspend their enrollments. New students were told that they should not accept admission into the now banned institutions (Government of Kuwait, Ministry of Higher Education, 2009).

Although some Bahrainis believed that the Kuwaiti decision was not related to assessment of educational quality, but rather a result of internal and inter-regional political rivalries, it is important to note that the Council of Higher Education of Bahrain also took drastic actions against some of these same institutions. During August 2011, the Council suspended five private higher education institutions for one year and one private university for a semester. Later, some of these suspensions were revoked, but clearly Bahraini higher educational institutions suffered a substantial loss in reputation.

Despite these findings, one should not necessarily assume that these institutions cannot be reformed. In several, but not all, of the cases discussed here, follow-up reports noted that the institutions under review did establish a functioning Board of Trustees and made an effort to improve working conditions for their faculty. Now that an impressive and transparent regime of supervision and accountability has been established throughout the region, we should expect to be able to determine whether governmental Western-style regulation are capable of improving and upgrading higher education.

Conclusion

The reports and official documents we have reviewed show that all GCC countries, except Qatar, have created national bodies to oversee the quality of education being delivered by private institutions. Moreover, these new governmental organizations are now beginning to subject public universities to the same accreditation procedures. Ruling authorities evidently feel the need for increased competition in the higher education sector to be coupled with the establishment of robust governmental regulatory agencies. Our analysis suggests that quality assessment regulations are particularly important to pressure smaller colleges to provide a higher quality university education. In the absence of rigorous reviews of an institution's academic integrity, some educational entrepreneurs will be tempted to cut corners and offer a cheap, but academically inferior, product. In fact, many of the negative evaluations are from relatively small, for-profit higher educational institutions that provide a limited set of degree programs in business and information technology. In these institutions, there is often limited attention paid to the academic quality of the student body. Authoritarian administrative controls by their owners have imposed onerous working conditions on faculty that make the delivery of high quality teaching and research unlikely. In addition, these institutions' expectations of direct accountability to students and their parents are sometimes weaker because the cost of education is covered by government scholarships for most national students.

The more ambitious universities and colleges that offer a larger menu of alternative degree programs and seem more committed to an introductory period of liberal arts education for their first-year and second-year students have been able to create a more sustainable, high quality educational experience. Such institutions (even if they are for-profit) tend to delegate the institution's governance to well qualified administrators with respectable academic credentials, who in turn rely on faculty for the design and implementation of the curriculum as well as the evaluation of student performance. The research output of faculty in these new private institutions is still limited, but if some of the more established private or semi-private institutions begin to offer postgraduate degrees, particularly PhDs, they will have to reduce classroom teaching for some of the faculty in return for greater research productivity.

It is still too early to tell whether or not the combination of increased competition and these regulatory interventions will be successful in raising the quality of education. It is still too early to come to definitive conclusions since all of the new higher educational regulatory bodies are less than 15 years old and all of the new colleges and universities are young as well. Nevertheless, the GCC states have introduced robust regulatory processes, and the assessment reports that have and will be generated will provide an ability to assess the reasons why some higher educational institutions succeed and others fail.[6]

Notes

1 This problem can also apply to apples. Consumers normally will not know whether or not the apple was produced safely. Thus, we rely on governmental authorities to ensure that the fruit is not poisoned with substances that could endanger our health.
2 Other American-type universities in the Arab world have also sought and received accreditation from either the Middle States Commission on Higher Education (American University in Cairo and the American University of Beirut) or the New England Association of Universities and Colleges (the Lebanese-American University).
3 For KSA's accreditation processes, see Chapter 7.
4 The Abu Dhabi Educational Council (ADEC) does not have a special body to license or accredit tertiary institution located in the emirate. Its Policy, Planning and Performance Management Division (PPPM) oversees the quality of education by coordinating with the CAA, the Federal Ministry of Higher Education and Scientific Research Commission.
5 The Kuwaiti ministry does not accredit degrees until the first cohort of students have graduated. It relies on information provided by the cultural office of the Kuwaiti embassy and then a committee of members from Kuwait University, the Council of Higher Education in Kuwait, the Institute of Higher Education, and the Public Authority of Higher Education is constituted to decide whether or not the degree should be accredited so that the student graduates can present a reputable degree to employers inside Kuwait.
6 However, we must also be cognizant of the risk of over-regulating. Submitting to multitudes of accreditation processes may become an end in itself. It is sometimes felt to be too cumbersome, too frequent and in some cases to serve political ends. This, however, is not unique to the GCC higher education but is the consequence of global competition.

References

Awadh, Farah (2007). *Al Wasat News*, February 28.
Chamberlin, E. (1933). *Theory of Monopolistic Competition.* Cambridge, MA: Harvard University Press.
Government of Bahrain, National Authority for Qualifications and Quality Assurance of Education and Training (2013). *Review Reports.* Available at: http://en.qaa.bh/reviewreports.aspx (accessed June 17, 2013).
Government of Bahrain, National Authority for Qualifications and Quality Assurance of Education and Training (2014). Available at: www.qqa.edu.bh/en/qaaetunits/sru/pages/dhr.aspx (accessed December 29, 2014).
Government of Dubai, Knowledge and Human Development Authority, University Quality Assurance International Board (2014). Available at: www.khda.gov.ae/Pages/En/FZQA.aspx (accessed December 29, 2014).
Government of Kuwait, Ministry of Higher Education, Private University Council (2014). Available at: www.puc.edu.kw/en/ (accessed December 29, 2014).
Government of Oman, Oman Academic Accreditation Authority (2010). *Report of an Audit for Al Zahra College for Women.* Available at: www.oaaa.gov.om/Review/zcw_report_final.pdf (accessed December 29, 2014).

Government of Oman, Oman Academic Accreditation Authority (2014). Available at: www.oaaa.gov.om/Default.aspx (accessed December 29, 2014).

Government of the United Arab Emirates, Commission for Academic Accreditation (2010). *Strategic Plan, 2008–2014: Revised 2010.* Available at: www.caa.ae/caa/DesktopModules/CAA_Strategic_Plan.pdf (accessed February 13, 2015).

Government of United Arab Emirates, Commission for Higher Education. Ministry of Higher Education and Scientific Research (2011). *Annual Report.* Available at: www.caa.ae/caa/images/AnnualReport2011.pdf (accessed December 29, 2014).

Government of United Arab Emirates, Commission for Higher Education, Ministry of Higher Education and Scientific Research (2011a). *Standards for Licensure and Accreditation.* Available at: www.caa.ae/caa/images/Standards2011.pdf (accessed December 29, 2014).

Hirschmann, A. (1970). *Exit, Voice and Loyalty: Responses to Decline in Firms, Organizations, and States.* Cambridge, MA: Harvard University Press.

INQAAHE (International Network for Quality Assurance Agencies in Higher Education) (2014). Available at: www.inqaahe.org/ (accessed December 23, 2014).

Kelly, M. (2011). Balancing cultures at the American University of Kuwait. *Journal of Arabian Studies: Arabia, the Gulf, and the Red Sea* 1: 201–229.

Stiglitz, Joseph (2001) Information and the change in the paradigm of economics. Nobel Prize Lecture, December 8. Available at: www.nobelprize.org/nobel_prizes/economic-sciences/laureates/2001/stiglitz-lecture.pdf (accessed December 23, 2014).

7 Reforming higher education in Saudi Arabia

Reasons for optimism

Amani K. Hamdan[1]

Introduction

Saudi Arabia is investing more than ever in higher education, with approximately 12 percent of the national budget (US$160 billion) earmarked for its development (Alankari, 2013: 3). This increased investment is justified by the government's growing realization that the working-age population will increase from 3.99 million in 2004 to 8.26 million by 2020 (Aljughaiman and Grigorenko, 2013). This highlights how the education system in the largest Arab economy (in terms of total GDP), with the highest oil exports, the largest conventional petroleum reserves, the highest population of foreign workers, and one of the highest birth rates is evolving. The Saudi government invests USD $22 billion a year in university students, allowances and scholarships. Latest statistics indicate that 1,058,155 male and female students, enrolled in 28 public universities, each cost the government US$19,000 a year. The number of students abroad has reached 147,000 (74 percent are males and 54 percent are in the United States), and the percentage of Saudi high school graduates who enter university is, at 92 percent, the highest in the world (AlShehri, 2014).[2]

In the last decade, the number of students enrolled in tertiary education, accommodated by 28 public and ten private universities, reached 1.2 million. Thus the focus in Saudi Arabia's education system is not only on increasing the number of colleges and universities and student enrollment, but according to the Ministry of Higher Education (MoHE) the focus is more on improving the capacity of educational institutions to compete and participate in the global economy by maintaining international quality standards. The knowledge economy perspective of the Saudi economic planners stresses the importance of the market and the economy; higher education is meant to help insert Saudi nationals into globalized commodity production as creative professional workers as well.

The Saudi Arabian government provides significant support to post-secondary students. Those who attend public universities pay no tuition and receive a monthly allowance. More than 48 percent of students in private universities are funded by the government's "internal" scholarships and approximately 85 percent of Saudi students studying abroad are supported by government funding through the King Abdullah Scholarship Program (KASP), which covers travel,

DOI: 10.4324/9780203796139-7

tuition and living expenses for recipients, their spouses and their children. Another important fact to consider when analyzing higher education is Saudi Arabia's rigorous commitment to gender segregation – except for King Abdullah University of Science and Technology (KAUST), a postgraduate university established in 2008, located 350 kilometers south of Jeddah. Women and men study in separate campuses. King Fahd University for Petroleum and Minerals (KFUPM), which is in Dhahran, is an all-male university, and Princess Nora University (PNU), which is in Riyadh, is an all-female university.

As we shall see, this commitment to gender segregation has an impact on the ability of women to gain access to the labor market for the high number of young Saudi women with higher education (Aljughaiman and Grigorenko, 2013; Jamjoom and Kelly, 2013). When women are only allowed to work in schools, hospitals and banks that strictly serve women, this limits their employment opportunities. Moreover, as stated by Aljughaiman and Grigorenko (2013: 309):

> although women are not restricted from all engineering fields – they can study internal design engineering and computer science engineering – other kinds of engineering like chemical engineering, petroleum engineering, electrical engineering, and so forth are not open to girls because there are no employment opportunities available for them in these fields.

By controlling women's access to labor market education, the Kingdom is not preparing Saudi women for the global economy; it perpetuates the socially accepted status quo (Baki, 2004).

In addition to providing large-scale subsidies and imposing gender segregation, a third factor that distinguishes Saudi Arabia's higher education is its strong emphasis on Islamic teaching:

> While there is a particular focus on scientific and technological development in order to improve international competitiveness of the Kingdom, there is also a significant allocation of funds for programs aimed at deepening Islamic values, morals, and allegiance to family, society and nation, and appreciating and preserving national achievement.
>
> (Smith and Abouammoh, 2013: 4)

The establishment and growth of universities in Saudi Arabia raises a variety of economic, social and cultural issues. Arguably the most salient is the question of quality and accessibility to all. Drawing on publicly available information on Saudi education as well as the researcher's personal observations and experiences from working in Saudi private institutions, this chapter argues that the emergence and growth of universities has led to significant changes in the status quo, including tangible and meaningful improvements to the accessibility and quality of Saudi higher education. At the same time, more time is required to evaluate the extent to which HE is participating in building a knowledge-based economy. While the government has one goal for education (promoting the knowledge economy), there are other goals intrinsic to the educational project, such as promoting critical thinking so that graduates can more effectively reshape their environment.

This chapter will also provide the reader with a comprehensive description of the significant and rapid structural transformations and reforms in higher education in Saudi Arabia over the past decade. It will attempt to assess the educational, institutional, economic and socio-cultural viability of these changes, considering that HE essentially only began in 1957 with the first Saudi university (Al-Eisa and Smith, 2013: 28). Critics (Smith and Abouammoh, 2013; Mazi and Altbach, 2013) agree that although SA is demonstrating remarkable energy in improving its HE system; there is a great need for strategic planning underpinned by conceptual discipline and procedural rigor; success can only be achieved with timely and strategic implementation and deployment of necessary human capital, administrative infrastructure, technology systems, grounding in local needs, and collaborative networks.

General context

Currently, KSA's population is estimated at 28.8 million, eight million of whom are non-native. This figure is projected to rise to 44.8 million by 2025, with approximately 49 percent under the age of 20 (MoHE, 2012). These demographic changes are already having significant implications for the education system. More specifically, the high birth rate means that universities are under pressure to take extra measures to meet the growing demand for student enrollment.

Saudi Arabia's demographic characteristics are unique to the Gulf region. According to the World Bank (2013b), the Saudi population's growth rate was at 1.75 percent (2010 estimate) and in 2009 there were 28,686,633 Saudi nationals and 5,576,076 migrant workers (*Saudi Arabia Demographics Profile 2013*, 2013). The high population growth rate has led to a rapid rise in the general youth population and in the number of high school graduates. Indeed, according to the MoHE (2010: 10), "the percentage of citizens less than 24 years of age is more than 62% and the number of high school graduates had increased by 443% from 1993 to 2008." This expansion in the number of high school graduates is imposing unprecedented pressure on the Kingdom's post-secondary institutions. Numerous studies have confirmed that the rising demand for HE in Saudi Arabia is challenging and highlighting the inability of the HE system to keep up with appropriate program options and job market preparation (Mosa, 2000, as cited in Alkhazim, 2003: 483; ICDL, n.d.: 1). During the 2000–1 academic year, around 60,000 of the high school graduates who applied to higher-education institutions in Saudi Arabia were unable to find placements. In 2001, between 25,000 and 30,000 Saudi students studied abroad at their own expense, and a further 6,000 studied abroad with government support (MoHE, 2001, as cited in Alkhazim, 2003: 483). These numbers have dramatically increased since then, and the estimated number of students who are being supported by the government with full scholarships for international studies has now reached 150,000 spread across 75 countries. Some of these students pursue educational opportunities elsewhere in the Arab world in such countries as the United Arab Emirates, Bahrain and Qatar. Others are studying in the West, especially in the United States, the United Kingdom, Canada and Australia.

The need for expansion: the need for foreign workers

According to the latest national statistics (2010), the Saudi population of 28 million included over eight million non-nationals, who together comprised about 33 percent of the labor force. The oil-driven economic boom of the 1970s and 1980s increased the number of foreign workers, and at one point this group comprised around 95 percent of the private sector's labor force (Okruhlik, 2005: 155). This large migrant workforce underlines the need to offer more opportunities for Saudis to address the skills shortfall through higher education. The expatriate labor force is the largest in the region, but its relative presence (in terms of percentages of the population or the labor force) is significantly lower than Kuwait, UAE and Qatar.

While foreign workers play a valuable role in the Saudi economy, they do so at a significant cost. Most of their income is repatriated to their countries of origin, a phenomenon that represents an outright loss to the Saudi economy. The sheer scale of this outflow is immense: worker "[r]emittances for the first eight months of 2009 totaled $15 billion" (Baxter, 2010: §1). Furthermore, the expertise that these employees gain while working in Saudi Arabia is irretrievably lost to the Kingdom when they leave. This expertise could instead be cultivated among Saudi citizens, who would eventually take their place as the core of the Kingdom's elite workers.

Economic expansion has ironically created an unemployment problem for Saudi nationals, which makes one of the long-term goals to get educated Saudis to replace expatriate professionals. Increasing Saudi participation in the labor market is therefore vital if KSA is to curtail its dependence on migrant workers. Expanding public and private higher educational institutions is seen as playing a pivotal role in effecting this change, and despite the fact that the expansion of higher education has opened many job opportunities, foreign workers and expatriate professors and lecturers continue to fill the majority of positions. It is not clear that the MoHE has any specific plans to reduce this reliance on foreign academic workers.

Increasing the number of HE institutions and enrollment

The drive to expand this sector has led to a steep rise in both the number of higher education institutions and in enrollments (MoHE, 2011). The scale of this expansion can be seen in Tables 7.1 and 7.2.

The enrollment rate in 2011 was 37.8 percent, higher than the world average of 26 percent and the regional average of 21 percent within Arab countries taken

Table 7.1 Growth of universities in KSA (2005–14)

	2005	2014	Growth
Public	11	29	123%
Private	4	10	100%
Total	15	39	113%
Population	22.7	28.1	19.4%
Number of universities per million people	0.7	1.2	71.4%

Source: Ministry of Higher Education (2014).

as a whole (MoHE, 2011). Since King Abdullah succeeded to the throne in 2005, improving the higher education system has become the government's top priority. One of the most prominent education reform initiatives is the King Abdullah bin Abdulaziz Public Education Development Project, also known as *Tatweer*. Another initiative, which is considered a national priority to foster international competence of a nation, is the King Abdullah Scholarship Program (KASP); this initiative funds the international programs that sponsor over 147,000 Saudi male and female students in 45 countries.

The Saudi government's strategy for higher education has a significant domestic component. The education authorities are primarily attempting to satisfy the overflow in demand for post-secondary education by expanding the number of universities and colleges within the Kingdom (MoHE, 2010). This expansion involves the establishment of both public and private universities, a process that has entailed the partial privatization of higher education. Over ten private universities and 21 colleges have been established since 2001 (when there were only seven universities in the country, all of them public and operated by the MoHE), accommodating more than 35,000 students (Mazi and Altbach, 2013). By 2010 this number had increased to 28 public universities, nine private universities run by private investors, 423 colleges of pure and applied sciences (see Tables 7.3 and 7.4), and 20 privately run colleges (see Table 7.5) (MoHE, 2010: 10). All offer bachelor degrees with only a few offering postgraduate diplomas and degrees. Public–private partnerships is a term that best reflects the situation of private-sector involvement in KSA, where the government's decision to subsidise land rental loans and tuition fees

Table 7.2 Growth of colleges in KSA (2005–14)

Year	2005	2014	Growth
Public	301	395	31%
Private	13	39	200%
Total	314	434	38%
Population	22.7	27.1	19.4

Source: Ministry of Higher Education (2014).

Table 7.3 Public universities in KSA

University	City	Year founded
King Saud University	Riyadh	1957
King Abdulaziz University	Jeddah	1967
King Faisal University	Al-Ahsa	1975
Umm al-Qura University	Mecca	1949
King Fahd University of Petroleum and Minerals	Dhahran	1963
Islamic University	Medina	1961
Al-Imam Mohammad Ibn Saud Islamic University	Riyadh	1974
King Khalid University	Multiple locations	1999
King Abdullah University for Science and Technology	Jeddah	2009
Taibah University	Medina	2003
Taif University	Taif	2003
Qassim University	Buraydah	2004
University of Ha'il	Hail	2005
Jazan University	Jazan	2005
Al Jouf University	Al-Jawf	2005
King Saud bin Abdulaziz University for Health Sciences	Riyadh	2005
Al Baha University	Al Baha	2005
University of Tabuk	Tabuk	2006
Najran University	Najran	2006
Northern Borders University	Arar	2007
Princess Nora bint Abdulrahman University	Riyadh	2005
University of Dammam	Dammam	2007
Prince Salman University	Al Kharj	2006
Shagra University	Shagra	2009
Almajmaah University	Majmaah	2009
Hafr Albaten University	Hafr Albaten	2014
Jeddah University	Jeddah	2014
Beesha University	Beesha	2014

Source: Ministry of Higher Education website, www.mohe.gov.sa/en/default.aspx.

indicates the extent to which it is prepared to support private universities (Al-Dali *et al.*, 2013: 130).

The Saudi government is also responding to the growth in demand for HE by sponsoring selected students to study overseas (especially in Western institutions). Even though increasing amounts of travel and tuition funding are being used to send students abroad to Western countries, the government's core priority is to expand the domestic university and college sector, in particular through the creation of new institutions and domestic scholarships. In addition, as part of its drive to increase capacity, the MoHE offers 10,000 scholarships per year for domestic study, which cover 50 percent of the cost of tuition in most Saudi Arabian private universities. Half the tuition is covered for selected students to attend private universities and colleges in the Kingdom and full

Table 7.4 Private universities in KSA

University	Subjects offered (based on university websites)	City	Year founded	Co-ed or single-sex
King Abdullah University for Science and Technology	Engineering, computer science, science	Jeddah	2009	First co-educational institution in KSA
Prince Sultan University (College in 1999)	Business administration, computer science, engineering, English language, interior design, law (women only)	Riyadh	2003	Separate male and female campuses
Arab Open University	Business administration, elementary education, IT and computing	Riyadh, Dammam, Jeddah	2006	Separate male and female campuses
Prince Mohammad bin Fahd University	Business administration, engineering, computer science, interior design	Al Khobar	2006	Separate male and female campuses
Alfaisal University	Business administration, engineering, medicine, science, technology	Riyadh	2008	Male only
Al Yamamah University	Business administration	Riyadh	2003	Separate male and female campuses
Effat University	Architecture, business administration, computer science, early childhood education, engineering, English and translation	Jeddah	1999	Female only
Dar Al Uloom University	Business administration, education, English language, IT, law	Riyadh	2009	Male only
Dar Al-Hekma University (www.daralhekma.edu.sa/)	Business administration, graphic design, management information systems, interior design, law, nursing, special education	Jeddah	1999/2000 (College) 2013 to a university	Female only

Source: Ministry of Higher Education website, www.mohe.gov.sa/en/default.aspx.

Table 7.5 Private colleges in KSA

College	Subjects offered	City	Year founded	Co-ed or single-sex
Prince Sultan College for Tourism and Business (www.pscabha.edu.sa/)	Business administration, tourism and hospitality	Abha	1999/2000	Male only
Al Baha Private College of Science (http://bpcs.edu.sa/)	Computer engineering, computer science	Al Baha	2001	Separate male and female campuses
College of Business Administration (www.cba.edu.sa/)	Business administration	Jeddah	2004	Separate male and female campuses
Soliman Fakeeh College for Science and Nursing (www.drfakeehhospital.com/)	Medicine, nursing	Jeddah	2004	Separate male and female campuses
Riyadh College of Dentistry (www.riyadh.edu.sa/)	Dental assisting, dental hygiene, dental lab technology, dentistry, pharmacy, medical laboratory	Riyadh	2004	Separate male and female campuses
Ibn Sina National College for Medical Studies (www.ibnsina.edu.sa/)	Dentistry, medicine, nursing, pharmacy	Jeddah	2005	Separate male and female campuses
Qassim Private College (www.qc.edu.sa/Arabic/)	Computing, dentistry, languages	Qassim	2006	Separate male and female
Prince Fahd bin Sultan College	Business administration, engineering	Tabuk	2006	Separate male and female campuses
Prince Sultan College for Tourism and Management (www.pscj.edu.sa/)	Business administration, tourism and hospitality	Jeddah	2007	Male only
Batterjee Medical College (www.bmc.edu.sa/)	Emergency medicine, general medicine, health administration, imaging and radiology, medical laboratories, nursing, physical therapy	Jeddah	2006	Separate male and female campuses
Saad College of Nursing and Applied Health Sciences (www.saadcollege.com/)	Nursing	Al Khobar	2007	Female only
Arriyadah College of Medical Sciences	Nursing	Jeddah	2007	Male only

College	Programs	Location	Year	Gender
Almarifah College for Science and Technology	Computer science, information systems, medicine, nursing, pharmacy	Riyadh	2009	Male only
Buraydah College for Applied Medical Sciences (www.bpc.edu.sa/)	Business administration, clinical laboratory science, computing, dentistry, engineering, environmental health sciences, languages and translation, law, nursing, nutrition, pharmacy, physical therapy, radiology, rehabilitation medicine, special education	Buraydah	2009	Separate male and female campuses
Mohammad Al Mani College for Medical Sciences	Pharmacy	Al Khobar	2009	Separate male and female campuses
Global Colleges	Computing, medicine, nursing	Riyadh	2009	Male only
Al-Farabi Dentistry College	Dentistry, nursing	Riyadh	2009	Separate male and female campuses
Al-Ghad International Medical Science Colleges (www.alghadcol.com/)	Emergency medicine, health management, medical laboratories, nursing, radiology	Jeddah, Riyadh, Dammam, Abha, Qassim, Tabuk, Najran, Medina, Almonawwarah, Hafr Al Batin	2009	Separate male and female campuses
Sulaiman Al Rajhi Colleges	Medicine	Al Bukayriyah	2009	Male only

Source: Ministry of Higher Education website, www.mohe.gov.sa/en/default.aspx.

coverage for students in all public universities through postgraduate education in all disciplines.

Private higher education in Saudi Arabia: a growing partner?

In recent years, Saudi Arabia has increasingly moved toward adopting a Western-style institutional model. For instance, the emerging private educational institutions are largely run on a Western model and prefer to hire Western staff and faculty to run their programs. The private Saudi universities, in seeking to build a prestigious reputation by pursuing American accreditation, attempt to attract teaching staff from North America, Europe and Australia with high salaries and benefit packages (such as a child education allowance in international schools up to US$30,000, travel, free accommodation, and health insurance). These benefits are strictly for foreign academics; Saudi nationals receive only a stipend. The argument is that these packages are supposed to be highly attractive for academics to work and live in Saudi Arabia. Private institutions also hire foreign consultants in an attempt to replicate Western curricula. Some observers argue that these measures are meant to appeal to Saudi families that would prefer their children (and particularly their daughters) to attend local institutions with international characteristics instead of having them go abroad beyond the reach of their family's protection and supervision.

The emergence of private universities in Saudi Arabia and their role in the abrupt yet necessary expansion of higher education are of international scholarly interest. As Mazi and Altbach (2013) argue, Saudi private institutions are of mixed quality: some have achieved good standards and local, regional and international reputation, while some for-profit institutions have not. In 2013, the MoHE closed two private institutions in Jeddah and Riyadh because they did not meet the standards set by the General Committee for Licensing and Approvals of Colleges, while some private institutions gained full accreditation or semi-accreditation, such as Prince Sultan University, Effat University, Al-Riyadh College of Dentistry and Pharmacy, College of Business Administration, and Dar AlHekma College, which became a university in 2005. A number of key questions flow from KSA's willingness to support the substantial privatization of this sector.

The decision to establish private universities followed a national debate that concentrated on the issue of employability (see Bosbait and Wilson, 2005, for an elaboration on this issue). Studies such as Bosbait and Wilson's have indicated that Saudi graduates lacked skills needed in the job market and thus were unemployable, which is the reason given for the private sector heavily relying on foreign workers for years. "The belief developed that traditional university graduates were not sufficiently attuned to the practical skills required for Saudi's future economy and that private education sector was better placed to deliver this outcome" (Al-Dali *et al.*, 2013: 28). One of the reasons for the government's plan to expand access to private higher education was that rapid economic growth had created a cluster of middle-class families with not only the ability but also a strong desire to pay for a better education for their children.

Another significant factor for the government's willingness to support private higher education was the growing dissatisfaction with the caliber of graduates' key workforce-related skills, such as critical thinking, problem solving, personal responsibility, as well as independence and a strong work ethic. The shortage of business skills among Saudi nationals is also a major factor driving the importation of large numbers of foreign workers. Thus, Nolan (2012: 14) suggests that "education reform was cited as a pillar of the efforts to diversify the Saudi economy, to 'Saudize' the Kingdom's companies and to address labour market inefficiencies and growing youth unemployment." The belief among many policy-makers, that existing public universities generally do not produce graduates who meet the requirements of Saudi Arabia's growing economy, is often given as a major reason for the decision to expand the private education sector (Al-Dali, *et al.*, 2013 Alkhazim, 2009; AlMunajjed, 2008). Indeed, the government recently acknowledged the importance of higher education institutions responding to economic imperatives in an official report:

> All the specializations in private colleges and universities are linked to the *needs of the labour market*, both current and future ... [they] have been selected very carefully so as to ensure the distinction of their products and their fulfilment of national development requirements.
>
> (MoHE, 2008: 12, emphasis added)

For instance, at a private university in the Eastern Province, the choices of majors offered to students were based on a needs survey of the job market, which included a large-scale job-market analysis. Thus, it is clear that the aim of privatization is to offer programs and degrees that will not only attract students but also qualify them for professional employment. More specifically, private universities are trying to overcome some of the barriers in order to make Saudi degree holders as appealing to employers as foreign workers with similar credentials. One of the most deeply rooted barriers to employment is associated with Saudi Arabia's "banking concept of education" (Freire, 2003) – an instructional approach that emphasizes memorization at the expense of critical thinking skills. This raises an interesting issue. To get workers "ready" for a knowledge economy, they cannot just learn or memorize skills. They have to develop their intrinsic intellectual abilities. So there might not be a conflict between acquiring high-level skills and a non-utilitarian liberal education.

Quality and accessibility

Governance and accountability in post-secondary institutions

The Saudi authorities have demonstrated considerable interest in holding universities accountable for the quality of the education they deliver. This interest is in part a reflection of the goal of building the national and international reputation of the Kingdom's post-secondary institutions (Darandari and Cardew, 2013: 78). It appears that the government is turning to a range of accountability systems – for universities in general, not only for private universities – to achieve this purpose.

One aspect of accountability is the government's supervision of universities. All higher education institutions are under the umbrella of the MoHE, which in turn is under the control of the Higher Education Council. The MoHE determines and enforces all the rules, regulations and practices of higher education institutions in Saudi Arabia, including those of privately owned institutions. The public–private distinction is somewhat blurred by this governance structure because the MoHE supervises both types of institution. Both public and private universities are required to follow the MoHE's rules and guidelines when seeking approval for new programs. Alkhazim (2009) suggests that this situation makes it seem like the private universities are de facto public universities. Others have referred to it as a public–private partnership since governance and financial support are managed by the MoHE (Al-Dali *et al.*, 2013). This state of affairs contrasts with that of the other member nations of the Gulf Cooperation Council (Al-Dali *et al.*, 2013), where "[p]rivately owned educational institutions [...] are not strictly controlled by the state" (Brandenburg, 2010: 6). A few private education institutions had received NCAAA (National Commission for Assessment and Academic Accreditation) accreditation for the programs they offer. Also a few public universities are on the list of accredited institutions and offer accredited programs. Recently four public universities (one of which is the newly established KAUST in 2009) appeared in relatively high positions in the Shanghai Ranking, which is not the subject of this chapter (Academic World University Ranking, 2014).

Teaching and learning

Higher education teaching and learning in Saudi Arabia has received international attention in the past decade. Traditional pedagogy, rote and didactic learning, and the emphasis on memorization rather than critical thinking and problem solving are major hurdles for quality HE. Teaching and learning heavily influences graduates' ability to engage in the workforce, and if not well trained they become an obstacle within the knowledge-based economy. This challenge of graduates' lack of skills can be overcome by a shared vision between individual teachers, department heads, colleges, institutional leaders, and the national government itself through the MoHE to ensure that graduates are equipped with the skills needed in the job market (Alnassar and Dow, 2013). Public and private universities and colleges started implementing a preparatory year to bridge the gap between secondary school and freshman year. In the preparatory year "there is explicit teaching of basic knowledge, explicit teaching of how to learn and the teaching of study techniques and skills" (Alnassar and Dow, 2013: 52). The MoHE has been trying to diversify and introduce innovation in teaching and learning strategies in the classroom, but the outcomes have yet to be evaluated (Aljughaiman and Grigorenko, 2013: 310). To a certain extent in recent years, because of MoHE efforts of encouraging faculty training inside their home universities and overseas, it seems that teacher-centred approaches have been replaced by student-centred approaches and learning outcome based assessment models. Teacher-centred approaches are how teachers traditionally have taught, where students are passive and powerless and teachers "own" knowledge and are transmitters of it; in contrast, student-centred approaches empower students, and teachers become facilitators and supporters of learning. Delivering high-quality teaching and learning in higher education is paramount for progressing and transforming HE and building the knowledge economy.

These educational reforms involve academics in the development of curricula or in university governance of academic standards. Many universities have established deanships of faculty development in which short programs are designed to support faculty members' professional development and further develop faculty skills (Al-Ghamdi and Tight, 2013). Moreover, some universities have established awards and incentives for excellence linked to faculty members' evaluation (Al-Ghamdi *et al.*, 2010). Therefore, building human capabilities – a term used by Amartya Sen instead of human capital in the context of educational reform, since it shifts the emphasis away from education as pure commodity production – should be the primary aim for Saudi universities (Frediani, 2010). What measures are currently taking place to improve the quality of education remains a focus for further exploration.

Importation of Western curricula and teaching staff

Saudi universities are seeking national and international credibility and visibility – first and foremost through their pursuit of foreign accreditation (Darandari and Cardew, 2013). The desire for reputational enhancement also extends into universities' curricular strategies. For instance, most if not all private higher education institutions in Saudi Arabia employ curricula transplanted from the West with few modifications, a practice that is continuing virtually unrestricted. Indeed, according to the MoHE: "because of the importance of benefiting from the experience of international universities, most private universities and colleges in the Kingdom have entered into contracts of cooperation and partnership with a number of prestigious international universities" (MoHE, 2010: 12).

The Texas International Education Consortium (TIEC), for instance, has designed several curricula implemented in the Saudi educational system "based on the American model for academic programs and administrative organization" (www.tiec.org/, 2010). As can be seen from its website, TIEC claims to offer a comprehensive package designed for clients who are seeking to establish new university programs, with services ranging from curriculum design to staff recruitment and the acquisition and installation of technological support.

However, it seems that many of these imported "packaged" curricula (which include textbooks and teacher resources) overlook the contexts, knowledge, skills and needs that Saudi Arabian students bring with them to university. The chosen textbooks are not culturally appropriate, and many topics tackle aspects of the American lifestyle that are irrelevant to Saudi students' lives and values or to Muslim Middle Eastern culture. Imported curricula make private higher education more imitative than creative (Mohrman, 2005). These institutions should make an effort to transition to using books created by local teaching staff, that are tailored to Saudi culture and to Saudi students' needs, but this will take time (Al-Dali *et al.*, 2013). Knowledge is socially constructed and sharing systems of meaning is significant to understand, value and accept that knowledge (Newell, 1999). Moreover, there should be an expectation that after two or three years the imported curricula will be reviewed and adjusted, where appropriate. The major challenge according to Al-Dali *et al.* (2013) is to create a faculty culture that understands the nature of the new practical curricula and diverse cognitive abilities of the students in today's higher education. This would entail granting faculty members a great deal of freedom to design their curriculum, yet this would depend on the level of education the faculty members have.

In saying this, it should be acknowledged that the imported curricula, which are mainly used in private universities, occasionally tackle subject matter generally overlooked in public universities. These courses sometimes cover crucial skills such as critical thinking and problem solving, logic and probability, professional development and competencies, communication (written, oral and technical), and leadership skills. Nevertheless, these courses need time to prove their effectiveness at challenging the deeply embedded tradition of rote learning in order to foster a culture of innovation and research (AlGhamdi and Deraney, 2013). It is the hope that all public universities will begin to adopt teaching curricula that promote critical thinking as well.

Efforts are taking place to reform public universities in terms of obtaining foreign accreditation. For instance, several engineering programs have been accredited by the Accreditation Board for Engineering and Technology (ABET); some business management programs have been accredited by the Association to Advance Collegiate Schools of Business (AACSB); some dentistry programs have been accredited by the Association for Dental Education in Europe (ADEE); and some Diploma of Education programs have been accredited by British Quality Education (Darandari and Cardew, 2013: 110–111).

Challenges facing the system

There is no education system – even in the most developed countries – that does not need improvement and Saudi Arabian higher education is no exception. Quantitative expansion (i.e., more students, more teachers, more schools and more funding) is not enough; the MoHE seems to have shifted to considering qualitative improvements as well (quality of textbooks, qualification of teachers), and that is significant (Aljughaiman and Grigorenko, 2013). Because Saudi higher education officials work with the vision of transforming their institutions into world-class universities and colleges, more rigorous and constructive research highlighting the challenges facing higher education is needed to offer and suggest solutions. The following sections will shed light on some of these major challenges.

Reliance on foreign academic staff

As mentioned, private universities showcase their drive to build a national and international reputation by their aggressive importation of Western staff (i.e., faculty). The need for rapid expansion to accommodate the surge in high school graduates helps to explain this phenomenon, as the importation of faculty staff is seen as the easiest and fastest way to build up these institutions. The importation of foreign staff has resulted in the vast majority of faculty members in Saudi private institutions being citizens of Western countries, though a significant number of these individuals are of Arab descent. The number of foreign faculty members has surged since the establishment of private universities, and non-Saudis currently hold 90 percent of the faculty positions (Onsman, 2010). The MoHE (2012) offers similar statistics: around 30 percent of faculty staff in public institutions are non-Saudi. The reliance on expats is supposed to be a temporary phenomenon (Al-Ghamdi and Tight, 2013; Shediac and Samman, 2010). It is assumed that more Saudi male and female graduates of KASP will fill many positions at universities and colleges in the Kingdom that are now occupied by foreigners. Yet, the plan is to have a portion of staff and faculty from different nationalities supporting Saudi faculty members as academic staff, which will create a multicultural environment in higher education institutions.

The heavy reliance on foreign academic staff in institutions of higher learning in SA is especially regrettable given the fact that many Saudis who have been sponsored by the MoHE to earn doctoral degrees domestically or overseas, are unable to find academic positions at home (Alsherean, 2012). This reliance on non-Saudi professors with a population that keeps growing rapidly has also contributed to excessive turnover rates. This phenomenon can be observed not only in Saudi Arabia but across the entire Gulf region. Despite the generous salaries and benefits, several factors lead many foreign academics to not stay for long. These include social conditions such as restrictions on academic freedom and free speech, the relative lack of support for research, and mobility restrictions on female staff (neither Saudi nor non-Saudi women are permitted to drive in the Kingdom). The high turnover rates are contributing to the "lack of rootedness" (Noori, 2010: 10) within Saudi Arabian universities.

Accessibility for women

Beyond the prevalence of foreign staff, another major challenge is increasing the ratio of female staff to students, since 60 percent of Saudi university students are female and with the segregation of campuses by gender more women should be appointed. Women's education has expanded enormously since its advent in 1959, when women went to private homes, *Kuttab* (Quranic schools), to memorize the Holy Quran (Jamjoom and Kelly, 2013). This expansion is a result of government initiatives to educate women by providing financial bonuses for the spread of education in all cities, villages and nomadic areas, putting the principle of equal opportunity into practice and enabling a full intake of female students at all educational levels (Jamjoom and Kelly, 2013: 120). Also, increasing social awareness around the necessity of education for women who are going to be mothers became a mission for women's education. A paradigm shift in recent years has emphasized the importance of educating women to participate in the workforce (Jamjoom and Kelly, 2013; AlMunajjed, 2012).

Observing teaching in Saudi Arabia's universities has brought attention to the fact that there is little emphasis placed on constructive approaches to curricula for female students and on empowering young women. For instance, despite the fact that private universities are seeking to emulate the West in even more obvious ways than public universities – by importing American and European curricula, hiring foreign staff, and courting international accreditation agencies – they have not decided to emulate the West in terms of placing a strong emphasis on improving women's access to higher education. This is especially the case for private institutions, which continue to marginalize women in comparison to both male citizens and non-Saudi (Arab and non-Arab) men. In fact, the establishment of private universities has only led to limited improvements in access to higher education for Saudi women, as many fields of study continue to limit or entirely forbid the admission of women. The recognition of women's rights in ways that draw on Islamic principles is a fundamental truth that is inspiring a new generation of Saudi women to demand recognition of their role as active participants in all aspects of society (Ghanea, 2004: 722).

Doumato (2010: 11) notes that there are senior positions, including five deanships, filled by women, but "the question remains, however, how these jobs will be created and in what sectors of the economy, as well as what kind of logistic accommodations will be devised so that sex-segregation on the job can be maintained." The only public university headed by a female professor is Princess Nora University in Riyadh and two in the private institutions of Effat University and Dar Alhekma in Jeddah. All three are female-only institutions. No one can deny the progress women have made in the historical trajectory of higher education in Saudi Arabia, but perhaps the most significant challenge for higher education today, elaborated by Jamjoom and Kelly (2013), is the tension between how Saudi cultural values view women and the significant contribution that women can and should make to the social and economic future of the Kingdom.

In recent years, Saudi women have witnessed great improvement in their status on the social level; nonetheless, much progress remains to be seen in the coming years. Women now account for 25 percent of enrollment in postgraduate degrees at Saudi universities (Alankari, 2013: 4) and comprise over 62 percent of enrollment in BA programs. In KASP, a fifth of Saudi students abroad are female (Smith and Abouammoh, 2013). So one can be positively optimistic about the impact these developments will have on women's issues in Saudi

Arabia. However, since the advent of private higher education, only a few new fields of study have opened their doors to women. These include computer engineering, journalism, law (at two private colleges only), interior design (although only one exists at a public university), accounting, business administration, marketing and finance. Effat University in Jeddah, the only private university that is headed by a woman, started as a college and was upgraded to become one of the first private universities in the country. It is the only private university to offer a Bachelor of Engineering degree for female students in the fields of architecture, electrical and computer engineering, and computer and information systems. Still, many fields of study are limited to men only, such as geology, piloting and some fields of engineering. Substantial reform of women's access to higher education is required if there are to be any meaningful increases in the proportion of Saudi women employed in technical and vocational areas, which currently stands at 26 percent (UNESCO, 1999, as cited in AlMunajjed, 2008). Increasing the number of female university graduates will certainly contribute to social and economic development in Saudi Arabia (Smith and Abouammoh, 2013: 185).

The emergence of universities has had a limited positive effect on access for women. Especially noteworthy is the establishment of KAUST, the first co-educational public–private university in Saudi Arabia, offering a variety of graduate degrees for both genders. As previously mentioned, Effat University in Jeddah provides programs and facilities for women across three faculties – business, social sciences, and engineering – and has recently become the first private all-female university to gain accreditation from the National Commission for Assessment and Academic Accreditation (NCAAA), an organization established in 2004 that aims to upgrade the quality of private and governmental higher education to ensure clarity and transparency, and to provide codified standards for academic performance (MoHE, 2013). Al Faisal University is another private non-profit university that offers undergraduate degrees for both men and women in business, medicine, engineering, science and general studies. The university also offers postgraduate degrees in business administration, educational administration and biomedical sciences.

Low levels of research and creativity in private universities

Another significant challenge surrounds the lack of strategy in gathering data about higher education. According to Smith and Abouammoh (2013), there is limited qualitative data collected at either the national or institutional levels. The need to establish high-quality data collection and analysis systems is, therefore, also a major priority.

Rather than challenging the status quo, private universities are primarily promoting market-driven programming. Seven private universities offer Masters of Business Administration and executive MBA degrees, while none offer a non-vocational degree in the humanities or arts, with the exception of Dar Al Uloom University, which offers a degree in English. Furthermore, the Saudi tradition of rote learning and lack of emphasis on critical thinking is manifested in the near absence of innovative research in the Kingdom's universities, including in the new private institutions. "Enhancing research productivity in higher education is a key pillar of the Saudi national development Plan for achieving the social and economic aspiration of the Kingdom" (Al-Ohali and Shin, 2013: 98).

While SA is slowly developing a research-oriented academic culture, one of the only new research universities is King Abdullah University of Science and Technology (KAUST), which critics argue will emerge as a research power-house in the coming years (Mazi and Altbach, 2013: 19). KAUST is not counted as a public university, yet it is a unique and specialized university with different goals and mission (its four research areas focus on energy, the environment, bio-sciences and engineering). In other institutions, while there is some lack of research in the pure and applied sciences, it is most starkly evident in the social sciences and humanities. These are the fields that offer the greatest potential to challenge the status quo and, at a more basic level, to open the minds of youth to creative and critical thinking. In this regard, it should be noted that the teaching of secular philosophy continues to be dismissed and even banned. This prohibition extends to Islamic philosophy within both public and religious schools. In addition, most of the research that is generated in the social sciences and humanities is oriented toward policy rather than critical analysis of Saudi Arabian society (Al Lily, 2011a, 2011b).

Research funding reinforces the disparities between the pure and applied sciences on the one hand and the humanities and social sciences on the other. Funding for social science research does not even remotely compare to that available for research in the pure and applied sciences through entities like the technological organisation known as King Abdulaziz City for Science and Technology (KACST). This organization is Saudi Arabia's most recognizable entity involved in financing, supporting and fostering scientific research in a wide range of scientific and engineering fields (KACST, 2010). Saudi universities are pressured to favor the pure and applied sciences, which may be due to aspects of the traditional thinking that have proven to be antithetical to innovative thinking and research. This focus, however, on Science Technology Engineering and Math (STEM) research is not a unique phenomenon to SA; it seems to be an international trend and has received attention from scientists and researchers in the field (Bui, 2013). Most of the curricula in private institutions, notably in health sciences and all STEM degrees, are delivered in English (except for Islamic studies, three courses required for all disciplines and Arabic courses). Public universities are moving toward converting the science fields to English and keeping other subjects in Arabic.

Private universities are affected by additional factors that undermine their ability to develop into centers of academic excellence. Staffs in private institutions are required to spend approximately 19 or more hours per week on teaching, in contrast to the maximum of 14 hours per week required in public universities, because of the shortage of faculty members to the number of students. This significantly curtails the amount of time and energy available for research (MoHE, 2012; Alnassar and Dow, 2013). Faculty members' teaching load could rise up to three to five courses and 20 hours of teaching per term to make up for the shortage of faculty and the high influx of students.

Excessive emphasis on labor market needs

Another undermining factor is the almost exclusive emphasis in private universities on granting degrees that are oriented toward satisfying the labor market. Despite the economic value of this approach, this fixation on the labor market compounds the pressure to avoid innovative thinking and research, especially in the social sciences. Prestigious career-oriented subjects such as medicine, nursing, dentistry and applied health sciences are given more attention, while the social sciences are neglected. Indeed, none of the emerging private institutions includes the social sciences as a field of study. Some voices even call for the closure of the existing social science and humanities programs, as they apparently fail to provide training oriented to the labor market (Al-Dhakeel, 2009). Only three private universities have programs in languages or translation, with only one offering another humanities subject – special education.

The private universities remain a work in progress and thus, despite the fact that they are currently more imitative than creative, and despite the fact that they have not yet reached the level of challenging the status quo (that is, producing high number of graduates), they deserve some amount of credit for attempting to offer an additional option in higher education. In other words, it is still too early to judge their merits. There are certainly reasons for being optimistic that the private universities will achieve their educational quality goals. The fact that their curricula remain in a state of flux and are being subjected to international auditors' scrutiny is likely to lead to long-term academic benefits. Their generally smaller class sizes also provide more opportunities for interaction between staff and students. In addition, they are more likely to be at the leading edge of technology implementation in the classroom, including making extensive use of Blackboard. Finally, private universities appear to offer freedom of expression in all areas, as well as a wide range of extracurricular activities for students and broader access to different ideas through exposure to diverse cultures (i.e., those of the diverse faculty members).

The significant Western influences in private institutions remain controversial. This influence is in part a reflection of the fact that despite the Arab world's long tradition of scholarship, Western universities have more experience in offering formal higher education, as many have been in continuous operation for decades or even centuries. Saudi universities therefore have relied – and continue to rely – on Western models since they are seen as the fastest and easiest way of establishing the institutional structure necessary to launch new programs. On the other hand, the emphasis on Western models (and on faculty members imported from Western countries) is sometimes excessive to the point of excluding opportunities to develop new institutions in greater harmony with the Middle Eastern cultural, historical and religious context. For instance, offering opportunities for Saudi faculty members to find teaching posts as an exchange service with international universities would be beneficial and reflect the importance of knowledge exchange. It is this emphasis on Western faculty that, to some extent, seems to be a reflection of a misguided inferiority attitude that traces back to the era of European colonialism and cultural hegemony.

Moving forward

Since the advent of higher education, lucrative funding programs (such as the National 10-Year Development Plan) have given the government of Saudi Arabia strong direction over university governance structures (Al-Eisa and Smith, 2013: 29). An important question is whether the expansion of universities will take into account the need for diversity and researcher independence, which above all requires an expansion of people's thinking beyond the strictures of the widespread and powerful religious ideology. Moreover, reforming higher education according to international standards implies that some of this power will have to be shared to create autonomy; this would be a first step toward reaching international standards and thus ranking. Al-Eisa and Smith (2013: 33) argue that "Saudi higher education would need a paradigm shift from centralization to broader autonomy and from strict regulation to genuine competition among universities." The authors argue, however, that only a few well-established and reputable institutions would be ready for semi-autonomous governance and potentially make it to international ranking: King Saud University (KSU) – the oldest higher-education institution in Saudi Arabia, which recently attracted substantial donations and is building the largest endowment in the history of Saudi higher education – and King Abdullah University of Science and Technology (KAUST), have attracted high-caliber international faculty with productive research records. However:

> the impact of KAUST on SA higher education is yet to be measured ... the autonomous model of its governance would be tested and juxtaposed with it becoming a research excellence hub in the region as its mission is to improve research agenda in SA.
>
> (Al-Eisa and Smith, 2013: 29)

The Saudi system of higher education has many issues to resolve, but like any other developing and growing sector there has been improvement (AlShehri *et al.*, 2013: 143). The Saudi Arabian MoHE (2013) stated that Saudi Arabia has adopted a long-term strategic plan to ensure that the education system becomes a major driving force behind the transformation of an economy primarily dependent on oil revenues to one that reflects a diversified knowledge-based economy. It is important to acknowledge, however, that private higher education in Saudi Arabia is still in its infancy and these impacts have yet to be fully measured.

Saudi public and private HE institutions are in a constant state of capacity building, and various measures have been taken to benchmark with international standards to achieve this goal (Daranadari and Cardew, 2013).

Implications and recommendations

The early twenty-first century has seen the beginning of positive change and educational reform in Saudi Arabia. Many educational strategies have been implemented and more than ten universities and an even greater number of colleges have been established in response to a range of demographic, social and political challenges. These new universities are taking aggressive measures to ensure they meet rigorous international standards.

Moreover, the MoHE has established several bodies and specialist centers to encourage, support and evaluate the quality of HE institutions and the programs they offer: the National Commission for Assessment and Academic Accreditation (NCAAA); the National Centre for Assessment in Higher Education (NCAHE); the Centre for Higher Education Statistics (CHES); and the Centre for Higher Education Research and Studies (CHERS). CHERS is considered the cornerstone of strategic planning for the development of higher education institutions in Saudi Arabia. In this center, many policy objectives are carried out, such as drawing the frameworks for developing and increasing the number of universities as well as the restructuring of university specializations and advancing the harmonization of higher education outputs to national needs, including the requirements of the labor market (MoHE, 2013). The broad mandate of these centers is to ensure that the quality of teaching and learning, student outcomes, management and support services provided within institutions, and research satisfy high international standards (Daranadari and Cardew, 2013: 106). In addition, the massive scholarship program named after King Abdullah (KASP), which was introduced in 2005 and is entering its tenth stage in September 2014, is considered the "most comprehensive scholarship program ever supported by a nation state" (Smith and Abouammoh, 2013: 10).

Leadership in the academy is a central driver of academic excellence and, in turn, high institutional ranking (Al-Swailem and Elliot, 2013: 42). In 2009, the MoHE created the Academic Leadership Centre (ALC) to offer training for those in academic leadership roles to develop the effectiveness and quality of their leadership. Al-Eisa and Smith (2013: 34) suggest that a shift toward innovative and creative leadership styles is essential for a knowledge-based economy to thrive; recent HE initiatives that encourage entrepreneurship and small businesses build on this idea (Al-Ohali and Burdon, 2013). In June 2009, the MoHE also introduced a national program called the Accelerated Program for Excellence (APEX) to promote excellence in national universities. Some of the objectives of the program include:

* Aligning university efforts toward achieving world-class excellence in teaching, research and community services.

- Encouraging partnerships with local and international research and industrial organizations.
- Informing academic communities of what it takes to achieve world-class standards.
- Promoting excellence in research.
- Graduating students who have the skills to be employable and who are competitive with graduates from other countries.
- Using ranking indices and benchmarks in the rankings as guidelines to achieve excellence.

If policy-makers and MoHE officials use these suggested strategies as guidelines to direct reforms, then higher education in Saudi Arabia will be on track to reach its aims and rank higher on the research front. In the new atmosphere that the MoHE is trying to create, teaching and learning can no longer be about "filling students' minds with theoretical information" at the expense of teaching creative and critical thinking (Alnassar and Dow, 2013: 58). If any progress is to be made on increasing the quality and employability of Saudi graduates, then more focus is needed on expanding/enhancing teaching methods; improving students' communication, study and time management skills, and connecting students with their community. These objectives would greatly improve the educational atmosphere of public universities. According to Alnassar and Dow (2013: 59) private universities are better at teaching these skills and preparing students for the workforce, especially those connected with international universities. Drawing on more advantages such as fewer students in the classroom and bringing on board a wide range of international expertise of faculty members and administrators, these institutions will have a fast track on advancement and national and international recognition.

There remain several worthy questions for further exploration, however: Will private universities promote the humanities, social sciences and fine arts? Will these reforms improve educational outcomes? What are the socio-cultural and economic implications of these reforms for the Arabic-speaking population of the region? Can Western educators develop and deliver educational models that successfully combine global needs with local aspirations? Are the new universities economically sustainable? Can they develop forms of governance that promote stability and intellectual creativity? These questions – together with the question of whether these improvements are actually increasing access to higher education for women – are of great significance to Saudi Arabia's national debate on education reform.

There has been an increasing emphasis from the Saudi government on developing universities into internationally competitive centers for knowledge and research (Onsman, 2010). Universities have been challenged by government initiatives over the last five years with at least some degree of success in terms of "developing programs and adopting teaching methods that provide students with knowledge and skills necessary for their entry to the global labour market" (Onsman, 2010: 512). However, it is important to determine how much knowledge is contributing to industrial development in SA because of the overdependence on oil, and whether HE institutions will actually help diversify the economy, including industrial infrastructure, toward knowledge-based innovation (Al-Ohali and Shin, 2013: 102). It is too early to determine if private universities thus far have lived up to their claims of world-class status – the aim of many universities worldwide, and Saudi Arabia is no exception. Even though these universities are investing heavily in importing Western staff and curricula, few resources are being directed toward the substantive development of their programs.

Since many countries in Asia, such as China, South Korea, Taiwan, Hong Kong and Singapore, have been investing in their higher education for decades with dramatic success (Al-Eisa and Smith, 2013: 10), Saudi Arabia is seeing the value and necessity of reforming its higher education into realms beyond pedagogy like governance structures, curricula, management, professional development, and even industrial relations (Darandari and Murphy, 2013: 70). Despite some deficiencies, HE in Saudi Arabia has, according to Smith and Abouammoh (2013: 10), "enormous potential and is driven by enormous enthusiasm at all levels from government to individual academics … Such enthusiasm should be harnessed by strong and relevant strategies, supported by rigorous and timely feedback mechanisms." Saudi Arabian higher education will no doubt see the fruits of such investment soon, and concerned, educated Saudis and outside observers can look to the future with optimism.

Notes

1 This chapter was contributed by Dr. Amani Hamdan, College of Education, University of Dammam, Dammam, Saudi Arabia. All correspondence regarding it should be addressed to its author. Email: Akhalghamdi@ud.edu.sa.
2 Some critics argue that this last figure (92 percent) is too high and indicates a problem. Surely not all 92 percent of high school graduates, which does not include postsecondary vocational training, are ready for, or even want to do, college-level work (Pavan, 2013).

References

Academic World University Ranking (2014). Available at: www.shanghairanking.com/ (accessed August 20, 2014).

Alankari, K. (2013). Foreword. In Smith, L. and Abouammoh, A. (eds.). *Higher Education in Saudi Arabia: Achievement, Challenges, and Opportunities*. New York: Springer, 3–8.

Al-Dali, W., Fnais, M. and Newbould, I. (2013). Private higher education in the Kingdom of Saudi Arabia: Reality, challenges and aspirations. In Smith, L. and Abouammoh, A. (eds.). *Higher Education in Saudi Arabia*. New York: Springer, 127–136.

Al-Dhakeel, T. (2009). Doctora laekn atela [jobless doctor]. Alwatan, September 23. Available at: www.turkid.net/?p=1467.

Al-Eisa, E. and Smith, L. (2013). Governance in Saudi higher education. In Smith, L. and Abouammoh, A. (eds.). *Higher Education in Saudi Arabia: Achievements, Challenges, and Opportunities*. New York: Springer, 27–37.

AlGhamdi, A.K.H. and Deraney, P. (2013). Effects of teaching critical thinking to Saudi female university students using a stand-alone course. *International Education Studies*, 6(7): 176–188.

Al-Ghamdi, S. and Tight, M. (2013). Delivering high quality teaching and learning for university students in Saudi Arabia. In Smith, L. and Abouammoh, A. (eds.). *Higher Education in Saudi Arabia: Achievements, Challenges, and Opportunities*. New York: Springer, 49–61.

Al-Ghamdi, S., Al-Gaied, A. and Abu-Rasain, M. (2010). *Faculty Education in Saudi Arabia: A Suggested Model* (in Arabic). Riyadh: Research and Studies Center in Higher Education.

Aljughaiman, A.M. and Grigorenko, E.L. (2013). Growing up under pressure: The cultural and religious context of the Saudi system of gifted education. *Journal for the Education of the Gifted*, 36(3): 307–322.

Alkhazim, M. (2003). Higher education in Saudi Arabia: Challenges, solutions, and opportunities missed. *Higher Education Policy*, 16: 479–486.

Alkhazim, M. (2009). *Altaleem alali fee almezan* [*Higher Education in the Balance*]. Lebanon: Toawa.

Al Lily, A.E.A. (2011a). On line and under veil: Technology-facilitated communication and Saudi female experience within academia. *Technology in Society*, 33(1–2): 119–127.

Al Lily, A.E.A. (2011b). Teaching across gender lines: A Saudi technological innovation. In Selwyn, N., Oliver, M. and Eynon, R. (eds.). *Learning, Media and Technology: Doctoral Research Conference* (July 4, 2011). London: Knowledge Lab, 4–11.

AlMunajjed, M. (2008). *Women's Employment in Saudi Arabia: A Major Challenge*. New York: Booz & Co.

AlMunajjed, M. (2012). Where the real worth is. Arabian Business.com. Available at: www.arabianbusiness.com/where-real-wealth-is-457262.html (accessed January 22, 2014).

Alnassar, S.A. and Dow, K. (2013). Delivering high quality teaching and learning for university students in Saudi Arabia. In Smith, L. and Abouammoh, A. (eds.). *Higher Education in Saudi Arabia: Achievements, Challenges and Opportunities*. New York: Springer, 49–61.

Al-Ohali, M. and Burdon, S. (2013). International collaboration. In Smith, L. and Abouammoh, A. (eds.). *Higher Education in Saudi Arabia: Achievements, Challenges, and Opportunities*. New York: Springer, 95–102.

Al-Ohali, M. and Shin, J.C. (2013). Knowledge-based innovation and research productivity in Saudi Arabia. In Smith, L. and Abouammoh, A. (eds.). *Higher Education in Saudi Arabia: Achievements, Challenges, and Opportunities*. New York: Springer, 95–102.

AlShehri, F. (2014). 44 billion is the expenditure of Saudi government on university students yearly. *Makka*.

AlShehri, M.Y., Campbell, S., Daud, M.Z., Mattar, E.H., Sayed, M.G. and Abu-Eshy, A.S. (2013). The development of medical education in Saudi Arabia. In Smith, L. and Abouammoh, A. (eds.). *Higher Education in Saudi Arabia: Achievements, Challenges, and Opportunities*. New York: Springer, 137–150.

Alsherean, D. (writer and TV producer) (2012). *Althamena* [TV talk show]. In MBC (Producer). Riyadh: Middle East Channel.

Al-Swailem, O. and Elliot, G. (2013). The learning experiences of Saudi Arabian higher education leadership: Characteristics for global success. In Smith, L. and Abouammoh,

A. (eds.). *Higher Education in Saudi Arabia: Achievements, Challenges, and Opportunities*. New York: Springer, 37–49.

Baki, R. (2004). Gender-segregated education in Saudi Arabia: Its impact on social norms and the Saudi labor market. *Education Policy Analysis Archives*, 12(28): 1–12.

Baxter, E. (2010). Saudi employed 1.5m foreign workers during crisis. Available at: www.arabianbusiness.com/590683-saudi-employed-15m-foreign-workers-during-crisis.

Bosbait, M. and Wilson, R. (2005). Education, school-to-work transitions and unemployment in Saudi Arabia. *Middle Eastern Journal*, 41(4): 533–545.

Brandenburg, T. (2010). The political economy of internationalization of higher education in the Sultanate of Oman. Unpublished manuscript. Mainz, Germany.

Bui, L. (2013). Report: Humanities, social science education needed along with STEM. *The Washington Post*, June 19. Available at: www.washingtonpost.com/local/education/report-humanities-social-science-education-needed-along-with-stem/2013/06/18/76076df6-d83e-11e2-a016-92547bf094cc_story.html.

Darandari, E. and Cardew, P. (2013). Accreditation and quality assurance. In Smith, L. and Abouammoh, A. (eds.). *Higher Education in Saudi Arabia: Achievements, Challenges, and Opportunities*. New York: Springer, 103–117.

Darandari, E. and Murphy, A. (2013). Assessment of student learning. In Smith, L. and Abouammoh, A. (eds.). *Higher Education in Saudi Arabia: Achievements, Challenges, and Opportunities*. New York: Springer, 61–72.

Doumato, E. (2010). Women's rights in the Middle East and North Africa. Available at: www.freedomhouse.org/uploads/special_report/section/174.pdf.

Frediani, A. (2010). Sen's capability approach as a framework for the practice of development. *Development in Practice*, 20: 173–187.

Freire, P. (2003). *Pedagogy of the Oppressed*. New York: Continuum.

Ghanea, N. (2004). Human rights of religious minorities and of women in the Middle East. *Human Rights Quarterly*, 26: 705–729.

Jamjoom, F. and Kelly, P. (2013). Higher education for women in the Kingdom of Saudi Arabia. In Smith, L. and Abouammoh, A. (eds.). *Higher Education in Saudi Arabia: Achievements, Challenges, and Opportunities*. New York: Springer, 117–127.

King Abdulaziz City for Science and Technology (KACST) (2010). *City for Science and Technology*. Riyadh: KACST. Available at: www.kacst.edu.sa/en/Pages/default.aspx.

Mazawi, A.E. (2005). The academic profession in a rentier state: The professoriate in Saudi Arabia. *Minerva*, 43: 221–244.

Mazawi, A.E. (2009). Dis/integrated orders and the politics of recognition: Civil upheavals, militarism, and educators' lives and work. In Borg, C., Mayo, P. and Sultana, R.G. (eds.). *Mediterranean Studies in Comparative Education*. Malta: Impressions Ltd., 69–89.

Mazi, A. and Altbach, P.G. (2013). Dreams and realities: The world-class idea and Saudi Arabian higher education. In Smith, L. and Abouammoh, A. (eds.). *Higher Education in Saudi Arabia: Achievements, Challenges, and Opportunities*. New York: Springer, 13–27.

Ministry of Higher Education (MoHE) (2001). *Statistics of Higher Education in Saudi Arabia*. Riyadh: MoHE.

Ministry of Higher Education (MoHE) (2008). *Ministry of Higher Education National Report*. Riyadh: MoHE.

Ministry of Higher Education (MoHE) (2010). *Ministry of Higher Education's Plan to Achieve Excellence in Science and Technology*. Riyadh: MoHE.

Ministry of Higher Education (MoHE) (2011). *Ministry of Higher Education National Report*. Riyadh: MoHE.

Ministry of Higher Education (MoHE) (2012). *Ministry of Higher Education National Report*. Riyadh: MoHE.

Ministry of Higher Education (MoHE) (2013). Center of Research and Strategic Studies. Available at: www.mohe.gov.sa/en/aboutus/Institutions/Pages/Center-for-Research-and-Strategic-Studies.aspx (accessed January 24, 2014).

Mohrman, K. (2005). World-class universities and Chinese higher education reform. Available at: www.bc.edu/bc_org/avp/soe/cihe/newsletter/News39/text013.htm.

Newell, S.M. (1999). The transfer of management education to China: Building learning communities rather than translating Western texts. *Education and Training*, 41(6/7): 286–293.

Nolan, L. (2012). *Liberalizing Monarchies? How Gulf Monarchies Manage Education Reform*. Doha: Brookings Doha Center Analysis Paper.

Noori, N. (2010). Overlapping spheres of governance: Accreditation agencies and American-style universities in the Middle East. Unpublished manuscript. Cambridge, UK.

Okruhlik, G. (2005). The irony of *islah* [reform]. *The Washington Quarterly*, 28(4): 153–170.

Onsman, A. (2010). Dismantling the perceived barriers to the implementation of national higher education accreditation guidelines in the Kingdom of Saudi Arabia. *Journal of Higher Education Policy and Management*, 32(5): 511–519.

Pavan, A. (2013). A new perspective on the quest for education: The Saudi Arabian way to knowledge society. *Higher Education Studies*, 3(6): 25–34.

Saudi Arabia Demographics Profile 2013 (2013). Available at: www.indexmundi.com/saudi_arabia/demographics_profile.html (accessed November 2013).

Saudi Arabia: ICDL as an Official Academic Curriculum (n.d.). ECDL Foundation. Available at: www.ecdl.org/index.jsp?p=906&n=2271&a=4278 (accessed December 21, 2013).

Saudi Gazette (2010). Census shows Kingdom's population at more than 27 million. Available at: www.saudigazette.com.sa/index.cfm?method=home.regcon&contentid=2010112487888 (accessed November 24, 2012).

Shediac, R. and Samman, H. (2010). Meeting the employment challenge in the GCC: The need for a holistic strategy. Booz & Co. Available at: www.strategyand.pwc.com/media/file/Meeting_the_Employment_Challenge_in_the_GCC.pdf.

Smith, L. and Abouammoh, A. (eds.) (2013). *Higher Education in Saudi Arabia: Achievement, Challenges, and Opportunities*. New York: Springer.

Statistics and Facts on Saudi Arabia (2013). Available at: www.statista.com/topics/1630/saudi-arabia/ (accessed January 30, 2014).

World Bank (2012a). Public spending on education, total (%GDP). Available at: http://data.worldbank.org/indicators/SE.XPD.TOTAL.GD.ZS.

World Bank (2012b). Population growth annual % (2013). Available at: http://data.worldbank.org/indicator/SP.POP.GROW (accessed December 25, 2013).

8 Arabic in higher education
Questions of national identity and pragmatism

In every society and throughout history, the need to communicate among different speech communities has often led to one of the socially or geographically defined dialectal varieties of a common language to become the dominant medium of communication in inter-group interactions. The dominant variety usually corresponds to the dominant group's dialect and eventually becomes the linguistic norm for that particular language. Historically, this linguistic evolution is common to most standardized languages such as Standard English, French, Italian, Spanish and other European languages. The distance between the Standard and the spoken variety that children are exposed to first in their home environment varies depending on the language itself, the socio-economic and educational background of the parents, the attitudes prevalent in that speech community toward linguistic variation and different registers, as well as a multitude of other contextual factors. While linguistic variation is tolerated at the level of the spoken language, speech communities are less accepting of it in academic and written discourse. The case of Modern Standard Arabic (MSA), and its earlier antecedent, Classical Arabic, is similar in some respects and different in many others. While it is the official language of the 22 Arab states, MSA (which has evolved from Classical Arabic) does not belong to a socially, geographically, politically or economically dominant group. It is nobody's mother tongue but has been the unchallenged and recognized official standard variety of all Arab states until recent times.

Since the start of the post-colonial era, MSA has been facing important challenges, particularly in being the main language in education. These challenges are the result of pressures from both foreign languages and the spoken dialectal varieties. Educational systems in the GCC countries, like in most other Arab countries, are grappling with these language issues. However, added to this linguistic situation, the GCC's linguistic context is even more challenging due to rapid socio-economic transformations, the recency of the educational systems and demographic imbalances where expatriate populations range between 60 and 90 percent of total populations.

This chapter discusses some of the linguistic and socio-economic factors interfering with the promotion of MSA as the official and main language of education in the GCC. We will argue that despite numerous policy decisions and

DOI: 10.4324/9780203796139-8

official statements affirming that Arabic (in all its varieties but principally MSA) is a central component of national and Pan-Arab identity that must be promoted as the official language of the GCC nations, efforts to implement language policies in the GCC (and the Arab world in general) seem to face hurdles not only due to the powerful push from English as a global language but also due to linguistic and socio-pragmatic factors tied to both the Arabic language itself and attitudes toward different varieties of the language in Arab societies in general. These factors have led to a devaluation of proficiency in MSA as a useful commodity in the GCC even though it still has some of its symbolic and nostalgic value.

The status of MSA today

It is no secret that proficiency in Modern Standard Arabic (MSA) has declined among literate young generations in many of the GCC countries and elsewhere in the Arab world. Different studies across the GCC reveal that millennial generations recognize that they have weak Arabic literacy skills and hold relatively negative perceptions of MSA's value as a useful language in the labor market and knowledge society (Badry, 2011, 2012, 2015; BBC Arabic, 2014;[1] Findlow, 2006). A recent series of articles in the UAE's *National* newspaper highlights the debate going on in the Federal National Council (FNC) in the UAE about whether or not there is a need for a law to protect the Arabic language. Based on "The council's education, youth and media committee, which studied the declining use of the language and Arabic literacy skills, [it was decided that] a law was needed to protect the mother tongue" (Salem, 2014).

There are many factors responsible for the decline of Arabic which are sometimes simplistically attributed to the power of English under globalization without a careful consideration of other contextually intrinsic factors. The dominance of English in the last decades is not unique to the GCC. English is increasingly becoming the sought after additional language by most non-anglophone nations. Its status as the language of international communication in business, technology, research and media, has led policy-makers all over the world to stress the need for high proficiency in English by adding it as a medium of instruction in their educational systems (Grin and Korth, 2005; Strubell, 1996; Tankersley, 2001; Wannaqat, 2007). Whether it is in Europe, China, Singapore or South Korea, the place of English in the curriculum is being emphasized (Ahmad *et al.*, 2007; Baetens-Beardsmore, 1998; Choi, 2010; Farrell and Fenwick, 2007; Giri, 2007). For example, schools and universities in France and Spain, two colonial languages of the past, have taken steps to allow for more time for English in their school systems. In fact, English is no longer only taught as a subject but is also used as a medium of instruction for part of the curriculum to develop their millennial generations' English proficiency "for future study, work and life" (Zhu, 2004, cited in Feng, 2007: 148). Bruthiaux (2003: 9) attributes this power of English and its status as the global language to the emergence of the United States as sole superpower and the growth of international trade.... For better or worse, this geopolitical shift favors an American worldview along with its principal linguistic vehicle, English. Meanwhile, those with the ambition to take part in international exchanges tend – rightly or wrongly – to regard possession of English as the key to professional success and greater well-being.

In the face of this "English invasion," most countries in the West and East have been able to maintain their national/official language as their primary medium of instruction at all educational levels. Moreover, outside schools, the national language continues to be used everywhere, from street signs, official documents, national newspapers to all social interactions in business and family settings. This use of the mother tongue in a variety of communication domains reinforces its primacy among societies' members. In contrast, in many former colonies of the South, mother tongues have not been so lucky. Already dealing with complex linguistic diversity which was delegitimized by colonial languages, former colonies have had to use English (or other colonial languages) as a common lingua franca. In many cases, while English is officially treated as an additional language in education, in practice full literacy in mother tongues has become a secondary goal of education. It is a fact that in some contexts, official national languages have remained as part of the curriculum to varying degrees but their development and perception as prestigious and valued commodities can be described as a continuum ranging from development (e.g., Hebrew), benign peripherization (e.g., Arabic) to endangered status (e.g., many African and other indigenous languages in Latin America and Oceania).

Across the Arab nations, the status of MSA in educational systems is not uniform. Since their independence, beginning in the late 1950s, the position of MSA has been fluctuating between basic maintenance to benign peripherization depending on the various reforms decreed by policy-makers in the last 60 years and the country being examined. In the GCC, educational reforms seem to rest on short-term goals that do not take into account socio-linguistic, pragmatic and political realities on the ground. The perceived urgency of catching up to the knowledge economies of the advanced world by using English has played a role in the declining proficiency in MSA.

The nature of reforms and their impact on Arabic

In the GCC most stakeholders concede that there are risks associated with the increasing use of English in schools and its impact on MSA proficiency. Governments repeatedly reiterate the need to maintain Arabic in the face of the "flattening effect of globalization" (Cabinet releases). Newspapers and TV programs are replete with articles, editorials and programs raising concerns about the future of Arabic (Ahmed, 2012; Al Baik, 2008; Al Lawati and Al Najami, 2008; Al Najami, 2007; Salem, 2014; Zacharias, 2012). However, the educational reforms implemented on the ground do not seem to respond to these concerns.

Education reforms in the GCC have generally been motivated by short-term goals of "catching up" to the developed world. Using English, particularly in higher education, is seen as a short cut to accessing the knowledge needed to transform the region into a "knowledge economy" since "most scientific research is … reported in English" (Ahmed, 2012). To prepare students for university study in English has necessitated stressing its position at pre-university levels as well. Governments across the region have devoted important resources to improving the teaching of English, from hiring native speakers of English as teachers, to developing materials in English, using IT, introducing it earlier in public schools (Drummond, 2010) and adopting a CLIL approach (Content and Language Integrated Learning) in model schools such as the MAG school in the UAE, Independent schools in Qatar, or the reformed Basic Education in Bahrain and Oman or Kuwait. These pilot models are expected to be gradually expanded throughout the whole educational systems. In comparison, efforts to improve the teaching of Arabic have been rather insignificant. Teachers using Arabic as a medium of instruction complain that relative to their colleagues who teach in English, they are paid less and feel they have little support. They point out that not much is done to remedy the paucity of interactive Arabic materials, to integrate IT in their teaching, nor to offer them professional development opportunities.[2] As discussed in Chapter 5, the emphasis on English at pre-university levels was necessary to prepare graduates for universities where English is the medium of instruction in engineering, sciences and technology throughout the GCC tertiary systems. In some national universities it has also replaced Arabic in social sciences, business and communication studies.[3] In the private sector, English is the de facto language of instruction and university culture everywhere in the GCC (see Chapter 4)

The strong belief in a causal relation between English and development is evident in various strategic plans. For example, the UAE's former Minister of Higher Education, Sheikh Nahyan, who presided over the three public universities until 2013, emphasized the need for English and led the shift to English as medium of instruction. Swan reports that "[d]espite opposition, he [the Minister] was determined to make young nationals competitive on the global stage" and as the HCT provost, Dr. Drummond, stated: "Sheikh Nahyan had the vision and determination to switch instruction to English language to foster international capabilities and global competitiveness for UAE citizens" (Swan, 2013). In Qatar, the reforms recommended by the RAND Corporation also mandated an earlier introduction of English to prepare students for English medium universities. The other Gulf states opted for a less aggressive route in replacing Arabic in their pre-university systems but had the same English medium of instruction approach to higher education. For example, in Oman, the reforms adopted starting in 1998 maintained Arabic in the pre-university public school system although English as a subject was introduced earlier as a foreign language starting with the first grade. At university level, engineering, sciences, business and IT majors have adopted English as their medium of instruction across most public universities and all private universities. Kuwait University seems to be the only university not requiring advanced English proficiency in its admission policies (e.g., a TOEFL of 310 compared to 500 at least in other GCC universities).

This prioritization of English is quite often supported by parents' demands that their children be prepared in English for higher education and jobs in the English-dominated global market. Increasing numbers of nationals in the GCC are sending their children to private schools and universities to be educated in English. For those parents who want their children to have a truly bilingual education their options are very limited as it is difficult to find schools that give equal importance to both Arabic and English in their curriculum (Abdel-Jawad and Abu Radwan, 2011; Badry, 2015).

The push for English at all tiers of the educational system, without equal attention to MSA, has consequences that go beyond linguistic behaviors as there are

> no more powerful means of "encouraging" individuals to assimilate to a dominant culture than having the economic, social and political returns stacked against their mother tongue. Such assimilation is not freely chosen if the choice is between one's mother tongue and one's future.
>
> (UNDP, 2004: 33)

These educational practices have led to many public discussions about the challenges that stand in the way of the Arabic language becoming a twenty-first century language for Arabs across the Arab world and globally (Al Jazeera.net, 2012). Opinions and editorials sounding the alarm that Arabic is "dying" abound in newspapers and TV programs (Al Baik, 2008; Al Jazeera TV; Al Najami, 2007; Lewis, 2010). Almost every year initiatives are launched by governments, academies and associations holding meetings in Beirut, Cairo, Dubai and Qatar, to discuss the necessity to protect and safeguard the Arabic language. There are centers and associations for the protection of Arabic in majors Arab cities and language charters have recently been proclaimed in Dubai and Qatar.

Pressures are coming from legislators, parents and intellectuals who are questioning educational reform outcomes. In a recent article, published by *The National*, entitled "Abu Dhabi parents: 'Teach our children in Arabic'" it was reported that the majority of the 50,000 parents surveyed in Abu Dhabi are calling for a reversal of the current approach of using English to teach math and science and to use Arabic instead. Dr. Masood Badri, ADEC's head of research and planning, concedes that "Arabic is not being given attention" in schools and confirms that "[p]arents feel their language and culture are being neglected. This is true" (Ahmed, 2012). He goes on to justify this neglect by attributing it to scant Arabic materials and resources in scientific subjects which rationalizes the use of English. The public's pressure is being echoed at higher levels of government. In the UAE, some FNC (Federal National Council) members are calling for laws that would make instruction in Arabic compulsory for government universities. Jamal bin Huwaireb, cultural consultant for the Dubai government, recently "launched a similar Twitter campaign calling on authorities to use

Arabic as the main medium of teaching, and the idea has caught fire" (Bilingual education crucial for the UAE, 2013).

Mounting pressures from stakeholders have forced policy-makers to reconsider the aggressive push for English in education and the negative impact such policies have on the preservation of national and Arab cultural identity across the GCC (more so in Qatar and the UAE than elsewhere). In 2012–13, changes began to be implemented. In the UAE, a new minister of higher education was appointed and public higher education is being restructured (see Chapter 4). One of the first steps of the new reforms was to replace Western leadership with nationals. There are also plans to increase the proportion of the required Arabic courses from the present 15 percent of Zayed University's curriculum and add a new course on the UAE in Arabic as a requirement for all students (personal communication).[4] ZU also launched "The Institute for the Arabic Language" that is looking into Arabization of curriculum. It also opened an early childhood bilingual program linked to its Abu Dhabi campus. At pre-university levels, ADEC has begun to offer training programs for Arabic teachers and Dubai Educational Council (DEC) is launching a certification program for Arabic teachers in schools. All these efforts are still in their initial stages.

In Qatar in 2012, the Supreme Education Council (a government body), in a reversal of the 2003–4 decision which had made English the medium of instruction at Qatar University, ordered the university to reinstate Arabic as a medium of instruction in law, international affairs, media and business administration (English vs Arabic, 2012). Although no official explanations for this reversal were made public, it followed mounting attacks in the media against QU. The imposition of English as medium of instruction in the public university had closed doors for many public high school graduates whose English proficiency was below admission requirements. This decision effectively shut out a sizeable number of young Qataris from higher education mainly because of their low English proficiency. Reinstating Arabic also responded to a combination of political realities after the Arab Spring as well as practical matters. The English policy had effectively led to the redundancy of Qatari faculty and reduced new faculty's chances for employment in the only public university of the country.[5] Recognizing the need for better proficiency in Arabic among future graduates, Georgetown University's School of Foreign Service in Qatar (SFS-Q) launched a program in Arabic language teaching to address this problem. Al Tonsi, one of the leaders of this program, explained that:

> The new initiative will enable a student of business to continue learning about his or her major but also much expand the ability to read and write in the clearest of Arabic. The same is true for a media student or a political science student. They will then know business or media or political science not just in English, but also in Arabic.
>
> (SFS-Q website)

SFS-Q's website describes the initiative, stating that "a range of special purpose courses, content courses and literature courses will be designed, in addition to new teaching materials and textbooks, new assessment methods and an expansion of extra-curricular activities." A similar program is in place at ZU (UAE) where students in all majors are offered "a language lab course." According to ZU's provost, this lab teaches students from all English medium majors (engineering, business, sciences and IT) the Arabic translation of key concepts in their disciplines. QU's return to Arabic, the SFS-Q initiative and the ZU efforts to promote Arabic are limited in their scope and English continues to be the medium of instruction for all science, engineering and technology majors.

Despite all calls and the few initiatives to do something about Arabic, it is likely that these efforts will have limited success, partly due to a disconnect between policy pronouncements and realities on the ground where employment opportunities in business, technology and science clearly favor the use of English over Arabic and where meta-messages sent throughout society associate English with the future and MSA with the past.

These calls notwithstanding, dominant discourses in the Gulf continue to ignore the importance of recognizing the impact of multiglossia and consider MSA as the only "true" Arabic. It is not unusual to hear that "good Arabic" is a "pure" language that must be developed only from within and reject external influences. There are purists who believe that any foreign intrusion into Arabic is a threat to its authenticity and see danger when young speakers code switch or borrow foreign words in their speech. Such discourses ignore the fact that all languages (including Arabic when it was a "global language" in its past) evolve by borrowing from other languages, using a variety of internal processes and external borrowings to change with their societies' changing environment. In an article published on Al Jazeera.net, Al Jundi defends the superiority and uniqueness of the Arabic lexicon in that its word formation process of "Ishtiqaq" (derivation), which is unique to Semitic languages, allows it to coin a wealth of new words to refer to scientific and technological concepts without having to borrow from external sources. He points out that the productivity of the root and pattern system allows Arabic "to evolve without changing" and supports his argument by citing numerous examples of words denoting new meanings that are derived from original Arabic roots.

Opponents of this purist approach rightly highlight the fact that the lag of Arabic in scientific and technological terminology is due to the Arab nations' lag in these fields rather than to the Arabic language itself. In a conference recently held in Cairo about the crisis of the Arabic language, presenters debated whether the problems facing the use of the Arabic language today are real or perceived. It was remarked that like all other languages of the world, there is nothing unique to Arabic needing to expand in order to express new concepts and developments. Another point raised in these discussions was that Arabic weaknesses stem from orientalist colonialist representations of Arabs and Arabic which have been internalized by Arabs themselves leading them to approach Arabic (MSA) as a "difficult language." What is evident today is that regardless of whether this perception has been nurtured by orientalist and colonialist influences or not, it is generally true that high proficiency and fluency in MSA is not very widespread among Arabs.

Equally important in the mix of factors affecting the future of MSA as an academic language are linguistic, affective and socio-pragmatic factors which must be considered in any effort to make MSA a language of knowledge production in the twenty-first century.

Linguistic and affective factors

Arabic as a diglossic language

One of the factors that can explain some of the difficulties facing the development of proficiency in MSA is the diglossic or rather the multiglossic nature of Arabic. Diglossia refers to linguistic contexts in which two varieties are used by the same speakers of a linguistic community for clearly separate functions (Ferguson, 1959). In the Arabic diglossic context, MSA (acquired through literacy) is reserved for use in formal situations and all written communications while dialectal (spoken) Arabic (the native variety) is expected to be used in informal intimate and everyday interactions. Historically, the diglossic distribution of MSA (or its historical antecedent, Classical Arabic), and the dialectal varieties has been a relatively stable phenomenon partly due to very low rates of literacy across the Arab world in the past. Knowledge of Classical Arabic and later MSA has been limited to a minority of religious scholars and intellectuals since everyday interactions are in the dialectal variety. For religious purposes memorization of the Quran (written in Classical Arabic) is sufficient to recite it in prayers.

Access to literacy coupled with Pan-Arab nationalist sentiments across the Arab world in the post-colonial era helped spread MSA among wider segments of the population and led to shaking the stability of its diglossic functional distribution. MSA became a strong symbol of national identity and Pan-Arab national unity and began to be mixed with the dialectal varieties. In informal and even semi-formal oral communication, code-mixing (of MSA, dialectal Arabic and a foreign language) has become the norm today. Moreover, the spread of Arabic satellite media and increased contact between Arabs from different regions of the Arab world often leads speakers of one region to accommodate others in cross-dialectal communication thus giving rise to what is today known as Educated Spoken Arabic (ESA). ESA is a collection of intermediate varieties that mix MSA with dialectal grammatical and lexical features and minimize the use of idiosyncratic colloquialisms to increase the chances of comprehension across dialects. Today, these many intermediate varieties have led to a fluctuating multiglossic socio-linguistic environment across the Arab world.

In a study of the varieties used in three Arabic-speaking satellite TV stations, Al Shamrani (2012) found that while MSA tends to be used by news broadcasters, there was a mix of the two varieties by guests in interview programs, revealing that even in contexts formerly reserved for MSA, dialectal forms are being used. The study also found that in entertainment and sports programs, dialectal Arabic was predominant. Even in those formal oral contexts where MSA is expected, it is customary to hear speakers start in MSA and gradually fall back into a mixed code (i.e., an ESA variety), either due to limited fluency in MSA or for pragmatic reasons to maximize comprehension.[6]

Such mixing between the dialects and MSA is not new. Ferguson (1959) called it a middle variety and described it as:

> a kind of spoken Arabic much used in certain semiformal or cross-dialectal situations [with] a highly classical vocabulary with few or no inflectional endings, with certain features of classical syntax, but with a fundamentally colloquial base in morphology and syntax, and a generous admixture of colloquial vocabulary.
>
> (Ferguson, 1959: 340, cited in Al Shamrani, 2012)

Educated Spoken Arabic (ESA) is the contemporary version of this middle Arabic that is used by educated Arabs in cross-dialectal, official and semi-official contexts. The spread of literacy and the globalization of communication has helped it become a widespread phenomenon (Badawi, 1973; Meiseles, 1980; Mitchell, 1986).

One could draw a parallel between the development of ESA and the earlier process which led to the birth of what we know today as Classical Arabic when it emerged as the common variety among pre-Islamic Arab tribes. Before Islam, Arabian Peninsula tribes spoke different dialects of Arabic which they adjusted to facilitate communication in contact situations such as trade and poetry competitions (e.g., Suq Okadh). Their accommodation gave rise to a "koine," defined as a linguistic variety based on dialects sharing the same base language and characterized by a neutralization of major regional and social features between them. It is this koine that was used in pre-Islamic poetry, later in the Quran and subsequently codified and standardized as Classical Arabic by the Arab grammarians for writing and speaking in formal contexts. At present, however, suggestions to recognize ESA as a potential real variety that deserves consideration and holds promise of resolving issues related to diglossia triggers strong emotional negative reactions among Arabs in general and purists in particular. In the Arab psyche there is only one "real" Arabic, Classical Arabic (CA) and its descendant MSA.[7] Any other form is perceived as a degenerate corruption of Arabic. Religious sentiments emanating from the desire to keep the sacred language of the Quran alive play a major role in these attitudes.

Affective factors

The multiglossic context of Arabic is sometimes wrongly equated with differences found between any standard language and its vernaculars. In English, for example, although there are clear differences between Standard English (American or British, for example) and its various spoken varieties, Standard English is functionally appropriate in both spoken and written registers and in formal and informal contexts. Native speakers of English could learn to speak a standard variety as a native language and outside of school. In contrast, MSA is nobody's native language. It is limited to formal contexts and written communication and violating this functional distribution feels unnatural and a subject of mockery (Haeri, 1997). Another difference is linked to status associated with Standard forms. While Standard English (or French), for example, is associated with higher social classes and educated elites, Standard Arabic is not. In fact, often it is the opposite. Arab elites have generally been educated in European languages and do not have high proficiency in Arabic. Modern secular higher education, originally introduced by colonization, relied heavily on foreign languages as media of instruction as mentioned above.[8] As a result, highly educated elites generally continue to use a foreign language for all formal and academic functions. Haeri's case study of Egypt illustrates this point.[9]

> Often the higher one's social class, the less likely it is that one will learn it [MSA] well. Upper class Egyptians, for example, generally attend foreign language [schools] ... and although multilingualism is a mark of their class, Classical Arabic is not necessarily one of the languages they learn.
>
> (Haeri, 2000: 68–69)

Contrary to expectations where knowing the standard variety confers some form of power, proficiency in MSA is a valued commodity in narrow circles such as poetry, literary and religious domains. These domains have emotional and nostalgic values but little market value in today's Arab societies. It is proficiency in English (or French) that opens important social and business doors that cannot be opened with proficiency in MSA alone although it may be a plus. Educated young Gulf Arabs generally admit to having low proficiency in writing in MSA and prefer to use English in written communication in formal contexts (Abdel-Jawad and Abu Radwan, 2011; Badry, 2011; Al-Issa and Dahan, 2011; Hopkyns, 2014). In fact, they willingly confess to their low writing skills in MSA. It is fashionable and a symbol status to admit that one's Arabic literacy skills are weak because it suggests that the person is "modern" and has been educated in a Western/private institution either at home or abroad. Speaking English is often associated with better education and is an ostentatious sign of upper social standing. A statement made by a 30-year-old quoted in *The National*[10] illustrates this paradox in language values when she said: "If I open my mouth and speak in English, people say, 'Oh she's amazing'. If I open my mouth and start speaking Arabic, it's like, 'Oh she's regular' " (Zacharias, 2012).

Impact of diglossia on literacy development in Arabic

In addition to the socio-linguistic and affective factors discussed above, linguistic differences between MSA and the home dialect are important and may be as significant as those that exist between what is considered two separate languages in other contexts from a purely linguistic perspective.[11] Psycholinguistic research reveals that the distance between MSA and dialectal varieties may explain some of the problems observed in reading acquisition among young

Arabic native speakers and that overlooking them in teaching methodologies may explain some of the attested low levels of literacy development of Arabic-speaking children.[12] Haeri (2000: 71) claims that expecting Arabic-speaking children to learn to read and write in MSA in the early grades of schooling is analogous to "a situation in which Italian children today were faced with classical Latin as their medium of education." The differences are at all levels of language, from lexical, phonological, morpho-syntactic to semantic (Abu-Rabia, 2000; Ibrahim, 2011; Saiegh-Haddad, 2003). Although the MSA lexicon and that of the dialects share common roots in large part, high frequency words are usually idiosyncratic to regional dialects. There are also many differences in morpho-phonological features. Experiments carried out on young children learning to read MSA revealed that recognizing these differences and building on them better prepares children for literacy in MSA. In an experimental study investigating "children's ability to perform phonological awareness tasks," Khamis-Dakwar (2007), for example, found that children who were exposed to MSA sounds that are not part of their dialect earlier performed better in early reading tasks than those in the control group.

There are additional particularities tied to the Arabic script that have been identified by linguists but not taken into consideration in the pedagogical approaches to teaching Arabic literacy. Learning to read in Arabic requires the development of perceptual and processing skills that may differ from those used in learning to read a Latin script on which most teaching reading approaches are based. The Arabic script represents vowels as supra-segmental diacritics which are not present in intermediate to advanced reading materials. After the initial stages of decoding, reading Arabic requires from the reader a degree of knowledge of the grammar of an inflected language[13] such as Arabic and an important lexical inventory to be able to guess the unrepresented vowels. The reader basically needs to "know" the words to be able to read them. Given the fact that the academic lexicon is either absent or quite different from what the young reader is familiar with, this is an added obstacle to guessing and deciphering unvowelized script. To overcome these "difficulties" the approach to teaching Arabic may be helped by drawing a reader's attention to the common typological properties of the Arabic lexicon such as its lexical derivation processes to establish connections between the two varieties and facilitate the transition from the dialect to MSA.

Pedagogical and socio-linguistic factors

Other pedagogical factors leading to lower proficiency in MSA are related to teaching methods that are heavily focused on grammatical accuracy much more than fluency, as well as attitudes linked to diglossic functional distributions of MSA and the dialects. The emphasis on correct grammar and eloquence raises expectations and inhibits spontaneous use of MSA by both students and instructors alike. It makes users pay more attention to form rather than content. In addition, using MSA in informal contexts is regarded by native Arab speakers as "unnatural" and pragmatically inappropriate.[14] Furthermore, a close examination of actual opportunities students have for listening, speaking, thinking, solving problems and interacting in MSA, when it is used as the medium of instruction is associated with "boring stuff." MSA is for doing grammatical exercises, speaking correctly, reading and memorizing texts on such subjects as religion, civic education and history. This partly explains why, although a considerable amount of time is allocated to learning MSA in GCC public education schools, social and affective constraints limit its practice and are not in line with findings in language learning studies that show that the more exposure to and varied use of a language, the better chance one has for becoming proficient in it.

The dominant prescriptive approach in language teaching focusing on correctness standards based on a language variety very few master has generally been counterproductive in Arabic literacy development. An alternative to this approach would be allowing the use of ESA especially in the early grades to minimize the distance between the spoken and the written varieties. While it is recognized only as a spoken variety, in reality, many written texts today are closer to ESA than MSA.[15] Furthermore, teaching methodologies used in teaching MSA are considered outdated as they are said to focus on rote learning and do not promote the critical thinking skills and inquiry methods needed in the twenty-first century. Traditional Arabic educational systems were even blamed for fomenting Islamist fundamentalism in the aftermath of the 9/11 events by Western powers.

Pragmatically, opportunities for using MSA even in its traditional domains of written communication have been reduced with the intrusion of global English as the lingua franca in a workplace dominated by expatriate workers from different linguistic backgrounds. Even written interpersonal interactions through social networking are predominantly in English as young Arabs find it "easier" to chat, message or use Facebook and Twitter in English, their dialect or "Arabizi" (a mixed code of Arabic and English written in a modified Latin alphabet that uses numbers for sounds specific to Arabic). In educational institutions, when Arabic is the medium of instruction teachers often resort to dialectal forms to explain the material being taught. Interpersonal interactions both inside and outside the classroom are in the dialect, thus further limiting exposure to MSA.

National identity versus pragmatism

The challenges discussed above are serious and have been the subject of many conferences and public discussions. The weak writing skills in MSA among young Gulf youths is well documented in many studies and news reports (Al-Issa and Dahan, 2011; Al Jazeera.net, 2012; Al-Kaff-Al-Hachemi and Underwood, 2013). These weaknesses are increasing among growing numbers of students and are particularly prevalent among higher socio-economic graduates who attend private universities.

While calls for using more Arabic in schools continue to rise from all stakeholders in practice, the percentage of national parents opting for private education continues to rise. Available statistics show that over half of UAE nationals, 57.4 percent (KHDA reports), enroll their children in private schools. In Kuwait it is around 50 percent according to recent news reports. Similar trends can be gleaned from news reports in other GCC countries. Students who graduate from public universities across the Gulf believe that they have been short-changed in their education because they did not have "enough English."[16] At the level of policy, more resources are devoted to the teaching of English at all levels. This discrepancy between the call for the protection of Arabic and actual practices is not unique to the GCC countries, however. Haeri's study of attitude differences toward MSA[17] found that men emphasized Arabic's significance

> in forging pan-Arab identity, in resisting colonial domination, and as a cultural and political weapon against more recent forms of foreign domination, [however] their actual use of Classical Arabic [MSA] forms did not match the overt importance they attached to this language.

She concluded that there is a "lack of match between what individuals assert to be the language that fits their cultural, political, and religious ideals, and their actual linguistic production" (Haeri, 2000: 69).

There are other factors that also cast doubts about the maintenance and development of MSA in the future. In his article "Language and identity in the Arabian Gulf," Holes (2011) notes the emergence of a "prestigious" Gulf Arabic variety across the region resulting from increased communication, increased literacy and globalization forces. This development suggests that the homogenization process in Gulf societies is actually strengthening the dialects and not MSA. Holes explains this phenomenon by stating that MSA:

> does not carry the type of prestige that matters in everyday interaction between ordinary Arabs, whatever their level of education. Prestige in this context comes from the status accorded to the dominant local variety of Arabic, so it comes as no surprise that it is the dialects of the large capital cities of the Arab world which carry this so-called "covert" prestige (as opposed to the "overt" prestige of Modern Standard Arabic).
>
> (138)

Holes gives examples of young Arabs who are reluctant and uneasy to use written Arabic because they do not feel competent in it. He reports on young students who say they "*never*" use MSA to communicate in writing. This inability or lack of desire to write in MSA among young Gulf youths in universities is a recognized phenomenon documented in many studies and reports and supported by personal experience in interactions with students throughout the years.[18]

Despite calls to promote literacy in MSA coming from all sectors of society, and despite the available financial resources being devoted by the GCC governments to "enrich" Arabic to become the language of knowledge production and transmission, the educational policies being implemented in the GCC have, in practice, downgraded Arabic in favor of English. Haeri (2000) describes this type of ambivalence toward Arabic which pervades the debates among intellectuals regarding identity issues in the post-colonial era by stating that:

> As anxieties about modernization, decolonization, independence, and political pluralism mounted in the course of this century, Classical Arabic came to stand, often simultaneously, as a language incapable of responding to the modern world, as the supreme vehicle for an indigenous and authentic modernity, as an essential ingredient of Arab identity regardless of religion, and as a language that insures a specifically Muslim identity. The non-classical varieties, likewise, came to be regarded as impediments to "progress" that needed to be overcome "exactly like poverty and disease" (N Mahfouz quoted in Dawwarah 1965:286). They also represent the "real self" (El-Messiri 1978), true symbols of local national culture, and transnationally divisive because unlike Classical Arabic, they differ from country to country.
>
> (Haeri, 2000: 63)

These apparent dilemmas can be understood as there are

> no more powerful means of "encouraging" individuals to assimilate to a dominant culture than having the economic, social and political returns stacked against their mother tongue. Such assimilation is not freely chosen if the choice is between one's mother tongue and one's future.
>
> (UNDP, 2004: 33)

However, achieving a balanced bilingual program that develops equal proficiency in both languages is feasible when language in education policies are based on realistic assessments of wider socio-political and global contexts surrounding the education enterprise. As Joshua Fishman (2012: x) in the preface to his book, *Do Not Leave Your Language Alone*, observes, "speech and writing communities the world over are not only expected to exert themselves on behalf of their own languages, but to feel remiss if they fail to do so when their language resources are threatened." A major means of such exertion can be through serious language planning efforts, which we turn to next.

Language planning

When nations decide to promote a linguistic variety for specific functions they resort to language planning (LP). Language planning refers to interventions at socio-political and linguistic levels regarding the corpus and functions of a language variety in a given state/nation (Ferguson, 2006). The socio-political involvement deals with the status of the language as the official language mainly in official discourse, government, business and education while the linguistic intervention focuses on standardizing the selected variety through interventions at all linguistic levels (grammar, lexicon, writing, spelling, etc.). In standardization, language academies and other linguistic bodies are generally entrusted with the mission to set the parameters for acceptable variations and changes to be allowed in a standard language. This canonization is usually achieved through dictionaries and grammatical treaties. Setting these standards, however, is not always without controversy and is the subject of debates between those who believe in preserving the purity and authenticity of the language and those who see language as a living organism which must adapt to changing environments by being more open to external influences. These two perspectives are widespread throughout the world's linguistic communities but once a variety is adopted as the Standard, education is one of the important institutions entrusted with implementing the state's language policy and teaching the Standard. In the Arabic context, school is the main if not the *only* institution responsible for the development of MSA proficiency among Arabic speakers.

Standardization and corpus planning in the Arab world have been the purview of Arabic language academies. Qahtani (2002) provides a historical overview of the five academies that have successively been set up across the Arab world: Damascus, 1919; Cairo, 1932, Baghdad, 1947; Rabat, 1964; and Amman, 1976 to oversee what is generally referred to as Arabization. Their mission is to preserve and protect the Arabic language and make it the common language of all Arabs. One of the major goals of the academies is to reduce the influence of the colloquial varieties and stop foreign borrowings into MSA. Arabization encompasses both the status and corpus dimensions of language planning. Its major objective is to enable MSA to become the official language by intervening linguistically to expand the Arabic lexicon using lexical derivational processes and defining standards of correctness at all linguistic levels (phonology, morphology and syntax). Throughout their years of existence, the academies have produced volumes of new terminology, particularly in the sciences but their efforts have not succeeded in stemming the influx of foreign lexical items into Arabic, nor have they been able to maintain a clear separation between the dialects and MSA. Even though MSA remains dominant in formal writings, language users resort to literal translations of English lexemes to fill lexical gaps, sometimes yielding funny sounding and opaque combinations in Arabic.[19] In addition, the academies' attempts to replace borrowed words from English (or other foreign languages), such as telephone, computer, feedback and brainstorming, regularly used by Arabs, with unfamiliar derived words, ignore the natural tendency of all languages to evolve through contact and integration of loan words. Overall, the academies' output has generally been judged as less than satisfactory and, despite their efforts, they have not succeeded in developing tools to stop outside influences nor have they made Arabs stop using Arabized terminology, borrowed lexical items and dialectal phonologies.[20] At the grammatical level, Arabs' formal interactions generally adopt the simplified inflections of ESA in communicative contexts where MSA is usually expected. The overly prescriptivist approach of the academies and the lack of coordination among them have been unable to check the unplanned and sometimes chaotic lexical innovations across the Arab world that increase the risk of dividing the MSA landscape further into increasingly differentiated regional varieties.[21]

In addition, historically, languages have survived and evolved when they were used as instruments for knowledge production in a multiplicity of disciplines. To reach this objective, translation of books from the more advanced civilizations is more effective in filling possible knowledge gaps rather than importing that knowledge in its original language. In the Arab world, translations of scientific and technological books are scarce compared to translations from English into other languages. For example, the 2003 UNDP report states that the entire Arab world translates less than 20 percent of the amount of translated works into Greek or Spanish every year (Zakhir, 2008). To remedy this state of affairs, the Gulf region has established centers and encourages projects on translation such as the Abu Dhabi "Kalima" project, the translation research institute at NYU Abu Dhabi in the UAE and the Translation and Interpreting Institute in Qatar (Lindsey, 2013).

Arab states' political and socio-economic realities may be considered an added obstacle to standardization and planning. Political rivalries among Arab states make it more difficult to recapture Arab peoples' "imagined community of Arabness" with the one Arabic language being its major force. In addition, there is no agreement between those who believe that only MSA is the "real" Arabic, those who argue that Arabic needs to be receptive to change while maintaining its standards and those who promote dialects and downplay the importance of MSA (Fassi-Fehri, 2013). This lack of consensus hampers efforts towards code selection and codification of one standard variety.

Language reforms and the wider socio-political context

One of the priorities of Arabization in post-independence language-in-education policies in the newly independent Arab states had to do with replacing the colonial language with Arabic but it faced several challenges in education. These included the translation and production of appropriate textbooks in MSA, the development of modern and culturally relevant curricula, and the availability of teachers who are proficient in MSA and trained in modern teaching methodologies. In the Arabian Gulf region, however, public educational systems did not inherit a colonial school system (see Chapter 4) but they imported existing educational traditions from other Arab states, such as Egypt, Lebanon, Syria and Jordan. At the beginning, GCC educational systems adopted Arabic as their medium of instruction and imported curriculum and teaching staff from other Arab countries. By the end of the twentieth century, the fast-paced integration of the GCC economies and societies into the global market and massive influx of expatriates to staff all sectors of the economy led to a greater need for English as the language of communication. Important changes in education policies were initiated and Arabic was replaced by English as a medium of instruction in science, mathematics and technical subjects in public education. The opening the GCC educational space to private institutions reinforced the dominance of English (see Chapters 4 and 5).

The above discussion demonstrates that weakened position of Arabic in education was not only the result of globalization pressures but also the status of Arabic as an instrument of knowledge transmission because most current scientific and technological knowledge wasn't available in it.

Alternative approaches: considering context in bilingual education policies

Cummins (2000) observes that in order to understand the conditions that lead to successful bilingual education, research and policy need to examine not only linguistic and psychological factors but also the important socio-political environments surrounding the school. In his discussion of the US context and the under-achievements of "social groups that have experienced long-term devaluation of their identities in the broader society," Cummins (2000: 34) points to the "need to shift to a sociological and sociopolitical orientation" to understand and find effective solutions to the problems facing education. While the context discussed by Cummins is different from the GCC countries in many respects, a number of parallels can be drawn. Both sets of students (minorities in the US and Arab students in the GCC) face a devaluation of their linguistic and cultural identities in both the school and social environments. As Cummins argued, "students' identities are affirmed and academic achievement promoted when teachers express respect for the language and cultural knowledge that students bring to the classroom" (2000: 34). In the GCC educational systems, despite the significant number of hours where students are exposed to Arabic, either as a subject or medium of instruction, academic proficiency in Arabic receives less quality attention compared to efforts poured onto English. Arabic teachers have less access to material resources or support, no IT facilities or professional development and training. Even the recent reinstatement of Arabic as a language of instruction in some of the public universities is limited to some of the "less valued disciplines" in the labor market. While this is a step in the right direction, it does not address the fundamental issue of its market value that led to its marginalization in the first place. Language in education policies must encompass the whole educational system, from kindergarten to university, and must address the important socio-pragmatic and pedagogical aspects tied to Arabic discussed above.

Another assumption that needs to be reviewed is the belief that because students speak a dialect of Arabic, then MSA can be considered their first language.[22] As the discussion earlier demonstrated, there are important differences between the dialect the child used at home and MSA to be used for literacy in school. These differences are at all levels of language. For a literacy pedagogy to succeed it needs to start with the premise that Arab children come to school unfamiliar with MSA and that they need strategies to help them transition from their dialect to the Standard as the research cited above has demonstrated. This entails radical changes in Arabic teaching methodologies and teacher training. For example, Younes (2014), in discussing teaching Arabic to non-native speakers, proposes an integrated approach that introduces students of Arabic as a foreign language to both MSA and dialectal Arabic simultaneously. While this is an active ongoing debate about how to prepare learners of Arabic in the United States to function appropriately in an Arabic-speaking context, it may be worthwhile to consider such an approach even in the Arab context.

The need to recognize the relation between MSA and the dialects is imperative in the GCC since a significant number of children do not even have enough exposure to their Gulf Arabic dialect as their caregivers (nannies and sometimes foreign mothers) are from outside the GCC and are not fluent speakers of Gulf Arabic. For these children, the gap between the home and school language is even wider but it is not recognized as such (Al-Kaff-Al-Hashemi and Underwood, 2013; Al Sumaiti, 2012; Scheele *et al.*, 2010). Furthermore, research shows that even when possessing conversational competence in a language, this does not automatically translate into academic language competence. To become a proficient user of academic language, young learners need focused attention and practice in the literate register (Cummins, 2000; Riches and Genesee, 2006; Garcia, 2009). Various studies from different linguistic contexts reveal that it takes between five and nine years of schooling to develop academic proficiency. Another finding from bilingual acquisition studies is that second language learning builds on and benefits from an acquired threshold level of academic skills in the first language (Cummins, 2000). When Arabic literacy is made a priority in the early years of schooling, learners are better equipped with transferable skills for the acquisition of academic proficiency in a second language.

The introduction of English earlier in the curriculum is based on the popular belief that in second language acquisition, "younger is better." While the age variable has been widely discussed in the literature, its impact seems to be interrelated with a host of linguistic, psychological, social and environmental factors that are outside the scope of this chapter (see for example, Singleton, 2001; Swain and Lapkin, 2005). The research findings suggest that developing high academic proficiency in a second language can be achieved at any age provided that the other conditions are favorable to it. Furthermore, research also shows that academic skills acquired through the first language facilitate the acquisition of those skills in the second. For example, data analysis of several studies reported by Cummins supports Beykont's findings that:

> the rapidity with which bilingual students approached grade norms in English reading by Grade 6 was strongly related to their level of Spanish reading at Grade 3. The better developed their Spanish reading was at Grade 3, the more rapid progress they made in English reading between Grades 3 and 6.
>
> (Reported in Cummins, 2000: 35)

It would therefore be more beneficial for young learners to first develop a certain level of proficiency in MSA before they are exposed to the second language. Even more alarming, the push for introducing English earlier and spending more time on it in class has generally not produced the academic proficiency levels in English expected among high school graduates either.[23] Test scores on various standardized English reveal that a very small percentage of the graduates have the requisite skills in English for university studies tests (see Chapter 5).

Conclusions: where do we go from here?

Although the reforms adopted by Gulf states expanding the use of English throughout their educational systems may not have intended to devalue knowledge of Arabic and in Arabic, nonetheless, they are "embedded within larger social management systems that buttress fundamental assumptions about the source and the substance of legitimate knowledge, and are thus closely tied to a more overarching politics of knowledge" (Leeman and Martinez, 2007: 36–37). It is a fact that pressures on Arabic from English are similar to those being exerted on most other languages under globalization (Probyn, 2005). English has become the de facto world language of science, technology and business. Arabs, like others, need to master English to become active participants in knowledge production of the twenty-first century. The worry is when English displaces the national language in the educational system, as is the case in many of the Gulf states. Today, Arabic tends to be associated with past greatness of a culture that has lost prominence in contemporary knowledge production even among Arabs themselves. The adoption of English in higher education has reinforced the perceived link of Arabic to the past and old traditions and English to the future and knowledge societies. Moreover, various UNDP and other IGOs' reports highlighting the "inadequacies" of Arabic education in the last decades have reinforced perceptions that link Arabic to outdated and unsuccessful teaching methodologies that are used to justify the marginalization of Arabic in education at all levels.

In the socio-political, attitudinal, pedagogical and linguistic context discussed in this chapter, the revolving revolutions characterizing GCC educational reforms tend to search for quick fixes to complex linguistic realities. The different policies that have been put in place show a lack of long-term planning and their reversals are based on short-term assessments. In addition, the top-down approach in the decision-making process where decisions are decreed based on political considerations, is not likely to yield educational outcomes that serve long-term national visions to make Arabic the language of the future.

The major challenge to Arabic in the GCC does not have to be the use of English in education as long as it is not the only valued language. For Arabic to find its place in knowledge construction, it must be used in university for research in twenty-first-century fields. One way to help change perceptions toward Arabic immediately among faculty and students is to allocate significant funding for research using Arabic as its medium of communication and transmission; another is to keep Arabic language programs in the mainstream of university curriculum rather than as a sideshow. Finally, Arabic instructors should be given the same rights and obligations as other faculty members in the same university.

On a macro level, there are many resources devoted to the protection of Arabic across the GCC and the Arab world which could achieve better results if they were unified to avoid duplication as well as competition as to which center outdoes the other. There are many academies, associations and conferences all working toward the protection and promotion of MSA. The multiplicity of these efforts shows that there is awareness about the problem. However, they appear to be counterproductive rather than leading to workable solutions. A single academy with representatives from all regional dialects may lead to more unified approaches to solving problems associated with variety selection for literacy development in Arabic. Some of its urgent tasks may be to codify the language based on current usage rather than a prescriptive approach. All linguistic means, including derivation, borrowing, innovation, extensions, are legitimate ways to come up with a language variety that could be used in textbooks across the Arab world. To speed up the development of Arabic, available knowledge must be translated from foreign languages into Arabic and a clear dissemination road map across the Arab world, or at least the major regional groupings, should be developed. Only the use of Arabic as the main language of education can change today's reality. Today, MSA is one of the few remaining components of Arab identity across the 22 Arab states and its relevance as a language of knowledge production is threatened. Language planners need to exert themselves to find effective ways to empower MSA (or its descendent ESA) as a valued language in academic and professional discourse.

Notes

1 BBC Arabic (December 18, 2014). Talking points program. Guests and participants discussed the decline of Arabic and speculated on reasons behind the decline and possible recommendations.
2 Personal communication with science and math teachers in a MAG school in Dubai, Fall 2011.
3 See Chapter 4 for the discussion on the recent changes in policies about Arabic as a medium of instruction in non hard sciences at Qatar University. Private universities, however, continue to teach all disciplines in English.
4 Larry Wilson, ZU provost, June 2013.
5 However, the change created other problems with expatriate faculty who had been hired to teach in English.
6 A good illustration of this are speeches by leaders such as Jamal Abdel Nasser of Egypt or King Hassan II of Morocco. Starting with MSA and switching and or mixing the dialectal variety communicated better with the people both in terms of linguistic comprehension as well affective connectedness.
7 In Arabic there is only one term, "fuSHa," to refer to both CA and MSA. To distinguish between the two, the adjective "mu'aSera" (contemporary) is sometimes used.
8 A notable exception to this trend was Syria where Arabic remained the language of instruction in university in all fields. Also, traditional universities such as Al Azhar in Egypt or Al Qaraouine in Morocco continued to use Arabic as a medium of instruction.
9 This state of affairs can be generalized across the Arab world.
10 An Abu Dhabi newspaper in English.

11 Spoken dialects form regional groupings on a continuum from East to West where the two ends of the continuum are the most distant and may be mutually unintelligible. So, based on linguistic considerations alone, Arabic varieties at the end of this continuum could be considered separate languages synchronically.

12 For the discussion of the impact of diglossia on literacy development in Arabic, see Maamouri (1998); Abu-Rabia (2000); Saiegh-Haddad (2003); Khamis-Dakwar *et al.* (2011).

13 Inflected languages use case markings to express grammatical functions at the level of the word. For example, English is no longer a heavily inflected language except in its pronouns where the distinction between subject pronouns such as "he," the object pronoun "him" and the possessive pronoun "his" is maintained. In MSA, most content nouns are marked for their grammatical function in the sentence (subject, object, genitive, etc.)

14 When foreigners learn MSA in school and try to interact in it with native speakers, they are immediately judged as unaware of the rules of use. Similar comments are often made about some North Africans who resort to MSA to interact with Arabs from the East in informal contexts because the latter say that they don't understand them. They are said to "speak funny, because they use grammatical Arabic" (Nahawi).

15 ESA seems to be the post-modern evolution of Modern Standard Arabic. A rich corpus collected from newspapers and satellite TV stations such as Al Jazeera and Al Arabiya can serve as the basis for standardization in today's corpus linguistic approaches.

16 This is constant complaint from students I teach in an MATESOL program. Although they admit to low proficiency in Arabic as well, they don't seem to mind it as much.

17 The distinction between Classical Arabic and MSA is not relevant to the present discussion and these two terms can be used interchangeably. Classical Arabic refers to the language of the Quran and it is the variety that has evolved into Modern Standard Arabic used today in formal contexts.

18 My students have conducted several surveys of students over the last eight years looking at biliteracy in English and Arabic and the results consistently reveal that students recognize that they have very low literacy skills in MSA.

19 For example, the English compound words "brainstorming" and "feedback" are literally translated as "al 'asf addihni" and "taghdia muakisa," using compounding which is an unproductive morphological process in Arabic, rather than coining new words by employing the very productive root pattern derivation process of Semitic languages.

20 Eastman in Al Qahtani (2012).

21 When one compares Media Arabic in North Africa, to that used in the Levant or Gulf regions, one can identify differences in semantic extensions are applied. North Africans tend to map their concepts onto French semantic fields while in the Middle East, English serves as a base.

22 This is of course not always the case. It is not always the case that Arab children speak any dialect as their native language. Very often parents insist on preparing their children to enter kindergarten in English and therefore expose them to it from the start. Also many children are raised by foreign nannies who speak Pidgin Arabic and some English. See Badry (2015) for a discussion of this issue.

23 Personal communication with ZU Provost, Dr. Larry Wilson, June 20, 2013.

References

Abdel-Jawad, H. and Abu Radwan, A.S. (2011). The status of English in institutions of higher education in Oman: Sultan Qaboos university as a model. In Al-Issa, A. and Dahan, L.S. (eds.). *Global English and Arabic*. Bern: Peter Lang, 123–151.

Abu-Rabia, S. (2000). Effects of exposure to literary Arabic on reading comprehension in a diglossic situation. *Reading and Writing: An Interdisciplinary Journal*, 13: 147–157.

Ahmed, A. (2012). Abu Dhabi parents: "Teach our children in Arabic." *The National* online, October 14. Available at: www.thenational.ae/news/uae-news/education/abu-dhabi-parents-teach-our-children-in-arabic#ixzz3LJFBFJ3f.

Ahmad, F., Omar, O. and Muhamad, M. (2007). Meeting the challenges of global economy in vocational education and training. In Farrell, L. and Fenwick, T. (eds.). *Educating the Global Workforce: Knowledge, Knowledge Work and Knowledge Workers.* London: Routledge, 102–114.

Al Baik, D. (2008). It is not acceptable to drop Arabic language from our lives. *Gulfnews*, March 16.

Al-Issa, A. and Dahan, L. (eds.) (2011). *Global English and Arabic*. Bern: Peter Lang.

Al Jazeera TV (2009). Television broadcast in Arabic: ma wara'a al khabar "Behind the news." April 18. Discussion with Dr. Salem Sari and Dr. Jasem Sultan.

Al Jazeera.net. (2012). التعريب بين الحاجة وحفظ الهوية. مؤتمر بقطر يدعو للنهوض بالعربية. Retrieved from http://www.aljazeera.net/news/pages/9de63a07-4d66-4c8a-8263-16af 7036529d (accessed June 30, 2015).

Al-Jundi, F.Y. (2013, June 12). لغتنا العربية. لغة العلوم والتقني فداء ياسر الجندي. Retrieved from http://www.aljazeera.net/news/pages/284a275f-9682-4362-8e4a-a85a299dfcd9 (accessed May 12, 2014).

Al-Kaff-Al-Hashemi, B. and Underwood, M. (2013). Challenges of learning Arabic in the UAE – even for Emiratis. *The National* online. Available at: www.thenational.ae/uae/education/challenges-of-learning-arabic-in-the-uae-even-for-emiratis#ixzz2r1TPcwOK TRACT.

Al Lawati, A. and Al Najami, S. (2008). In depth: Sorry, I don't speak Arabic. *Gulf News*, March 20.

Al Najami, S. (2007). Bilingual education hangs in the balance for schools. *Gulf News*, October 18.

Al Shamrani, H. (2012). Diglossia in Arabic TV stations. *Journal of King Saud University – Languages and Translation*, 24: 57–69.

Al Sumaiti, R. (2012). Parental involvement in the education of their children in Dubai. Dubai School of Government. Policy Brief #30.

Badawi, E.S. (1973). *Mustawayat al-A'rabiya al-mu'asira fi Misr* [Levels of Contemporary Arabic in Egypt]. Cairo: Dar Al-Ma'arif.

Badry, F. (2011). Appropriating English: Languages in identity construction in the United Arab Emirates. In Al-Issa, A. and Dahan, L.S. (eds.). *Global English and Arabic*. Bern: Peter Lang, 81–122.

Badry, F. (2012). Education in the UAE: Local identity and global development. In *Essentials of School Education in the UAE*. Abu Dhabi: ECSSR Publications, 85–106.

Badry, F. (2015). UAE bilingual education: Searching for an elusive balance. In Mehisto, P. and Genesee, F. (eds.). *Building Bilingual Education Systems: Forces, Mechanisms and Counterweights*. Cambridge: Cambridge University Press, 197–214.

Baetens-Beardsmore, H. (1998). Language shift and cultural implications in Singapore. In Gopinathan, S., Kam, H.W., Pakir, A. and Saravanan, V. (eds.). *Language, Education and Society in Singapore: Issues and Trends*. Singapore: Times Academic Press, 85–98.

Bilingual education crucial for the UAE (2013). *The National*. Available at: www. thenational.ae/thenationalconversation/editorial/bilingual-education-crucial-for-the-uae#ixzz2NJSfaxAc.

Bruthiaux, P. (2003). Contexts and trends for English as a global language. In Humphrey,

T. (ed.). *Language in the Twenty-First Century*. Selected Papers of the Millennial Conferences of the Center for Research and Documentation on World Language Problems, held at the University of Hartford and Yale University, 9–23. Available at: http://site. ebrary.com/lib/aus/docDetail.action?docID=10041620 &page=15 (accessed March 14, 2009).

Choi, P.K. (2010). Weep for Chinese universities: A case study of English hegemony and academic capitalism in higher education in Hong Kong. *Journal of Education Policy*, 25(2): 233–252.

Cummins, J. (2000). *Language, Power and Pedagogy: Bilingual Children in the Crossfire*. Clevedon: Multilingual Matters.

Drummond, J. (2010, June 28). Bilingual classes at heart of shake-up. FT.com, June 28. Available at: www.ft.com/cms/s/0/c3d168da-82c8-11df-b7ad-00144feabdc0.html.

English vs Arabic: Qatar University decision continues to stir controversy (2012). *Doha News*, January 29. Available at: http://dohanews.co/post/16690774138/english-vs-arabic-qatar-university-decision-continues#ixzz2XIi7gkb8 (accessed June 1. 2015).

Farrell, L. and Fenwick, T. (2007). Educating a global workforce. In Lesley, F. and Tara, F. (eds.). *Educating the Global Workforce: Knowledge, Knowledge Work and Knowledge Workers*. London: Routlege, 13–26.

Fassi-Fehri, A. (2013). *Language Policy in Arab Countries* (in Arabic). Beirut: Dar Al-Kitab Al-Jadida Al Muttahida.

السياسة اللغوية في البلاد العربية. عبد القادر الفاسي الفهري

.دار الكتاب الجديدة المتحدة أيلول/سبتمبر

Feng, A. (ed.) (2007). *Bilingual Education in China: Practices, Policies and Concepts*. Clevedon: Multilingual Matters.

Ferguson, C.A. (1959). The Arabic koine. *Language*, 616–630.

Ferguson, G. (2006). *Language Planning and Education*. Edinburgh: Edinburgh University Press.

Findlow, S. (2006). Higher education and linguistic dualism in the Arab Gulf. *British Journal of Sociology of Education*, 27(1): 19–36.

Fishman, J. (2012). *Do Not Leave Your Language Alone: The Hidden Status Agendas within Corpus Planning in Language Policy*. London: Routledge.

Garcia, O. (2009). *Bilingual Education in the 21st Century: A Global Perspective*. Chichester: Wiley-Blackwell.

Giri, R.A. (2007). The power and price of English: Educating Nepalese people for the global workforce. In Lesley, F. and Tara, F. (eds.). *Educating the Global Workforce: Knowledge, Knowledge Work and Knowledge Workers*. London: Routledge, 211–224.

Grin, F. and Korth, B. (2005). On the reciprocal influence of language politics and language education: The case of English in Switzerland. *Language Policy*, 4(1): 67–85.

Haeri, N. (1997). Symbolic capital: Language, state, and class in Egypt. *Current Anthropology*, 38(5): 795–816.

Haeri, N. (2000). Form and ideology: Arabic sociolinguistics and beyond. *Annual Review of Anthropology*, 29: 61–87.

Holes, C.D. (2011). Language and identity in the Arabian Gulf. *Journal of Arabian Studies: Arabia, the Gulf, and the Red Sea*, 1(2): 129–145.

Hopkyns, S. (2014). The effects of global English on culture and identity in the UAE: A double-edged sword. *Learning and Teaching in Higher Education: Gulf Perspectives*, 11(2). Available at: http://lthe.zu.ac.ae.

Ibrahim, R. (2011). Literacy problems in Arabic: Sensitivity to diglossia in tasks involving working memory. *Journal of Neurolinguistics*, 24: 571–582.

Khamis-Dakwar, R. (2007). *The Development of Diglossic Morphosyntax in Palestinian Arabic-Speaking Children*. New York: Columbia University.

Khamis-Dakwar, R., Froud, K. and Gordon, P. (2011). Acquiring diglossia: Mutual influences of formal and colloquial Arabic on children's grammaticality judgments. *Child Language*, 1–29.

Leeman, G. and Martinez, J. (2007). From identity to commodity: Ideologies of Spanish in heritage language textbooks. *Critical Inquiry in Language Studies*, 4(1): 35–65.

Lewis, K. (2010). Bilingual education for pupils aged 4. *The National*, June 21.

Lindsey, U. (2013). A potential renaissance for Arabic translation. Available at: www.al-fanar.org/2013/06/a-new-dawn-for-arabic-translation/.

Maamouri, M. (1998). Language education and human development: Arabic diglossia and its impact on the quality of education in the Arab region. Discussion paper prepared for The World Bank, The Mediterranean Development Forum.

Meiseles, G. (1980). Educated spoken Arabic and the Arabic language continuum. *Archivum linguisticum*, n.s. 11.

Mitchell, T.F. (1986). What is educated spoken Arabic? *International Journal of the Sociology of Language*, 61(1): 7–32.

Probyn, M. (2005). Language and the struggle to learn: The intersection of classroom realities, language policy, and neocolonial and globalization discourses in South African schools. In Lin, A.M.Y. (ed.). *Decolonisation, Globalisation: Language-in-Education Policy and Practice*. Clevedon: Multilingual Matters Limited, 153–172.

Qaḥṭānī, S. H. (2002). Al-Taʿrīb wa-naẓariyat al-takhṭīṭ al-lughawī: dirāsah tatbīīqīyah ʿan taʿrīb al-musṭalaḥāt fī al-Saʿūdīyah. Beirut: Markaz Dirasat al-Wahdah al-Arabiyah
التعريب بين الحاجة وحفظ الهوية. مؤتمر بقطر يدعو للنهوض بالعربية.

Riches, C. and Genesee, F. (2006). Cross-linguistic and cross-modal aspects of literacy development. In Genesee, F., Lindholm-Leary, K., Saunders, W.M. and Christian, D. (eds.). *Educating English Language Learners: A Synthesis of Research Evidence*. New York: Cambridge University Press, 64–108.

Saiegh-Haddad, E. (2003). Linguistic distance and initial reading acquisition: The case of Arabic diglossia. *Applied Psycholinguistics*: 115–135.

Salem, O. (2014). Law planned to preserve Arabic language in the UAE. *The National*, November 25. Available at: www.thenational.ae/uae/law-planned-to-preserve-arabic-language-in-the-uaewww.thenational.ae/uae/law-planned-to-preserve-arabic-language-in-the-uae.

Scheele, A.F., Leseman, P.P.M. and Mayo, A.Y. (2010). The home language environment of monolingual and bilingual children and their language proficiency. *Applied Psycholinguistics*, 31: 117–140.

Singleton, D. (2001). Age and second language acquisition. *Annual Review of Applied Linguistics*, 21: 77–89.

Strubell, M. (1996). Language planning and bilingual education in California. *Journal of Multilingual and Multicultural Development*, 17(2): 262–275.

Swain, M. and Lapkin, S. (2005). The evolving sociopolitical context of immersion education in Canada: Some implications for program development. *International Journal of Applied Linguistics*, 15(2): 169–186.

Swan, M. (2013). Sheikh Nahyan led push to education for all. *The National*, March 14. Available at: www.thenational.ae/news/uae-news/education/sheikh-nahyan-led-push-to-education-for-all#ixzz2PnTxBazm.

Tankersley, D. (2001). Bombs or bilingual programmes? Dual-language immersion, transformative education, and community building in Macedonia. *International Journal of Bilingual Education and Bilingualism*, 4(2): 107–124.

UNDP (United Nations Development Programme) (2004). Cultural liberty in today's diverse world. New York: UNDP.

Wannaqat, U. (2007). Learning through L2-Content and Language Integrated Learning (CLIL) and English as a Medium of Instruction (EMI). *The International Journal of Bilingual Education and Bilingualism*, 10(5): 663–682.

Younes, M. (2014). *The Integrated Approach to Arabic Instruction.* London: Routledge.

Zacharias, A. (2012). Enticing expats to learn Arabic is key to charter's success. *The National*, April 8. Available at: www.thenational.ae/news/uae-news/enticing-expats-to-learn-arabic-is-key-to-charters-success#ixzz2NJkHYKCk.

Zakhir, M. (2008). The history of translation. Available at: www.translationdirectory.com/articles/article1695.php.

9 Higher education revolutions
Short-term success versus long-term viability?

The preceding chapters have shown how, in a relatively short period of time, GCC governments were able to build a national system of public higher education alongside a variety of private institutions that have made higher education more accessible to those seeking it. This accessibility has been particularly beneficial to women who now can study at home compared to the past when few parents allowed their daughters to pursue higher education abroad. In addition, the children of expatriate workers, both males and females, who have grown up in the GCC no longer have to leave the region in order to receive a college degree.

In addition to accessibility, the introduction of private universities has also forced public universities to become more accountable and has led to reforms in their curricula, delivery methods, admission requirements and administration. The competition resulting from these changes has also introduced quality assurance measures and processes throughout the educational landscape. A less impressive change resulting from the educational revolution has been in the area of research production although the recent emphasis on developing research centers and the establishment of think-tanks is creating open spaces that are supposed to encourage critical discussions and participation in global research networks.

At the same time, these revolutionary educational reforms are not without controversy. Their embrace of the new predominantly utilitarian mission of the university is problematic for a coherent evolution of Gulf societies based on their present realities and their own visions for the future. The revolutions which have swept the GCC higher education raise two key questions:

1 Can the type of educational reforms adopted in the GCC accomplish the overarching goals of modernizing and joining the global world while maintaining and preserving cultural and linguistic identities of the GCC societies?
2 Can changes at the level of higher education work in isolation from transformative changes at other educational and socio-political levels?

We have attempted to show in this book that the high expectations placed on education to revolutionize GCC societies are not likely to be realized, if other

DOI: 10.4324/9780203796139-9

policies and practices outside the higher educational system do not support the desired changes. While education is a major means for development, it must be supported by changes at other levels of social, economic, and political structures and processes. If it is to succeed, it must provide citizens with fair "opportunities for education, employment, civic participation, and social and cultural fulfill-ment as human beings, in the context of a fair distribution of the society's resources among all its citizenry" (Boulding and Parker, 2005: 179).

This chapter assesses the degree of alignment of educational practices at the level of their content, delivery and administration with GCC nations' constitu-tions and their declared early twenty-first century visions. In our analysis, we rely on data from published official declarations and documents as well as mission statements, goals and curricular trends of major universities in the region. These sources are complemented with interviews of university execu-tives when possible. Our analysis is based on the findings described in the previous chapters of this book and draws on our personal experiences as aca-demics and administrators in UAE higher education.

National visions and the role of educational reforms

The five GCC countries (Bahrain, Kuwait, Oman, Qatar and the UAE) focused in this book, not only share a common past but they also have a common vision for their future. A reading of the GCC constitutions and the various visions pro-mulgated in the last two decades shows that they share important aspirations. All five nations aspire to become knowledge societies, attain great economic devel-opment and become leaders rather than followers in the globalized world. In their constitutions, they also affirm their belonging to the Arab nation and declare Arabic as their official language. The early articles of the constitutions of the five GCC countries all make it clear that the modern states are part of the Arab nation, linked to its history and cultural heritage through language and reli-gion. This commitment to the Arab identity is also confirmed in strategic devel-opments that are outlined in visions and goals for the next decades. For example, Sheikh Mohammad, the ruler of Dubai, prime minister of the UAE and one of the leading actors in Dubai's fast-paced development, stated in his book, *My Vision: Challenges in the Race for Excellence* (Al Maktoum, 2006) that in order for the UAE to join the developed world, it needs to acclimate itself to the rapid changing reality of the world, embrace change and transform its thinking from the past to the future to become a leading nation in the twenty-first century. He also stressed that the UAE must preserve its identity as a member of the Arab nation[1] and be guided by its core values, convictions and principles derived from belonging to the Arab civilization. The important role given to Arabic as the national language is also reaffirmed in the UAE vision for 2021 which asserts that "Arabic will re-emerge as a dynamic and vibrant language, expressed every-where in speech and writing as a living symbol of the nation's progressive Arab-Islamic values" (Cabinet releases, 2010; Youssef, 2010). Projecting into 2021, which will mark the nation's jubilee, the vision identifies several goals. The following are some of the themes relevant to this study as articulated by the UAE government in its vision 2021:

> 1.4 Vibrant culture: The UAE's distinct culture will remain founded on progressive and moderate Islamic values and endowed with a rich Arabic language, to proudly celebrate Emirati traditions and heritage while reinforcing national identity.
>
> 2.2 We want the nation to draw strength from its traditions of openness, peaceful coexistence and understanding. In this way Emiratis will always resist the value-flattening effects of globalisation, and will always be enriched rather than threatened by their nation's openness to the world.
>
> 3.1 The UAE will harness the full potential of its National human capital by maximising the participation of Emiratis, encouraging entrepreneurship, and nurturing home-grown public and private sector leaders while attracting and retaining the best talent.
>
> (Cabinet releases, 2010)

The same aspirations and challenges are identified by all GCC countries in their visions. They all recognize human and social development as prerequisites for economic development. The Qatar National Vision (QNV2030) promulgated in 2008, for example, states that, "Despite rapid economic and social gains, as well as political change, Qatar has maintained its cultural and traditional values as an Arab and Islamic nation that considers the family to be the main pillar of society." It recognizes that one of the major challenges to achieve its long-term goals is to modernize while preserving its traditions under globalization pressures (Qatar National Vision, 2030). The Kuwaiti 2031 vision states as one of its aims: "Providing [a] climate for balanced human development, safeguarding social values and national identity, preserving the community's values and its Arab and Islamic identity."[2] Similarly, the Bahraini vision 2030 (also decreed in 2008) focuses on economic development, and stresses "The Kingdom of Bahrain's interaction with the human civilization and its Arab belonging to satisfy the requirements of continuous development that conforms with the international standards, as stated in the Kingdom's constitution" (Kingdom of Bahrain).[3] Oman's 2020 vision focuses on diversification of the Omani economy which can be achieved by promoting:

> a Higher Education system that: a) keeps pace with developments and changes in today's world; b) meets the requirements of sustainable development in the Knowledge Era, while preserving the cultural identity of Omani society; and, c) contributes to the progress and development of humankind.
>
> (Ministry of Higher Education-Oman)

To achieve these stated visions, education is expected to be both the engine of the desired transformations and the keeper of traditional values and Arab culture.

This has led all GCC countries to implement a series of educational reforms which are discussed in the next sections.

Educational reforms

Both in terms of their goals and the means used to implement them, educational reforms adopted throughout the GCC are strikingly similar in both their underlying assumptions and implementations. They share the following underlying assumptions:

1   improving education quality can be achieved through the transplantation of the Western university model;
2   adopting English as the medium of instruction is the most efficient shortcut;
3   presuming that educational reforms do not negatively affect the Arab-Islamic identity of the region;
4   achieving economic development and nationalization of the labor force through education can be isolated from other important policies that govern employment and social practices.

These assumed transformative powers of education are consistent with those discussed in various international governmental organizations and reiterated by successive Arab Human Development Reports (UNDP, 2002, 2004, 2005). Higher education reform is envisaged to play the key role in transforming GCC societies both economically and socially. It is expected that tribal affiliations will become less important; a greater number of more empowered women will enter the labor market; and the countries' reliance on professional expatriate labor will be reduced. It is also assumed that all these fundamental shifts in social and economic practices will occur while preserving and strengthening Arab and Muslim heritage, culture and traditions and protecting the Arabic language in the face of English dominance.

Improving education quality by transplanting the Western university model

As discussed in Chapter 3, the transplantation of the Western university model is part of the globalization of education all over the world. This trend, which has been accelerated by the globalization of the economy and, more particularly, by the generalization of information technologies, has facilitated global interconnectedness and encouraged the homogenization of higher education. Institutions in the periphery tend to adopt Western curricula, Western produced textbooks and materials, and patterns of organization and standardization (Spring, 2009). There is also homogeneity in the way these institutions submit themselves to American and British systems of accreditation agencies to improve their institutions' and programs' rankings on the global stage. However, transplanted models are also affected by local forces and are born out of political decisions decreed by local governments that impose their own specific regulations. Naturally, governmental interventions shape the actual functioning of the imported institutions and as such cannot lead to mirror images of the Western institutions which they copy. Local influences have manifested themselves in governance issues, adjusting to students' competencies, teaching conditions and encouragement of research across the GCC.

In addition to the transplantation of the Western university structure and curriculum which are widespread worldwide, Westernization in GCC higher education has gone further by relying on Western faculty and administrators to implement and lead their reforms. This dependence on Westerners started with private universities and spread to public institutions at all levels. For example, most reforms of the primary and secondary educational system were developed and supervised by external partnerships and Western consultants. At the university level, Arab top executives were replaced by Western administrators in many public universities especially in the UAE, and the reforms to revamp educational programs in most GCC countries were also led by Western experts and organizations (Mills, 2008a).

There are many assumptions that can explain governments' decisions to rely on Western experts to reform education. It is believed that importing Western curricula is the most expedient way to respond to globalization's fast-paced need for wide-ranging economic transformations. Policy-makers consider that they are in a race against time to join the globalized world and that the fastest way to reach development is to import the knowledge and expertise available in the developed West. According to a higher education adviser in the UAE,[4] given the priority of professional education and the constraints of time to accomplish such training, it is not realistic to expect university education to accomplish everything in four or five years. This view was shared by other university provosts who stated that the main objective of university education is to provide professional training to young nationals so that they can serve their country. A former Zayed University provost pointed out that the university was exploring ways to "align and link everything ZU does with national needs," in order to "support the business community and economic development of the country" (personal communication, March 2009). In another interview with New York Institute of Technology (NYIT) Abu Dhabi dean, it was emphasized that the goal of NYIT is to provide professional education that trains students "for a clear career orientation." The dean did concede that the issue of contextualizing the curriculum had to be resolved in the future. For example, courses on federal taxation required by NYIT in New York are irrelevant for business students in the region where there are no taxes. The same priorities of preparing graduates for the labor market were stressed in interviews in Kuwait with university administrators.

The second reason often cited to justify the adoption of the Western educational model in the region is linked to the serious criticisms leveled against the Arab educational system in the entire Arab world (Mazawi and Sultana, 2010). Drzeniek-Hanouz and Yousef (2007: 8) point out that one of the reasons the UAE did not have a better standing among the 40 most competitive economies in the world was due to "low rankings on indicators related to health and education when benchmarked against the group of advanced economies." They pointed out that "aside from quantitative targets, the quality of outcomes in tertiary schooling needs to be enhanced to reverse the low valuation of educational credentials by the private sector." The World Bank report on education in the MENA region levels similar criticisms. Arabic education has become synonymous with rote learning, outdated teaching methods and a teacher-centered approach (Boyle, 2006; World Bank, 2009). Its failures are usually attributed to its being out of sync with the skills requirements of the modern job market because of a curriculum and pedagogy that do not develop the necessary skills of flexibility, critical thinking and analysis, and lifelong learning. Since these skills are considered to be the hallmark of the Western educational system and the reason for the advancement of Western societies, transplanting the Western/ American educational models and importing top executives to lead the reforms of the educational system are seen as the solution to what is ailing the Arab educational system and a shortcut to producing Arab graduates with the required qualifications to spearhead the development of their countries (Drzeniek-Hanouz and Yousef, 2007; UNDP, 2003; Mazawi, 2007). It is expected that recruiting international consultants, mainly from the United Kingdom, the United States and Australia, to direct both public and private institutions will remedy Arab education failings and raise the quality of Arab university graduates' modest output as researchers, innovators and producers of knowledge (Bollag, 2006; Mills, 2008a, 2008b).

The nature of the reforms and the short-term failure to change labor market outcomes has led many academics and parents alike to question their effectiveness. They point to the relatively high unemployment rates among national graduates and what they consider as young generations' weakening ties to Arabic culture and Arabic proficiency. Mounting criticisms of the direction of earlier reforms, particularly in the UAE and Qatar where the reforms were the most aggressive, has resulted in the reversal of some of their components such as a partial return to Arabic as a medium of instruction in the humanities and social sciences and the nomination of national administrators to lead public and even some private universities. By April of 2013 sweeping changes in the administration of UAE public universities were carried out by the new minister of higher education. Qatar University also reversed its policy of English medium instruction by reinstating Arabic in all but hard science colleges (see Chapter 5). These abrupt shifts serve to highlight key problems with the reform process: the exclusion and lack of participation of important national stakeholders in the planning stages of educational reforms opened the door to criticisms of the reforms. In some cases governments reacted by decreeing reversals of parts of the policies in unpredictable and unplanned ways, thus creating further instability in the educational system and resulting in new problems of their own.

Adopting English as the medium of instruction is a pragmatic solution

As discussed in Chapter 8, there has been relatively little attention in official discourses about the implications of a language policy that stresses the need for English proficiency rather than a dual language proficiency in both Arabic and English (Al Baik, 2008; Al Najami, 2007; Nahyan, 2009).[5] The emphasis on English as the language of modern education reflects an acceptance of the developed/developing binary division of the world and stems from the belief that it is possible to catch up to the developed countries by using English to access the knowledge available in it (Tikly, 2004; Drummond, 2010; Lewis, 2010; Swan and Lewis, 2010). There seems to be little concern about the impact that using English to educate may have on the maintenance, let alone the development, of Arabic as a language of knowledge in the future, as aspired to in the vision statements discussed above. The contradiction between the adoption of English as the language of instruction and the declared goals of developing Arabic to become the language of twenty-first-century knowledge seems to be set aside for more pressing pragmatic considerations. Interviewed university executives[6] concede that more attention should be given to Arabic culture and language in university education. However, they stressed that the priorities in education today are to prepare university graduates for a labor market that requires English. They shared the opinion that, today, there is a clear emphasis in the Middle East on professional education and that to prepare graduates for the knowledge society they need to master English, the language of science, research, business and technology and develop the skills required in the labor market. In effect, this association between English and "useful education" helps "standardize Western measures of skill technology, innovation and productivity in ways that are quickly recalibrating regional economic and political relationships" (Tikly, 2004: 16). Setting the priorities from this perspective impacts not only the neglect of the mother tongue but it also means that students must devote more time to learning English and professional skills with very little space in the curriculum reserved for the acquisition of local knowledge to ground them in their culture and history.

The consequences of these implemented educational policies are all the more important given the demographic makeup of the society and family structure. The need to import a large labor force and a reliance on the expatriate experts to build infrastructure and lead economic development have seriously impacted GCC societies' communication patterns and channels, although to varying degrees.[7] The influx of expatriates has given rise to globalized urban centers where Western culture and the English language have become ubiquitous and their influence inescapable inside and outside the home. From a very early age, children watch American programs on TV and are spoken to in English by their parents or their foreign nannies at home. Outside the home, English functions as the lingua franca in communication between expatriates from different linguistic and cultural backgrounds and with nationals. Western cultural messages dominate the social landscape in shopping malls, restaurants, movie theaters and hospitals. Nationals must know some English to obtain even the most basic services in their own countries.[8] In some cities such as Dubai or Doha public spaces, local culture and language have become confined to souks and heritage villages that have been developed to represent culture not only for tourists but also for young generations of nationals (Khalaf, 2002, 2005).

Although the impact of globalization is not uniform across the region and seems to depend on the degree of integration with the global market and dependence on imported skilled manpower, the infiltration of English into life patterns of young generations seems to be similar across the GCC, particularly in urban centers. Several studies conducted among university and high school students in the GCC reveal that young Gulf nationals and Arabs residing in the UAE, Qatar and Oman feel the real impact not only in terms of their linguistic practices where English dominates their diverse interactions but also in their thought patterns. The reliance on English for almost everything in their lives has aroused concerns and made university students themselves ambivalent about their mother tongue (Al-Issa and Dahan, 2011). Such linguistic practices are clearly misaligned with GCC vision statements emphasizing Arabic language and culture as an integral part of their identities.

Reforms' impact on the construction of national identity

Mission statements of GCC public universities and the different types of private or branch institutions are similar in their visions and goals although they may highlight different aspects having to do with reducing the "flattening effect of globalization" on national identity. For example, the more ambitious semi-private universities do recognize the need to combine the global with the Islamic/historical/cultural/local knowledge in their educational outcomes, unlike branch and public universities that tend to emphasize preparing students for careers in a globalized world. The larger semi-private institutions also acknowledge the value of a liberal arts education model which is generally one of the important features of the American-style university education. However, the focus on professional education remains dominant in most universities in the region. In defense of this professional focus in higher education, one of our interviewees stated that "Arabs need to adapt to the global context and not allow [their] history to prejudice their outlook on the present environment."[9] He went on to explain that in order for universities to provide the desired local knowledge, students would have to spend more years in university study given their initial low competencies in English and other study skills.[10] Similarly, in response to a question on how the university is ensuring that students receive a liberal arts education when the focus is on professional training, the dean of the school of humanities at AUK suggested that their approach is to blend acquisition of liberal arts education, local knowledge and professional training throughout the curriculum. She went on to explain that this blending is accomplished by offering a professional education and targeting problem solving skills to find solutions to local market problems. Such a perspective seems to suggest that localizing university education means focusing on professional training and providing the skill set in demand by the local labor market.

Other administrators acknowledged that there is a problem with the way university education is presently handling its grounding in the local Arab culture and environment. A university provost stated:

> Our students have told us they don't know much about their own history and we are trying to respond to that. The question is what *minimum level of knowledge students should have about their own country and culture* [emphasis added] and to build that into the general education curriculum so that, that level of awareness is assured. Even beyond that, communicating in Arabic is something that even our students who have grown up here are not able to do effectively in some cases. Increasing the level of sophistication and knowledge in the use of communicating in Arabic is an important part of what we are trying to accomplish.
>
> (Personal communication, March 2009)

The concerns about how university education can balance between its two goals of grounding itself in local culture and preparing students to participate in the global economy of their countries was expressed over and over again by university professionals (faculty and administrators) interviewed in Kuwait, Qatar and the UAE. The pressure to graduate students who can directly enter the job market is too great to allow for the allocation of time to a more liberal arts curriculum. This is particularly problematic given the low skill sets that entering students bring with them from high schools (see Chapter 5).

Two further elaborations are in order here. First, what exactly does one mean by liberal arts education and, second, what does one mean by grounding in local culture? In its definition of the purpose of general education offered in a liberal arts approach to education, the Harvard Task Force Report (Harvard University College of Arts and Sciences, 2007: 1) states that it should prepare citizens to "[E]ngage with forces of change—cultural, religious, political, demographic, technological, [and] planetary." This is generally accomplished by having students take general courses in humanities, social sciences, mathematics, composition and natural science disciplines, before moving on to specialize in their particular field (Latzer, 2004). However, in the GCC context, the benefits of such program of study are constrained by the relatively low academic English proficiency of freshmen. Depending on their TOEFL scores, students may have to spend a year or more in pre-college courses of instruction in order to prepare them for the four-year collegiate course of study. Thus, the normal four-year course of study for students in the West can often be extended to five, or even six, years. The result is that less time is spent on the type of courses that can provide students with "the tools to face [the cultural, religious, political, demographic, technological and planetary] challenges in an informed and thoughtful way" (Harvard Task Force, 2007: 1). As a result, general education has to devote more time to developing linguistic proficiency in English to access professional level training rather than a more humanistic education.

UNESCO defines humanistic education as one that promotes critical thinking about one's own society, culture and historical traditions to prepare citizens to be active defenders of human rights, equitable societies and the environment (Spring, 2009). Offering an education that does challenge the traditional status quo is understandably a sensitive route that universities must carefully negotiate, and doing it in Arabic might be even more difficult. But preparing graduates to make appropriate choices and be critically engaged in the development of their societies requires it. In addition, the fact that the majority of faculty are expatriates, with no real job security, often makes them avoid discussing "sensitive issues" for fear of being negatively labeled as not respecting local cultures and traditions.[11]

The GCC states are relatively young nations that have witnessed phenomenal transformations during their short history. They are faced with a multitude of existential questions which have been further intensified by recent regional upheavals. Since the 9/11 events, the region has come under world scrutiny and such questions are being debated within prevalent competing paradigms ranging from liberal, progressive, conservative to Islamist ideologies. Dominant conservative and liberal perspectives are often at odds over how to reconcile Western values and lifestyles brought in by globalization with an understanding of "progressive and moderate Islamic values [that are] endowed with a rich Arabic language, to proudly celebrate ... [national] traditions and heritage while reinforcing national identity" (Cabinet releases, 2010: Theme 1.4). The debates touch on issues relating to all aspects of social and political life ranging from environmental and gender issues, morality, cultural affiliation, religious practices, Islamic and Western banking systems to political alignments. All of these questions are regular topics of discussions on TV programs and newspapers in the region (e.g., Mathew, 2008; Al Jazeera TV, 2009; Al Arabiya TV, 2009; BBC Arabic, 2014). While university education cannot provide a magic solution to these issues, it should offer students skills and knowledge to participate in this debate and reflect on competing discourses. The evidence from the general education curriculum of both private and public universities shows little evidence that this discourse is taking place. A liberal arts education that makes students acquire knowledge of their national history, cultural heritage and society could enable students "to think and act critically and reflectively *outside* the channels of a career or profession" (Muller, 2000: 41). So far, higher education reform has missed the opportunity to use general education to create a new generation of critical thinkers who can productively construct their own national identities and civic engagements.

Defining knowledge in the new mission of the university

In describing what they called the "Education Gospel" Grubb and Lazerson (2006) point to the similarities across many parts of the world, from the United

States to China, passing through Europe, sharing a common discourse about education. This discourse "first stresses the failures of schools and universities and then proceeds to reform them with more economic and utilitarian goals" (295). There is a widespread acceptance of this gospel by all stakeholders in the education process. This doctrine rests on the belief that in light of the "knowledge revolution" that has taken place in the last decades, work qualifications have also changed with the labor market demanding "higher order skills" which can only be obtained through higher education if individuals want to participate in the knowledge economy. The framing of the value of education in terms of its "economic production function" is widespread worldwide and is attributed to the corporatization of higher education (Olssen and Peters, 2005; Spring, 2009). Nedeva (2008: 86) observes that the "rhetoric about repositioning universities as global players in the 'knowledge society' and major contributors to 'economic competitiveness' and 'wealth creation' is widespread both horizontally and vertically." Horizontally, across nations, university education missions stress their role as knowledge producers and the same discourse is held vertically at all levels within each nation. IGOs such as the World Bank and the OECD and national governments expect HEIs to offer citizens and societies a competitive advantage on the global stage. These expectations have affected not only the type of skills being targeted but also the mission of the institution itself. The emphasis on efficiency, accountability and competitiveness are gradually transforming university education into marketable services and subjecting it to the capitalist laws of the market. Such changes are leading many education researchers to question HEI's new role (see, e.g., Epstein, 2008; Dale, 2008; Naidoo, 2008; Ursin, 2008). For example, Etzkowitz (1998, cited in Nedeva, 2008: 88) argues that the growing commercialization of higher education is creating an "entrepreneurial university," which integrates economic development into the university as an academic function along with teaching and research. It is this "capitalization of knowledge" that is at the heart of a new mission for the university, linking universities to users of knowledge more tightly and establishing the university as an economic actor in its own right.

While criticisms of the reframing of the university's mission to serve this "third mission" to respond to corporate funding demands are beginning to be heard in the West (Nedeva, 2008; Brown *et al.*, 2008), the rest of the world has embraced the university's new mission and its commercialization as the sacred gospel to be duplicated. Universities in the Arabian Gulf and elsewhere have approached reforming education from an either-or perspective. The binary alternatives of either importing Western curricula and language to close "the knowledge gap separating the Arab and Islamic nations from the advancement of contemporary global civilization" (Abdallah S. Jum'ah, quoted in Verde, 2010) or lagging behind is a false dilemma.

Developing countries' education may be better reformed if it seriously considers the concerns raised about the corporatization of universities to avoid its pitfalls. In addition, an educational system that worked in the West with different social and historical configurations may not necessarily yield the same outcomes in a different socio-historical context and a rapidly changing and diversified global landscape.

The fast-paced and dynamic changes of increasingly global economic and social structures and knowledge capital require that higher education pay more attention to lifelong learning critical thinking skills. For example the World Bank (2003) suggests that the new type of learning should "emphasize creating, applying, analyzing, and synthesizing knowledge and engaging in collaborative learning across the lifespan" (World Bank, 2003: xvii–xviii cited in Farrell and Fenwick, 2007: 15). While this may be true, the debate remains about how to define a type of knowledge that has local relevance. According to Muller (2000), there are two orientations regarding the categories of knowledge. He argues against:

> accepted dichotomies between an education for knowledge and an education for skills, a curriculum of the past and one of the future, the emphasis on understanding or memorization because they tend to "portray the world en route from one to the other [and] will certainly not aid our understanding of what knowledge and skills our millennial citizen will find most worthwhile."
>
> (Muller 2000, 54)

The problems of governance and sustainability

The need to develop a university and college system that addresses local needs while providing students with the technical and intellectual means to make their way in a rapidly globalizing economy requires us to look at the governance of higher education institutions. One cannot develop the humanities and social scientific academic infrastructure to creatively engage students in exploring important social and cultural issues without creating an administrative system that can unleash the creative scholarly energy of the faculty.

As we noted in Chapter 6, many of the new private institutions that have been created over the past two decades suffer from what we might call a participatory governance deficit. In extreme cases, faculty members are employed to teach a large number of courses whose syllabi and methods of assessment are predetermined. Sometimes, accreditation demands inadvertently exacerbate this problem by insisting on the quantification of educational outcomes. This leads to the adoption of standardized tests and limits the ability of institutions to provide engaging courses of study. This problem is especially severe for the small institutions that primarily provide business and information technology degrees. It is likely that the very competitive environment that these for-profit institutions face make it much more unlikely that their owners will encourage the empowerment of their key workers.

While it is not uncommon for faculty to assist in the management of degree programs as well as to evaluate the educational accomplishments of their students, it is less common for academic workers in most of the GCC institutions to contribute to important decisions on efforts to reform the curricula.[12] More often than not, these decisions come from above in unpredictable ways. This is particularly the case in public institutions that are run directly by ministries of higher education or councils under these ministries. Very few universities and colleges in the GCC have functioning Faculty Senates. This is partly a result of the hierarchical political systems of the Gulf, but it is noteworthy that the newer higher educational institutions often have a more disempowered expatriate faculty than the older public institutions.

The elite branch campuses face a series of different issues that call into question their long-term ability to integrate the study of local social issues into their curricula. In some cases, the campus is required to provide an identical curriculum to that offered by the home campus. This can obviously limit the ability of the campus to creatively respond to local student needs. On the other hand, the prestigious nature of these institutions allow the campus administrators to limit teaching loads and encourage research, and some of these institutions have developed impressive research output in the few years of their existence.

The larger issue these campuses face revolves around efforts to maintain their legitimacy as most were created through decisions of a very small group of elites. On the GCC side, the ruler must commit to providing a high level of subsidies even though most of the students are not national citizens. On the university side, the university president is often responsible for the decision to create a branch campus even though the faculty of the home institution might be unenthusiastic. It is not at all difficult to imagine a change in university leadership leading to a reassessment of a home country's overseas commitments. Nor is it hard to foresee a new ruler in a GCC country re-evaluating the commitment of subsidies to an elite university that services a very small number of its own national citizens. The isolation of GCC citizens from the educational reform process is particularly noteworthy in these cases.

Can education reform alone achieve the nationalization of the labor market?

One of the major challenges of the GCC planning authorities has been the effort to encourage the nationalization of the workforce. Despite heavy investments in education and the various qualitative reforms we have documented, there remains an almost total reliance on expatriates in most private sectors of the economy. As we have seen, the causes of this mismatch are often blamed on the quality of education and the orientation of students in humanities and non-scientific degrees that are considered not to be aligned with the required skill sets and qualifications demanded by the private sector. The evidence, however, points to a different conclusion: in the absence of a strong coordination between education, labor and economic policies, this mismatch is likely to continue.

Most GCC nationals graduating from university seek management positions and are unwilling to accept positions that they do not consider prestigious due to real social pressure on them. Nationals are expected to be rich and owners of businesses rather than mid or low level employees (this is especially true for

Kuwaiti, Qatari and UAE nationals). Such attitudes perpetuate the dependence on expatriates to occupy these positions, particularly in the private sector. In fact, an important outcome of higher education reform is that it has provided educational opportunity for expatriate youth and promoted their employment in the private sector at lower wages than nationals are willing to accept. Current labor laws and regulations end up not encouraging nationals to join the private sector who prefer public sector employment because it offers higher pay scales, shorter working hours, longer holidays, and retirement benefits. From businesses' perspective, there is reluctance to employ nationals because of regulations making it difficult to fire them and the perceptions that nationals either lack the needed skills or, just as importantly, the motivation to be productive workers. This has often led to the employment of shadow (or phantom) workers doing the job of the national in sectors of the economy where the states have imposed hiring quotas such as banking in the UAE, Qatar or Kuwait. Hertog reports that these hiring quotas

> have been difficult to monitor, have led to evasion and in some cases corruption between businesses and labor administrations. Various forms of "phantom employment" of nationals are widespread across the region, and quotas have probably increased the informal employment of foreigners.
>
> (Hertog, 2014: 7)

The lesson drawn from this unsuccessful experience has been that quotas have failed because nationals do not have the appropriate skills to function effectively in a global economy or do not have incentives to do so. Quotas alone cannot force businesses to really use labor services of national citizens. Neither can expansion of higher education alone make national students seek private sector employment.

The embrace of higher education across the GCC where in some countries close to 90 percent of high school graduates apply for tertiary education has led some cynics to see in this step a strategy to delay youths from entry into the job market and disguise the potential high unemployment rates among the youths. In some cases, such as in Oman, the current labor market is unable to absorb all tertiary education graduates and the prediction is that a brain drain is underway where Omanis are looking for careers in neighboring countries. Recently, however, education policies are encouraging vocational training colleges and institutes as an alternative to university education, particularly in countries such as Oman and Bahrain. The indication is that government policy-makers do want increasing numbers of GCC citizens to find private sector employment, but so far, national citizens continue to disproportionately work in the public sector for relatively high wages, while the private sector largely employs a disproportionate number of expatriate workers at lower wages.[13]

In the richer countries (Qatar and the UAE), more than 90 percent of the private sector labor force is expatriate, while more than 80 percent of employed nationals work in the public sector. National workers in the three lower income countries of the GCC (Saudi Arabia, Oman and Bahrain) are more likely to work in the private sector, but only Oman has over the past decade successfully reduced the relative presence of expatriates in the private sector and the relative number of nationals who work in the public sector (Kuwait may also be meeting these goals). The inability and unwillingness of nationals to enter the private sector has particularly affected well-educated women who desire to work and less well-educated national men. Unemployment rates for female nationals have climbed as larger numbers of young adult women improve their educational attainment. In the UAE, for example, the percentage of women in the labor force who cannot find work is 28 percent. In Saudi Arabia, this female unemployment rate is 35 percent (IMF, 2013).

What accounts for the seeming inability of higher educational reforms to transform the labor market? Part of the explanation is linked to recent and transitory trends. In the wake of the recent period of high oil prices, many of the GCC states are implementing large physical infrastructure projects that require the importation of vast numbers of low-wage workers from South Asia. More fundamentally, however, is the continuation of an incentive structure that favors relatively low wage expatriate employment in the private sector and high wage employment for nationals in the public sector.

Given these realities, education reforms alone cannot achieve the goal of attracting more nationals to the productive sectors of the economy without policy interventions to reform the patterns of job creation in the GCC. There is a need for the creation of higher-skilled mid-level job opportunities for the thousands of national university, college and vocational training graduates who expect more attractive wages than the private sector is presently paying to expatriates. A portfolio of coherent government interventions to address short-term employment constraints could include the introduction of a tax and subsidy program that can induce an increase in the relative share of nationals employed in the private sector. Such steps must be accompanied by changes in public sector wage-setting practices and private sector employment management policies so that wage differentials between the private and public sectors decrease. These measures should be coupled with what is referred to as "labor market active programs" such as the UAE's TANMIA.[14] If these reforms are implemented, then the higher education reforms we have documented are much more likely to succeed in increasing nationals' participation in the private sector of the economy toward achieving GCC nationalization goals.

Opening the doors to women: a chance for equality?

GCC governments across the region have entrusted education with social development and the empowerment of women. But unlike the limited impact that education has had in the area of nationalization of the labor force discussed above, a major achievement of higher education in the GCC is that it has laid the basis for women's emancipation. Across the GCC the percentage of women enrolled in HEIs is equal if not superior to men. This has been possible thanks to the availability of HE education at home as families are much more reluctant to send their daughters to study abroad. Literacy rates among females above the age of 15 are around 84 percent, and in 2009 more than 60 percent of graduates in Kuwait, Qatar and the UAE were women (Al Masah Capital Limited, 2012).

The personal and social benefits of women's education are undeniable. Worldwide research shows a clear correlation between women's education and health benefits for both females and their children. Increased education of women leads to a decrease in child mortality and fertility rates, increase in life expectancy and an increase in potential income (Adely, 2009). For most countries of the GCC, the rapid increase in the number of educated women has resulted in gender role imbalances as the percentage of women university graduates is greater than men's. Women's empowerment seems at times to have outpaced the often paternalistic traditions and expectations which still prevail in society (Al-Nasr, 2011).[15]

Despite these advances, women's educational successes have not been paralleled by corresponding participation in the labor market. Indeed, women's participation in the labor sector remains well below what one would expect. Despite governments' steps to encourage women to participate in their societies' labor market, out of the 10.2 million literate women above the age of 15 only 3.3 million are recorded as employed, bringing their participation in the GCC labor market to 26.9 percent, compared to 84 percent for males (Al Masah Capital Limited, 2012). IGOs have tended to explain this mismatch by invoking the role of cultural values and family traditions as a major cause. The questions often asked are: how important are Arab cultural and family values in explaining this mismatch? What is the role of economy planning and labor policies in women's low participation in the labor market? And, can other reforms in higher education reverse this reality?

There is no agreement as to the role played by culture, family and tradition. It is widely presumed that women's freedom to work outside the home is restrained by Arab traditional values in male-dominated societies. These traditions are often reinforced by laws that severely limit women's rights under the guise of religion. For example, in most Arab countries, laws still favor men over women in inheritance and their ability to make their own decisions relating to marriage, divorce and freedom of movement.

As restrictive as this reality is, Arab women's legal rights have progressed in the last decades. Women's equal rights to men have been formally recognized in most GCC constitutions such as "in Qatar, Kuwait (Kuwait Constitution Article 29), UAE (UAE Constitution Article 25), Bahrain (Bahraini Constitution Article 4), Oman (Oman Basic Law Article 17), [and] the Saudi Arabian Constitution guarantees 'human rights in accordance with Shari'ah' (Article 26)" (Al-Nasr, 2011: 44). GCC women have also gained some political rights, including voting and running for parliament in some countries. There are women ministers and municipality representatives in Kuwait and the UAE. Within higher education, Sheikha Moza al Misnad of Qatar, the mother of the present-day ruler, is the head of the Qatar Foundation, which supervises Doha's Education City. In

Kuwait, Sheikha Dana al Sabah is the founder and head of the Board of Trustees of the American University of Kuwait. In the UAE, Sheikha Fatma, the wife of the late UAE president Sheikh Zayed, and four women holding ministerial posts, are all role models that send powerful messages to GCC women and men.

GCC women have also made great strides in business. Like in the rest of the world they have become entrepreneurs, albeit at much slower rates depending on the specific country. Zeidan and Bahrami (2011: 102) report that "Saudi, Bahrain and the UAE seem to be at the forefront, while the women of Kuwait, Qatar and Oman have not been as active." According to the authors, women's participation in business activities still face several challenges including access to capital and relevant information, and cumbersome and sometimes gender-discriminatory regulations, particularly in Saudi Arabia. Other barriers have to do with a lack of self-confidence and, more importantly, women's prioritization of their family responsibilities and desires to establish a family and work balance. It is clear that such factors limiting labor force participation of women are not unique to Arab women but can be found everywhere across cultures (Adely, 2009).

In an ethnographic study conducted by Adely on Jordanian women and their perceptions of paid work outside the home, participants articulated a wide variety of reasons for their participation in higher education. For some it was seen in economic/financial terms as opening doors for better employment opportunities, while for others, the reasons were more personal such as improving their prospects for a better marriage. Adely (2009) suggested that there are many factors that influence women's decisions regarding education and work that go beyond the neo-liberal explanations and stereotypical conceptions of "a pathological" representation of the "Arab family," "Arab culture" and "Arab men and women" prevalent in IGO reports such as the 2005 Arab Human Development Report, which tend to perpetuate such discourse on Arab women's status. Adely concludes that such stereotypical representations ignore the rapid changes that are taking place not only at the level of the economy but also at the level of cultural beliefs. She writes that:

> The AHDR 2005, despite making important contributions to the conceptualization of development challenges in the Arab world, fails to account for the range of factors that shape decisions about education, waged labor, marriage and family. It oversimplifies the significance of global economic and political forces tied to contemporary development projects like formal education, and despite giving credence to the importance of developing human capabilities to make informed choices, it continues to rely on assumptions shaped by economic determinants and a liberal ideal of progress about what constitutes progress and quality of life. Thus the reader is unable to imagine alternate outcomes or desires.
>
> (Adely, 2009: 117)

It is clear that transformative changes taking place in Arab societies are also leading to changes in "Arab family" values, albeit at different rates. While some values, such as parents' role to decide for their children, both males and females, what to study, who to marry and where to work are still current practices, many others are in transition. Nonetheless, Arab attitudes toward the value of girls' education have dramatically changed. Across the Arab world, families are willing to make great sacrifices to send their daughters to school and university when it is accessible to them and they can afford it.

When it comes to work, there are many other factors that affect women's choices of employment. In a study of women's perceptions of work, Khalifeh (2011) found that interviewed Qatari women felt that both their society and their government encouraged them to enter the workforce. They expressed preferences as to which sectors are better working environments for them based on their need to balance work and family. They consider working in the public sector safer even though they recognize that work in the private sector leads to better pay and better opportunities for career advancement. For them the priority is to find a job that allows them to balance between family and work responsibilities, a balance that is possible in careers such as in education.

One of the accepted economic benefits of women's paid employment outside the home, worldwide, is the liberating force of being financially independent which empowers them to be more assertive. In the GCC, there are possible explanations as to why employment may not necessarily be perceived as that financially liberating force. GCC women can be financially independent without having to work. The welfare system in the wealthy GCC states subsidizes basic living for all its citizens, making employment for financial needs less of a necessity. It should be noted here that Islam grants wives the right to control their own financial resources and makes men alone responsible for household expenditures and family support. In addition, many national women can claim unemployment to receive supplementary government unemployment insurance. As a result many women may choose not to work if the family constraints on their freedom of movement are not too onerous.

The changes described above are not uniform throughout Arab societies or the GCC. It is true that there are still family/cultural constraints that do limit possibilities for those women who do want to work. Parents of unmarried young women do not favor their daughters moving away from home in search of employment unless they are in dire need of that extra income. In the GCC, as elsewhere, this constraint on women's mobility is exacerbated by job creation spatial patterns. Both government and private industry employment availabilities tend to be concentrated in the larger cities such as Dubai, Abu Dhabi, Doha, Kuwait City, Manama or Muscat. Educated women living outside of these centers are less likely to find work (specifically in the private sector) close to home unless they are willing to commute. There are also still cultural restrictions on the type of work acceptable for women. For example, women engineers are unlikely to be offered or themselves seek work that requires night shifts in manufacturing industry, construction sites or offshore oil rigs.

Socially, prevailing beliefs that male and female spaces should be segregated in societies that are male-dominated also limit women's opportunities to partake in their own development and the development of their societies. Separate educational institutions have made it possible for parents to send their daughters to school in an environment that otherwise would have kept them at home. At the same time segregated schools have perpetuated the mentality that women do not belong in public spaces controlled by men. In some contexts such as Saudi Arabia, gender segregation has also negatively affected the quality of education being delivered and received by women. On the job market, women are encouraged to work in domains where there is little interaction with males, such as teaching, thus limiting their opportunities for work. Social discourses about women's education tie the benefits of education to their role in the private space of the home and family as good mothers and wives rather than direct participants in the economic development of their societies. It is often said that by raising good citizens, educated mothers are in fact participating in the evolution of their societies. In short, through their education women are expected to be enablers and supporters of men to carry out their responsibilities. We should be mindful, though, that constraints on women are not necessarily unique to the "Arab family" or the GCC societies but can be found in all cultures and civilizations.

Nonetheless, the impressive participation of women in universities and colleges throughout the GCC signals a significant shift in the social practices throughout the region. Arab/Islamic culture is not static or inherently hostile to female empowerment. Most young women and their parents are now firmly committed to attaining high levels of formal education. The fact that significant increases in education have not yet resulted in sharp rises in labor force participation is partly due to the cultural barriers we have outlined in previous paragraphs. But we should also give due weight to economic factors that have limited both the ability and desire of young women to become professional workers. The incentive system that channels national workers into the public sector also negatively affects national women's desire to seek work in the private sector. The lack of government employment opportunities combined with lower wages in the corporate business world and a welfare system that encourages women to stay within the household economy are also responsible for low female labor force participation. Higher education attainment is one important factor promoting the increased autonomy and equality of women, but educational reforms by themselves cannot be expected to shift the subaltern status of GCC women.

Conclusion

There is little doubt that the road taken by educational policies in the GCC has revolutionized the education system in terms of its quantity and quality. There are however many questions about where this road is leading to. The determination of GCC leaders to transform their sheikhdoms into modern societies is impressive. They have bet on educational reforms to help them achieve their goals of becoming part of the twenty-first-century knowledge societies but in following education commodification trends prevalent in contemporary Western higher education, they run the risk of missing their goals of becoming leaders rather than followers. Even the embrace of a professional education to enable students to enter the entrepreneurial global economy seems to be questionable when measured by the actual participation and productivity of national graduates in the new knowledge economy of their respective countries. Such shortcoming may be the result of a turnkey approach to education that is not rooted in its local socio-cultural, historical and economic context. The reforms have considered education as "a key site of cultural reproduction" (Phillipson, 2000: 99) where authentic individual development is generally secondary. In his critique of this perspective, Sing observes that it "is narrowly economic and instrumental and often means little more than short term retraining and adaptation. Most governments are concerned more with national competiveness and economic growth than individual development" (Sing, cited in Spring, 2009: 67). GCC educational reforms are inscribed in this deeply flawed instrumental view of education that too often associates tradition with inertia and "modernity" with progress. As Ramadan (2009) points out, all traditions are constructed through movement; and modernity is a present tradition that deals with the challenges of contemporary times.

It is the obligation of any national education policy to guarantee its citizens the right to their past so that students can learn to critically evaluate their heritage and participate in their own social evolution. Rulers expect their universities and colleges to nurture citizens' sense of pride and appreciation of their cultural heritage. Their effort to construct a contemporary national identity, however, is frustrated by the importation of educational systems, curricula and academic workers. This can clearly limit the opportunities for students to study their own culture and society. A global university should engage students in a truly global culture to build a future society that starts with knowledge about its own traditions, social dynamics and environmental issues. This knowledge is just as essential and urgent as technological and scientific knowledge and can provide the tools necessary to "resist the flattening and homogenizing effects of globalization" expressed in the UAE charter. In this respect, using Arabic as one of the languages of instruction is essential because "when the written language becomes a means of representing and problematizing the issues facing the community ... [then it serves] as a tool for linking [students'] uses of language to their concerns within the local community" (Holmes, 2008: 363).

To pose the challenge of development as either following the Western model or remaining underdeveloped creates a false and unproductive dilemma. The universities and colleges of the GCC can offer their students all that is good about Western education while at the same time teach them about themselves and their environment. Given their wealth, they can afford to do it. It is fitting to close this chapter and book with one of the great leaders of the GCC and the founder of the UAE when he stated:

> I believe that he who does not know his past will not understand the present, nor will he be able to prepare himself for the future.
>
> (Sheikh Zayed)[16]

Notes

1 Arab nation refers to the imagined community of all Arab states forming one nation as Arabic has two terms for nation, one referring to the nation state, "qutr' or "dawla," and the other with a more Pan-Arab conceptualization with religious overtones, "Umma." Umma is linked to the past Arab/Islamic empires and later to attempts by nationalists such as Jamal Abdel Nasser of Egypt and the Baathist movements to unify the Arab world.
2 World Trade Organization (January 4, 2012). Trade Policy Review Report by the State of Kuwait.Wt/Tpr/G/258.
3 Kingdom of Bahrain, Ministry of Education website, available at: www.moe.gov.bh/en/vision_mission.aspx#.UpxEUiLp0is.
4 Interview with the higher education advisor to the Ruler of Sharjah, April 10, 2008.
5 Fears regarding the loss of Arabic among future generations in the Arab world is a constant topic of debate in Arab media.
6 We interviewed provosts and deans from the following universities, American University of Kuwait, Kuwait University, Qatar University, University of Sharjah, Zayed University, New York Institute of Technology, Abu Dhabi. We also gathered information from colleagues in Texas A&M Qatar, University of Bahrain, the Gulf University for Science and Technology, and Georgetown University Qatar.
7 The five countries could be placed on a continuum with the UAE being the most impacted and Oman the least.
8 See Badry (2011) for a discussion of the impact of global English and globalization on UAE identity.
9 Higher education advisor to a UAE ruler, personal communication, April 10, 2008.
10 When students matriculate into their major after the foundation year, they generally have to complete around 12 credits in English composition alone, which limits the number of courses they are required to take in their general education component.
11 Discussions on local politics and religion tend to be taboo subjects in class discussions.
12 There are, however, exceptions to this observation. In some semi-private universities such as AUS, faculty serve on curriculum committees to make recommendations to higher administration for changes or additions to their courses and programs. AUS also moved to develop a Faculty Senate and Faculty handbook that provides the faculty with many avenues for participating in the governance of the institution.
13 The data analysis in this paragraph heavily relies on a recent report on GCC labor markets prepared for the Gulf Cooperation Council by the International Monetary Fund (IMF, 2013).
14 TANMIA is an effort by the government of the UAE to provide job training that can match the needs of the labor market with the skills of potential national citizen workers. TANMIA is supposed to supplement and improve on the high level skills that national citizens should be obtaining through the higher education system. Other countries have similar programs, but some more heavily rely on quotas and administrative diktats.
15 Such imbalance is sometimes blamed on higher rates of divorce as educated women tend to be less submissive. Education of women has also led to profound social changes. Young couples are less likely to live in extended family arrangements.
16 Quoted in Codrai (1990).

References

Adely, F.J. (2009). Educating women for development: The Arab Human Development Report 2005 and the problem with women's choices. *International Journal of Middle Eastern Studies*, 41: 105–122.

Al Arabiya TV (2009). Television broadcast in Arabic: hiwaaru al-arab. 'the dialogue of Arabs.' March 26.

Al Baik, D. (2008). It is not acceptable to drop Arabic language from our lives. *Gulf News*, March 16.

Al-Issa, A. and Dahan, L. (eds.). (2011). *Global English and Arabic: Issues of Language Culture and Identity*. Oxford: Peter Lang.

Al Jazeera TV (2009). Television broadcast in Arabic: ma wara'a al khabar "Behind the news." Discussion with Dr. Salem Sari and Dr. Jasem Sultan. April 18.

Al Maktoum, S.M.b.R. (2006). *My Vision: Challenges in the Race for Excellence*. Dubai: Motivate Publishing Co. (in Arabic).

Al Masah Capital Limited (2012). Women in the GCC: Challenging the status quo. Report 19. Available at: http://almasahcapital.com/uploads/report/pdf/report_19.pdf.

Al Najami, S. (2007). Bilingual education hangs in the balance for schools. *Gulf News*, October 18. Available at: http://gulfnews.com/news/gulf/uae/education/bilingual-education-hangs-in-the-balance-for-schools-1.207122.

Al-Nasr, T.J. (2011). Gulf Cooperation Council (GCC) Women and Misyar marriage: Evolution and progress in the Arabian Gulf. *Journal of International Women's Studies*, 12(3): 43–57.

Badry, F. (2011). Appropriating English: Languages in identity construction in the UAE. In A. Al-Issa and L. Dahan (eds.). *Global English and Arabic: Issues of Language, Culture, and Identity in the Arab World*. Bern: Peter Lang, 81–122.

BBC Arabic (2014). Talking points program. Guests and participants discussed the decline of Arabic and speculated on reasons behind the decline and possible recommendations. December 18.

Bollag, B. (2006). America's hot new export: Higher education. *Chronicle of Higher Education*, 52(24): A44.

Boulding, E. and Parker, H. (2005). Women and development. In Snarr, Michael T. and Snarr, D. Neil (eds.). *Introducing Global Issues*, 3rd edn. Boulder: Lynne Rienner, 185–200.

Boyle, H.N. (2006). Memorization and learning in Islamic schools. *Comparative Education Review*, 50(3): 478–495.

Brown, P., Lauder, H. and Ashton, D. (2008). Towards a high-skills economy: Higher education and the new realities of global capitalism. In Epstein, D., Boden, R., Deem, R., Rizvi, F. and Wright, S. (eds.). *Geographies of Knowledge, Geometries of Power: Framing the Future of Higher Education*. New York: Routledge, 191–210.

Cabinet releases UAE Vision 2021 (2010). UAEinteract. February 7. Available at: www.uaeinteract.com/docs/Cabinet_releases_UAE_Vision_2021_(full_text)/39555.htm.

Codrai, R. (1990). *The Seven Shaikhdoms: Life in the Trucial States before the Federation of the United Arab Emirates*. Singapore: Stacey International.

Dale, R. (2008). Repairing the deficits of modernity: The emergence of parallel discourses in higher education in Europe. In Epstein, D., Boden, R., Deem, R., Rizvi, F. and Wright, S. (eds.). *Geographies of Knowledge, Geometries of Power: Framing the Future of Higher Education*. New York: Routledge, 14–31.

Drummond, J. (2010). Bilingual classes at heart of shake-up. FT.com, June 28. Available at: www.ft.com/cms/s/0/c3d168da-82c8-11df-b7ad-00144feabdc0.html.

Drzeniek-Hanouz, M. and Yousef, T.(2007). Assessing competitiveness in the Arab world: Strategies for sustaining the growth momentum. 2006–2007. Available at: www.weforum.org/pdf/Global_Competitiveness_Reports/Reports/chapters/1_1.pdf.

Epstein, D. (2008). Introduction: Geographies of knowledge, geometries of power: Framing the future of higher education. In Epstein, D., Boden, R., Deem, R., Rizvi, F.

and Wright, S. (eds.). *Geographies of Knowledge, Geometries of Power: Framing the Future of Higher Education.* New York: Routledge, 191–210.

Farrell, L. and Fenwick, T. (2007). Educating a global workforce. In Farrell, L. and Fenwick, T. (eds.). *Educating the Global Workforce: Knowledge, Knowledge Work and Knowledge Workers.* London: Routlege, 13–26.

Grubb, N.W. and Lazerson, M. (2006). The globalization rhetoric and practice: The education gospel and vocationalism. In Lauder, H., Brown, P., Dillabough, J. and Halsey, A.H. (eds.). *Education, Globalization and Social Change.* Oxford: Oxford University Press, 295–307.

Harvard University College of Arts and Sciences (2007). Report of the Task Force on General Education. Available at: www.sp07.umd.edu/HarvardGeneralEducationReport.pdf.

Hertog, S. (2014). Arab Gulf States: An assessment of nationalization policies. Gulf Labor Markets and Migration (GLMM). GLMM Research paper. N.1/2014.

Holmes, J. (2008). Culture and identity in rural Africa: Representation through literacy. *Language and Education*, 22(6): 363–379.

IMF (2013). Labor market reforms to boost employment and productivity in the GCC. Staff Report Prepared for Annual Meeting of GCC Ministers of Finance and Central Bank Governors.

Khalaf, S. (2002). Globalization and heritage revival in the Gulf: An anthropological look at Dubai Heritage Village. *Journal of Social Affairs*, 19(75): 13–42.

Khalaf, S. (2005). National dress and the construction of Emirati cultural identity. *The Journal of Human Sciences*. Bahrain: University of Bahrain.

Khalifeh, F. (2011). Qatari women: Employment challenges and the new generation of leaders. University of Phoenix, ProQuest, UMI Dissertations Publishing, 2011. 3535522.

Latzer, B. (2004). Common knowledge: The purpose of general education. *The Chronicle of Higher Education*, October 8. Available at: http://chronicle.com.ezproxy.aus.edu/article/Common-Knowledge-the-Purpo/12903/http://chronicle.com.ezproxy.aus.edu/article/Common-Knowledge-the-Purpo/12903/.

Lewis, K. (2010). Bilingual education for pupils aged 4. *The National*, June 21.

Mathew, F. (2008). Shoring up national identity. *Gulf News*, April 17.

Mazawi, A.E. (2007). "Knowledge society" or work as "spectacle": Education for work and the prospects of social transformation in Arab societies. In Farrell, L. and Fenwick, T. (eds.). *Educating the Global Workforce: Knowledge, Knowledge Work and Knowledge Workers.* London: Routledge, 251–267.

Mazawi, A.E. and Sultana, R.G. (eds.) (2010). *Education and the Arab "World": Political Projects, Struggles, and Geometries of Power.* London: Routledge.

Mills, A. (2008a). Emirates look to the west for prestige. *The Chronicle of Higher Education*, September 28. Available at: http://chronicle.com/article/Emirates-Look-to-the-West-for/8165 (accessed June 5, 2015).

Mills, A. (2008b). U.S. universities negotiate tricky terrain in the Middle East. *Chronicle of Higher Education*, 54(46): A1.

Muller, J. (2000). *Reclaiming Knowledge: Social Theory, Curriculum and Education Policy.* Florence, KY: Routledge.

Naidoo, R. (2008). Higher education: A powerhouse for development in a neo-liberal age? In Epstein, D., Boden, R., Deem, R., Rizvi, F. and Wright, S. (eds.). *Geographies of Knowledge, Geometries of Power: Framing the Future of Higher Education.* New York: Routledge, 248–265.

Nahyan: English to stay as medium of instruction in varsities (2009). Staff Report. *Gulf News*, November 22.

Nedeva, M. (2008). New tricks and old dogs: The "third mission" and the re-production of the university. In Epstein, D., Boden, R., Deem, R., Rizvi, F. and Wright, S. (eds.). *Geographies of Knowledge, Geometries of Power: Framing the Future of Higher Education*. New York: Routledge, 85–103.

Olssen, M. and Peters, M.A. (2005). Neoliberalism, higher education and the knowledge economy: From the free market to knowledge capitalism. *Journal of Education Policy*, 20(3): 313–345.

Phillipson, R. (2000). English in the new world order: Variations on a theme of linguistic imperialism and "World" English. In Ricento, T. (ed.). *Ideology, Politics and Language Policies*. Philadelphia: John Benjamins, 87–106.

Qatar National Vision 2030. Available at: www.gsdp.gov.qa/portal/page/portal/gsdp_en/qatar_national_vision/qnv_2030_document/QNV2030_English_v2.pdf.

Ramadan, T. (2009). Identity, Islam and the challenges of modernity. Paper presented at the "Who am I? Who are You?" conference, April 20–21, in HCT Sharjah, UAE.

Spring, J. (2009). *Globalization of Higher Education*. London: Routledge.

Swan, M. and Lewis, K. (2010). Billions invested into university research. *The National*, June 10. Available at: www.thenational.ae/apps/pbcs.dll/article?AID=/20100610/NATIONAL/100619985/1010.

Tikly, L. (2004). Education and the new imperialism. *Comparative Education*, 40(2): 173–198.

UNDP (United Nations Development Programme) (2003). *Arab Human Development Report: Building an Arab Knowledge Society*. New York: UNDP.

UNDP (United Nations Development Programme) (2004). *Arab Human Development Report 2004: Towards Freedom in the Arab World*. New York: UNDP.

UNDP (United Nations Development Programme) (2005). *Arab Human Development Report 2005: Towards the Rise of Women in the Arab World*. New York: UNDP.

Ursin, J. (2008). In quality we trust? The case of quality assurance in Finnish universities. In Epstein, D., Boden, R., Deem, R., Rizvi, F. and Wright, S. (eds.). *Geographies of Knowledge, Geometries of Power: Framing the Future of Higher Education*. New York: Routledge, 128–141.

Verde, T. (2010). Houses of wisdom. Saudi Aramco publication. Available at: www.saudiaramcoworld.com/issue/201003/houses.of.wisdom.htm.

World Bank (2009). The World Bank annual report. Available at: http://siteresources-worldbank.org/EXTANNREP2K8/Resources/YR00_Year_in_Review_Englishpdf.

Youssef, M. (2010). Cabinet sets nation new targets for 2021. *The National*, February 6. Available at: www.thenational.ae/apps/pbcs.dll/article?AID=/20100207/NATIONAL/702069832&SearchID=73393375552175.

Zeidan, S. and Bahrami, S. (2011). Women entrepreneurship in GCC: A framework to address challenges and promote participation in a regional context. *International Journal of Business and Social Science*, 2(14). Available at: http://ezproxy.aus.edu/login?url=http://search.proquest.com/docview/904521781?accountid=16946.

Index

Page numbers in *italics* denote tables.

ABET accreditation 138–9, *139*
Abouammoh, A. 154, 169, 173, 175
Abu Dhabi Educational Council (ADEC) 62–3
Abu Dhabi (UAE): branch and private universities *84–90*; collaborative research 127; elite branch campuses 55, 57, 62–4; private universities 82; public universities *106–7*; semi-private model 81–2
academic culture 23–4
academic freedom 125
Academic Leadership Centre (ALC), Saudi Arabia 173
academic partnerships 31–2
academic ranking 23, 81
academics: commonality 37–9; international exchanges 29–30; mobility 30–1
Accelerated Program for Excellence (APEX) 173–4
access to higher education 117; women 167–9
accountability 163–4
accreditation 20, 38, 104, 113; AACSB accreditation 138, *140*; ABET accreditation 138–9, *139*; accreditation bodies 137–8; context and overview 134–5; foreign 166; new regulatory institutions 140–4; problems of 216; reasons for 135–6; summary and conclusions 150–1; Westernization 136–40; *see also* quality assurance
Adely, F.J. 220
admission criteria 114
adolescent pregnancies *6*
Advance Collegiate Schools of Businesses (AACSB) 138, *140*

affiliation 70–81
Ahlia University 74
Al-Dali, W. 166
Al-Eisa, E. 172, 175
Al-Ghamdi, A.K.H. 165
Al Jundi, F.Y. 185
Al Maktoum, S.M.b.R 205
Al Misnad, Sheikha Mozah 111, 114, 125, 127
al Nahyan, Sheikh N.b.M. 115
Al-Ohali, M. 170
Al Qahtani, S.B. 193
Al-Qasimi, Dr Sheikh S.b.M. 80
Aljughaiman, A.M. 154
Alkhazim, M. 164
Alnassar, S.A. 164, 174
Altbach, P.G. 162, 170
American University of Dubai (AUD) 54
American University of Kuwait (AUK) 75, 80
American University of Sharjah (AUS) 80–1
American university model 34–6, 80–1, 137; *see also* Western models
analytic approach 8
Arab educational system, criticism of 113
Arab Human Development Reports 17, 40–2, 113, 127, 207, 220
Arab identity 205
Arab Spring uprisings 5
"Arab university," criticism of 7
Arabian Gulf University 109
Arabic *see* World Bank Modern Standard Arabic (MSA); as medium of instruction 98, 99, 117, 184; purity 185
Arabization 41, 117–18, 184, 193, 194
Arnold, M. 111

aspirations 205–6
Association of American International
  Colleges and Universities 34; members
  35
Australian University of Wollongong 54
Azad, A.N. 124–5

Badri, M. 183
Badry, F. 122
Bahrain 71, 74–5; accreditation 142–3;
  governance 146, 147; private higher
  education institutions *76–7*; public
  universities *110*, 116; quality of HE
  149–50; school reforms 120–1; vision
  206
Bahrain Economic Development Board 74
Bahrain Polytechnic 105
Bahrami, S. 220
banking concept of education 163
Banks, A. 5
Barr, N. 19
Basic Education Curriculum (BEC), Oman
  119
Baxter, E. 156
Becker, Gary 16
bilingual education 183, 184, 195–7
book: analytic approach 8; structure and
  overview 8–10; summary and
  conclusions 222–3
Booz & Co. report 6, 62
Bosbait, M. 162
Boulding, E. 205
Bourdieu, P. 25n9
Bowles, S. 22
branch campuses 35–6; Bahrain 74–5;
  Dubai 65–8; sustainability 91–2
British Empire 1
Bruthiaux, P. 180–1
budget allocation 16
business formation 49

capitalism 21–3
categorization: difficulty of 55; elite
  branch campuses 55, 57–64; universities
  and colleges 55–70, *56*
Centre for Higher Education Research and
  Studies (CHERS), Saudi Arabia 173
Centre for Higher Education Statistics
  (CHES), Saudi Arabia 173
Chapman, D. 125
class 13, 22
Classical Arabic 179, 186, 187
collaborative research 127
colleges *see* universities and colleges

Collins, C.S. 22
colonial languages 180–1
colonialism 1
Commission for Academic Accreditation
  (CAA), UAE 140–1, 145
common language 37–9
competitiveness 127, 136–7
"Comprehensive Development of Education
  in the Gulf Cooperation Council" 42–3
Cooke, M. 4
cooperation: elite branch campuses 60
corporatization 38–9, 146, 214–15
Council of Higher Education, Bahrain 149
"Creating Opportunities for Future
  Generations" 40
credibility 137, 165
critical thinking 24
cross-border collaborative arrangements
  137
cross-border homogenization 34–7
cross-border presence 31–4; categories *32*
cross-registration 60
cultural challenges 61
cultural hegemony 91
cultural identity 184
cultural loss 209
culture: effect on women 218–19, 221–2;
  local 212; Western models 210–11
Cummins, J. 195, 196
curricula: American influence 113;
  Arabization 184; cultural hegemony 91;
  Dubai 65; globalization 37–9; imported
  165–6, 208; Sharjah 81

de-Arabization 6
degree choices 18, 21
degree programs: market-driven
  programming 169–70; quality assurance
  148–9
degrees, recognition of 149
demographic behavioral change 5–6
demographic composition 3, 6
developed/developing binary 210
development, contributing to 15
dialects 187, 189, 191, 195–6
diglossia 186–7, 188–90
Doumato, E. 168
Dow, K. 164, 174
Drzeniek-Hanouz, D.M. 113
Dubai: accreditation 141; branch campuses
  65–8; education malls 64–8;
  neoliberalism 64–5; private higher
  education 54; universities and colleges
  66–7, *69*

Dubai Healthcare City (DHC) 65
Dubai International Academic City (DIAC) 65
Dubai International Financial Center (DIFC) 65
Dubai Knowledge Village (DKV) 65

economic diversification 174–5
economic failure, risk of 136
economic globalization 17, 49–51
economic growth 15–19
economic indicators 2
economic perspective 15–19
economic returns on educational investments 17–18
Educated Spoken Arabic (ESA) 186, 190
education: development of 7; expected duration of schooling 7; individual and collective benefits 16–17; and supply or workers 50–1; value of 214
Education City 57–64, 91; *see also* Educity
Education Cluster (EDC) 65
education expenditure *124*
Education Gospel 213–14
education malls 64–8
education reform 39–43, 51
educational exports 33–4
educational hubs 33, 74, 80
educational models 136–7
educational practice: context and overview 204–5; defining knowledge 213–15; governance 215–16; grounding in local culture 212; humanistic education 213; key questions 204; labor market nationalization 216–18; language proficiency 212–13; national identity 211–13; reforms 207–9; and role of education 213–14; socio-political environments 213; summary and conclusions 222–3; sustainability 216; use of English 210–13; vision and reform 205–7; Western models 207–9; women 218–22
Educity 33, 57–64, 91
Effat University 169
Egyptian educational model 98
El Hamed, A.L.Y. 42
elite branch campuses 35–6, 55, 57, 91–2; Abu Dhabi (UAE) 62–4, *84–90*; Qatar 57–62; and status of national universities 113–14; sustainability 216
elite institutions, funding 38–9
emancipation, education as 23
Emirates Industrial Bank (EIB) 123

employability 162–3
employers: expectations 135
Engels, F. 29
English: developing competence 41; impact on MSA 181; as language of communication 194; as medium of instruction 38, 70, 80, 81, 113, 115–16, 117, 148, 180–1, 182, 194, 210–13; resource allocation 182; status 180–3
enrollment rates *14*, 43–5, *44*; Dubai 65, 68; public universities 98; Qatar University (QU) *101*; Saudi Arabia 156–7
European imperialism 1
exit threat 135
expatriate workers 6–7, 49, 210, 217–18
expenditure, on research 122
external affiliations 70–81

faculty: elite branch campuses 64; factors affecting significance of research and satisfaction *126*; hiring practices 49–51, 113, 162; Kuwait University (KU) 99; language proficiency 117; professional development 165; Qatar University (QU) 115; quality assurance 145, 146; reliance on foreign staff 167; removal of foreign nationals 117–18; research capability 123–5, 127; working conditions 148–9, 170–1
Fagerlind, I. 23
family values 220–2
Ferguson, C.A. 187
Fishman, J. 192
foreign accreditation 166
Fouache, E. 64
franchise arrangements 70–1
Freire, P. 163
French, R. 82
Friedman, T. 29
funding: corporate 214; gender and mobility 109; industry funding 127; potential sources 43; public universities 104; research 123; scarcity 38–9

gas production 2
gender: educational reform 40–1; integration 80, 81; and mobility 30, 109; segregation 70, 80, 81, 99, 102, 154, 221–2; of students 14, 43, 45
gender role imbalances 218
General Committee for Licensing and Approvals of Colleges, Saudi Arabia 162

Georgetown University School of Foreign
   Service in Qatar (SFS-Q) 184–5
Ghabra, S. 111
Gintis, H. 22
global citizens 23–4
global competitiveness index rankings
   123, *124*
global expansion: composition of student
   body 12–13; context and overview
   12–14; enrollment rates *14*; pursuit of
   knowledge 23–4; regional shares of
   students *13*; student numbers 12;
   summary and conclusions 24–5; and
   Western domination 21–3
global rankings 37
globalization: American university model
   34–6; commonalities 37–9;
   conceptualizing 28–39; context and
   overview 28; cross-border
   homogenization 34–7; cross-border
   presence of universities 31–4; dynamic
   22; economic globalization 49–51;
   education reform in GCC 39–43; elite
   branch campuses 35–6; enrollment rates
   43–5, *44*; global rankings 37; impact
   211; institutions 31; international
   exchanges 29–30; international growth
   28–9; isolation of workforces 49–51;
   knowledge societies 42; language
   proficiency 183; mobility 30–1; policy
   39–40; role of Gulf states 39–49;
   student mobility 45–9; types of program
   31–3; Western models 207–9
Gonzalez, G.C. 119
governance 92–3; educational practice
   215–16; lack of data 147; Oman *109*;
   Qatar 61; quality assurance 144–5,
   146–8; reforms 209
graduate programs, Qatar 58–9, 60
graduates: social positions 21; wage
   premium 17, 18
Grigorenko, E.L. 154
Grubb, N.W. 213–14
Gulf Arabic 191, 195–6
Gulf Cooperation Council (GCC) 4–5
Gulf Cooperation Council (GCC) states:
   overview 1–7; role in globalization 39–49
Gulf states, variations between 2
Gulf University for Science and
   Technology (GUST) 75, 80

Haeri, N. 188, 189, 191, 192
Hammad Bin Khalifa University (HBKU)
   58, 60

Harvard Task Force Report 212
hegemony, cultural 91
heritage, retaining 4
Hertog, S. 50, 217
Higher Colleges of Technology (HCT)
   102, 116, 118
higher education: purpose of 24; social
   roles 15
Higher Education Review Unit (HERU),
   Bahrain 143, 147
hiring practices 49–51, 113
hiring quotas 217
Hirschmann, A. 135
Holes, C.D. 191
Holmes, J. 223
homogeneity 207
homogenization 34–7, 97
Huang, F. 31, 32
human capabilities 165
human capital 15–19
human capital theory 16–18, 22–3, 24
humanist viewpoint 23–4
humanistic education 213
humanities, neglect of 171

identity: Arab 205; and language 195;
   national 186, 190–2, 211–13; pan-Arab
   191; preservation 42, 184
illiteracy 98
immigration policy: and skill gaps 18
income status: effects of education 17, 18;
   and student numbers 13–14, *13*
independent governance boards 41
industrial partnerships 81–2
industry, research funding 127
information and communication
   technology (ICT) in schools 119–22
information asymmetry 135–6
institutional templates 41
institutions, globalization of 31
instrumentalist view 51
insularity 49
integration, gender 80, 81
intellectual freedom 127
international exchanges 29–30
international flows 28–9
International Governmental Organizations
   (IGOs) 15–16
international growth 28–31
International Network for Quality
   Assurance Agencies in Higher
   Education (INQAAHE) 137–8
international standards 137
international strategic interests 5

investment: efficiency of 18; measures of success 23; returns on 17–18; Saudi Arabia 153, 175; scientific training 18–19
inward mobility 45–9, *46*, *48*
Islam 154
Islamist movements 5
isolation: elite branch campuses 92; of national workers 49–51

Jamjoom, F. 154, 168
joint programs 32–3

Kelly, M. 143–4
Kelly, P. 154, 168
Khalifa University of Science, Technology and Research (KUSTAR) 82, 104
Khalifeh, F. 221
Khamis-Dakwar, R. 189
King Abdulaziz City for Science and Technology (KACST) 170
King Abdullah bin Abdulaziz Public Education Development Project 157
King Abdullah Scholarship Program (KASP) 153–4, 157, 173
King Abdullah University of Science and Technology (KAUST) 169, 170, 172
King Saud University (KSU) 172
Knight, J. 33, 74
knowledge: as capital 22; defining 213–15; pursuit of 23–4
Knowledge and Human Development Authority (KHDA) 68
Knowledge and Human Development Authority (KHDA), Dubai 65, 141
knowledge-based economy 15
knowledge revolution 214
knowledge societies 42
koines 187
Kuwait 75, 78–80; accreditation 143–4; degree programs in public HEIs *100*; private higher education institutions *78–9*; public universities 99–101, 116; school reforms 120; vision 206
Kuwait University (KU) 99–101

labor market: meeting requirements 123, 163, 171–2, 208, 209, 211–12, 213–14; nationalization 216–18; private sector workers 217–18; structure and functioning 49–50; women's participation 42–3, 154, 218–21
labor market active programs 218
language: age and acquisition 196–7;

colonial 180–1; dominance 179; and national identity 184, 186; and personal identity 195; purity 185; sacred 187; and social status 188, 191; standardization 193; survival 194; teaching methods 189–90; translation 194; written 190, 191, 193; *see also* Modern Standard Arabic (MSA)
language academies 193
language planning (LP) 192–4
language proficiency 117, 148, 212–13
language teaching: age and acquisition 196–7; resource allocation 182, 195
Lazerson, M. 213–14
leadership 173
learning outcomes: elite branch campuses 64
learning strategies, Saudi Arabia 164–5
legal rights: women 219
legitimacy: elite branch campuses 216; maintaining through tradition 5
legitimation: and human capital 22–3; through university education 20–1
levels of development 13
liberal arts education 212, 213
Lightfoot, M. 121, 122
linguistic context 179
literacy development: and diglossia 188–90
literacy: female 218

McGlennon, D. 123
Malaysia, international strategy 33
Marginson, S. 37
market-based system, Oman 68, 70
market competition 134, 135–6
market-driven programming 169–70
Marx, K. 29
Masdar Institute of Science and Technology (MIST) 81, 127
Massive Open Online Courses (MOOCS) 31
Mazi, A. 162, 170
meritocracy 19–21, 22
Meyer, J.W. 12, 20
Ministry of Higher education (MoHE), Saudi Arabia 156, 157, 158, 162, 163–5
mission and purpose, of higher education 15
mobility 29–30, 33, 45–9, 109; inward and outward *46*; women 221
Modern Standard Arabic (MSA): affective factors 187–8; bilingual education 195–7; campaigns for 183–4; context and

overview 179–80; and dialects 195–6; diglossia and literacy development 188–90; as diglossic language 186–7; impact of educational reforms 181–6; impact of English 181; language planning (LP) 192–4; measures to protect 184; national identity vs. pragmatism 190–2; pedagogical factors 189–90; pragmatism 210; proficiency 185, 191–2; protection and promotion 197–8; reading 189; resource allocation 182, 195; socio-linguistic factors 190; socio-political context 194–7; status 180–1; summary and conclusions 197–8; teaching 195–7; *see also* language

Moini, J.S. 111
Mok, K.H. 38–9
monarchs 5
mother tongue 181
Muller, J. 215

Nahyan, Sheikh 182
Naidoo, V. 33
national aspirations 205–6
National Commission for Assessment and Academic Accreditation (NCAAA), Saudi Arabia 173
National Education Review Initiative (NERI), Bahrain 120–1
national identity 184, 186, 190–2, 211–13
national universities 97–111; dates of establishment *98*; status 113–14
national workers, isolation 49–51
nationalism, Pan-Arab 186
nationalization: as driver of reform 122; labor market 216–18
natural resources 2
Nedeva, M. 214
neoliberalism 16; Dubai 64–5; influence 38; perspective on educational reform 40–1
New York University Abu Dhabi (NYUAD) 63, 91
Nolan, L. 163
Northern Emirate private universities *83*

Office of Institutional Research and Planning, Qatar 114
oil production, effects of 1–2
oil wealth: effects of 97–8; and regional stability 5
Olsson, M. 22
Oman: accreditation 141–2; external affiliations 70–1; governance *109*,

146–7; public universities *108*, 116; regulated privatization model 68–73; school reforms 119–20; universities and colleges *72–3*; vision 206
Oman Academic Accreditation Authority (OAAA) 141–2
Omanization 120
online learning programs 31
Onsman, A. 174
Organization for Economic Cooperation and Development (OECD) 16
outward mobility 45–9, *46*; destinations *47*
overseas study 158
ownership 92–3; and quality assurance 146–7

pan-Arab identity 191
pan-Arab nationalism 186
Paris Sorbonne University Abu Dabi (PSUAD) 38, 62–4
Parker, H. 205
Pennington, R. 122
Peters, M.A. 22
Piketty, T. 25n1
policy 39–40
political commitment 92
political cultures: differences 61; and quality assurance 147–8
political economic subordination 23
politics, role of 39
post-graduate programs 124
pragmatism: vs. national identity 190–2; use of English 210–13
pre-university level, language teaching 184
pre-university level reforms 119–22
Prior, David 61
private higher education institutions: Abu Dhabi (UAE) 82, *84*; Bahrain *76–7*; Kuwait *78–9*; Northern Emirate *83*; Qatar *59*; quality assurance 146–7; reasons for optimism 171; research and creativity 169–71; Saudi Arabia *159–61*, 162–3; Western influence 171–2
private schools 190–1
private sector workers 217–18
Private Universities Decree, Kuwait 75
Private University Council (PUC), Kuwait 75, 143–4
privatization: branch and private universities in Abu Dhabi *84–90*; categorization of universities and colleges 55–70, *56*; challenges 93; combined approaches 82; context and overview 54–5; education malls 64–8;

privatization *continued*
elite branch campuses 55, 57–64, 91–2;
external affiliations 70–81; financial
commitment 91; governance 61, 92–3;
impact of 92; industrial partnerships
81–2; ownership 92–3; political
commitment 92; private universities in
Northern Emirate *83*; regulated
privatization model 68–80; Saudi Arabia
163; semi-private model 80–90; summary
and conclusions 91–3; sustainability 91–2
Program for International Student
Assessment (PISA) 16, 118
Public Authority for Applied Education
and Training (PAAET) 101
public education system 98
public universities: Abu Dhabi (UAE)
106–7; anti-Westernization backlash
116–18; Bahrain 105, 109, 116; context
and overview 97; degree programs,
Kuwait *100*; enrollment rates 98;
establishment of national universities
98; funding 104; growth of 109; Kuwait
99–101, 116; mission and purpose 113;
Oman 104–5, *108*, 116; Qatar 101–2,
113–15; reforms 111–18; research
centers *128*; rise of national universities
97–111; Saudi Arabia *158*; school
outcomes and university requirements
118; summary and conclusions 128–9;
teaching and research 122–8; United
Arab Emirates 102–4, *103*, 115–16;
Western models 112–16
public–private partnerships 157
public/private sector workforce 50–1
purpose and mission 15
pursuit of knowledge 23–4

Qatar: collaborative research 127; Education
City 57–64; elite branch campuses 55,
57–62; governance 61; graduate programs
58, 60; pre-university level reforms 61;
private higher education institutions *59*;
public universities 101–2, 113–15; quotas
60–1, 91; reforms 57; school reforms 119;
student numbers 60–1; youth
unemployment 62
Qatar Faculty of Islamic Studies (QFIS) 58
Qatar Foundation 58, 60, 62, 127
Qatar National Vision 206
Qatar University (QU) 57, 58, 101–2,
113–15; colleges *101*
quality: concerns 55; elite branch
campuses 64

quality assurance 38; AACSB
accreditation *140*; ABET accreditation
138–9, *139*; academic quality 145;
access to reports 145–6; accreditation
and assessment agencies *138*;
accreditation bodies 137–8; choices
134–5; conflicting interests 146–7;
context and overview 134–5; criticisms
209; degree programs 148–9; faculty
working conditions 148–9; foreign
accreditation 166; governance 144–5,
146–8; international standards 137;
new institutions 144; new regulatory
institutions 140–4; and political culture
147–8; private higher education
institutions 146–7; problems of poor
quality 149–50; regulation and
accreditation 135–6; Saudi Arabia 162,
163–4, 173–4; standards 144–6; student
preparation 148–9; summary and
conclusions 150–1; Westernization
136–40; *see also* accreditation
Quality Assurance Authority for Education
and Training (QAAET), Bahrain 121,
142–3
quality audits 142
quality control mechanisms 137
quotas 60–1, 91
Quran, language 187

Ramzi, N. 125
Rand Corporation 57–8
RAND–Qatar Policy Institute (RQPI)
report 114–15, 119
Rassekh, S. 120
reading: Modern Standard Arabic (MSA)
189
reforms: factors for success 204–5; impact
on MSA 181–6; labor market
nationalization 216–18; pre-university
level 61, 119–22; Qatar 114–15;
similarities 207–9; United Arab
Emirates 115–16; and vision 205–7;
Western models 112–16
regional mobility 30
regional stability 5
regulated privatization model 68–80;
Bahrain 71; Kuwait 75, 78–80; Oman
71–5
regulation: new regulatory institutions
140–4; quality assurance 135–6;
Westernization 136–40
religion 34
rentier culture 42

rentier economies 5
research: collaboration 127;
  competitiveness 127; faculty capability
  123–5, 127; faculty perceptions of
  significance and satisfaction *126*;
  industry funding 127; lack of facilities
  123; public universities 122–8;
  spending, public universities 122
research centers *128*
research funding 123
resource allocation 18
Rhoads, R.A. 22
roles, of higher education 15
Romanowski, M.H. 125
Rubin, A. 119

Saha, L. 23
Sakr, A. 121
Saudi Arabia: accessibility for women
  167–9; challenges 166–9; context and
  overview 153–5; data collection 169;
  demand for HE 155–6; demographic
  characteristics 155; economic
  diversification 174–5; expanding HE
  156–62; expatriate workers 156;
  faculty 162; further questions 174;
  government emphasis 174–5; growth of
  universities and colleges *157*;
  implications of study 173–4;
  investment 153, 175; labor market
  needs 156, 171–2; moving forward
  172–3; overseas study 158; private
  higher education institutions *159–61*,
  162–3; public/private distinction 164;
  public universities *158*; quality
  assurance 162, 163–4, 166, 173–4;
  recommendations 174–5; reliance on
  foreign staff 167; research and
  creativity 169–71; student numbers
  153; support for students 153–4;
  teaching and learning 164–5; Western
  curricula 165–6; Western models 162
Schofer, E. 12
school outcomes and university
  requirements 118
schooling, expected duration *7*
"schools of the future" project, Bahrain
  120
schools, reforms 119–22
Schultz, Theodore 16
Science Technology Engineering and Math
  (STEM) research 170
scientific and technological capacities 123
scientific terminology 185

scientific training: under-investment 18–19
secularization 20
segregation 70, 80, 81, 99, 102, 154, 221–2
semi-private model: Abu Dhabi (UAE)
  81–2; Sharjah 80–1
Sen, A. 165
Senior Reform Committee (SRC), Qatar
  University 114
sex-segregation 70, 80, 81, 99, 102, 154,
  221–2
Seyyed, F.J. 124–5
Sharjah 80
Sheikh Mohammed Bin Rashed Al
  Maktoum IT Education Project (ITEP)
  119
Sheikha Mozar 111, 114
Shin, J.C. 170
Shoura system 5
Singapore 33
skill gaps 18, 163
Smith, L. 154, 169, 172, 173, 175
social homogenization 28–9
social legitimation 20–1
social mobility 20
social roles of higher education 15
social sciences, neglect of 171
social segmentation 6
social status: and language 188, 191
socio-political environments 213
standards: international 137; quality
  assurance 144–6; Western influence 38
STEM subjects, promotion of 40–1
stereotypes 2
strategic planning: Qatar University (QU)
  114–15; Saudi Arabia 172
students: access to higher education 117;
  career expectations 216–17; choice of
  degree 18, 21; composition of student
  body 12–13; employability 162–3;
  expectations of 23; gender 14, 43, 45;
  insufficient preparation 118, 148–9;
  international exchanges 29–30; inward
  and outward mobility 45–9, *46*; mobility
  30–1, 33, 45–9, 109, 158; motivation
  121; numbers 12, 43, 60, 65, 68, 81, 97,
  99, 101, 104, 105, 109, 153; outbound
  destinations *47*; regional shares *13*;
  socio-political position 23–4;
  transnational social stratum 21
study abroad 109
Supreme Educational Council (SEC),
  Qatar 117
sustainability 91–2, 150, 216
Swan, M. 182

teaching: language teaching 189–90;
  public universities 122–8; Saudi Arabia
  164–5
teaching loads 148
technical terminology 185
terrorism 57
Texas International Education Consortium
  (TIEC) 165
The Institute for the Arabic Language
  184
Tight, M. 165
Tonsi, A. 184
traditions: effect on women 218–19; and
  legitimacy 5; preservation 206
translation facilities 41, 194
transnational programs 32
Trends in International Mathematics and
  Science Study (TIMMS) 118
tribal identity 4
truth finding 23

undergraduate studies, prioritization of 123
unemployment 209
UNESCO 30
United Arab Emirates: accreditation
  140–1; public universities 102–4, *103*,
  115–16; vision 205–6
United Arab Emirates University (UAEU)
  102, 115–16, 118
United States, strategic interests of 5
universities and colleges: adoption of
  English 182–3; categorization 55–70,
  56; choices 134–5; as contested terrains
  24–5; cross-border presence 31–4;
  difficulty of categorization 55; Dubai
  66–7, 69; expectation of 135; objectives
  208; Oman *72–3*; prioritization of
  undergraduate study 123; scientific and
  technological capacities *123*; *see also*
  private higher education institutions;
  public universities
University City, Sharjah 80–1
university education: academic ranking 23,
  81; changing purpose 20; ethos 23;
  original purpose 19; perceived value of
  15; and social legitimation 20–1; socio-
  political position 23–4

university formation: as transnational
  process 20
University of Bahrain (UoB) 74, 105, 109
University of Sharjah (UoS) 80, 81

value: of education 214; of university
  education 15
van der Wende, M. 37
Vision 2020 119, 120
vision and reform 205–7, 211
vocational training colleges 217

Wallerstein, I. 22
wealth 2, 4
welfare 221
Western domination 21–3
Western influence: private higher
  education institutions 171–2
Western models: and education quality
  207–9; public universities 112–16;
  Saudi Arabia 162; *see also* American
  university model
Westernization: educational practice 208;
  regulation and accreditation 136–40
Wilson, R. 162
women: access to higher education 167–9;
  educational practice 218–22; labor
  market participation 42–3, 154, 218–21;
  legal rights 219; mobility 30, 221;
  participation 14
women's education: attitudes to 221–2;
  benefits 218
workers, isolation 49–51
workforce 50–1
working conditions 148–9, 170–1
World Bank 16, 120, 215; Report on
  Education 113
world systems theory 22

Younes, M. 195–6
Yousef, T. 113
youth unemployment 62

Zayed, Sheikh 223
Zayed University (ZU) 102, 116, 117–18,
  184–5
Zeidan, S. 220